I SAY A
PRAYER
FOR ME

To Dorine —
Be encouraged
always!

I SAY A PRAYER FOR ME

ONE WOMAN'S LIFE OF

FAITH AND TRIUMPH

STANICE ANDERSON

Stanice Anderson

1/11/03

West Bloomfield, Michigan

WARNER BOOKS

An AOL Time Warner Company

Published by Warner Books, Inc. with Walk Worthy Press

Real Believers, Real Life, Real Answers in the Living God™

Walk Worthy Press, 33290 West Fourteen Mile Road, # 482, West Bloomfield, MI 48322

Warner Books, Inc., 1271 Avenue of the Americas, New York, NY 10020

Visit our Web sites at www.walkworthypress.net and www.twbookmark.com.

 An AOL Time Warner Company

Printed in the United States of America

First Printing: November 2002
10 9 8 7 6 5 4 3 2 1

Library of Congress Cataloging-in-Publication Data

Anderson, Stanice.
  I say a prayer for me : one woman's life of faith and triumph / Stanice Anderson.
    p. cm.
  ISBN 0-446-53034-4
  1. Anderson, Stanice. 2. Christian biography—United States. 3. Narcotic addicts—
United States—Biography. I. Title.

  BR1725.A343 A3 2002
  248.8'629'092—dc21
  [B]   2002016891

Book design by Giorgetta Bell McRee

*To Michael Tucker, Jr., my son,
confidant, and friend.*

For I know the plans I have for you, declares the Lord,
plans to prosper you and not to harm you,
plans to give you hope and a future.
Then you will call upon me and come and pray to me,
and I will listen to you.
You will seek me and find me when you seek me
with all your heart.
I will be found by you, declares the Lord,
and will bring you back from captivity.

Jeremiah 29:11–14 (New International Version)

Acknowledgments

First and foremost, I thank God the Father, His Son, Jesus Christ, and the Holy Spirit for saving me and for providing absolutely everything needed to write, produce, and distribute the book He predestined you to now hold in your hands.

I began a list of all the family and friends who have made a tremendous impact on my life and thus this book, since it is a collection of stories that represents my life. However, because God is rebuilding my life, with the aid of so many people, such a list would have almost as many pages as this book. In addition, if I inadvertently left out any names, it would possibly hurt people and that is not my desire. So I say to my family and friends: "I love you and thank you for the encouraging words, prayers, and support. I thank God for you and pray that He who knows each of you by name and never forgets, bless you immeasurably more than you can ask, think, or imagine."

I will, however, attempt to individually thank the people and institutions that God directly used to impact this writing project.

Acknowledgments

Thank you to my friend, mentor and life-coach, Dorine "The Mother" Phelps, who helped prepare me for such a time as this. Dorine, for many years you have given me God-breathed counsel, rebuke, and the tools I need to become a woman of discipline, substance, and honesty, without which this book would not have been possible.

Thank you to my friend and writing world coach, author and former *Washington Post* reporter Patrice Gaines, who took me under her wing, encouraged me every step of the way, and introduced my work to Denise Stinson. Patrice, without your guidance, encouragement, and sharing with me your knowledge of the publishing world this book may not have happened.

To my friend and writing coach, Tom Fuller, I say thank you for taking the time to share with me all you know about the craft of writing. As you promised, you gave me the tools to help me realize my dream of becoming "a great writer who just happens to be African-American." Now it's up to me.

Although now with the Lord, I thank God for Reverend John Kinard, assistant pastor of John Wesley A.M.E. Zion Church in Washington, D.C., who when I placed a desperate call for help many years ago canceled all his appointments and got me into a drug treatment center.

I also want to thank *The 700 Club* and Operation Blessing. God used you to bring me to salvation and tangibly help me start my new drug-free life in Christ.

I also rejoice in how God has used my lifelong friends, Omie Brown, Traci Hill, Peggy Stroman, Edith Ellerbe, Toni Wright, and Linda Washington. After years apart, He ordered our steps and brought us back together again—all new creatures in Christ Jesus! Thank you for keeping me encouraged, circulating my stories to your families and friends, praying, and reminding me that God had His perfect season for this book's release. We are walking testimonies!

ACKNOWLEDGMENTS

Thank you my generous teachers and encouragers in the Word of God for showing me how to walk upright and in victory: Pastor and Co-Pastor El Chico and Joyce Williams (Recovery and Refuge Ministry, Durham, North Carolina), Archbishop Viril M. Myers and Pastor Peaks (Greater Zion Wall Missionary Baptist Church), Pastor Diana Nichols (Highways and Hedges Church, Durham), Bishop Harry and Pastor Michele Jackson (Hope Christian Church, Beltsville, Maryland); Pastor Nettie Finney and Rev. Allegra Henderson, and my church family (Christ's Spiritual Temple Baptist Church, Baltimore); Robin Turner (Bible Study Leader), Evangelist Clarence Simon (Baltimore), and Evangelist Lois McFarland (Tallahassee).

Thank you, Denise Stinson, publisher of Walk Worthy Press. God surely preordained our working together. You are a brilliant, beautiful, and bold sister in the Lord Jesus Christ. God has entrusted you with an enormous vision and I am grateful to be a small portion of it. Thank you for reminding me that this book deserved the best that we could give. It helped me not to settle for mediocrity and totally rely on God and allow Him to stretch me and teach me to soar with eagles. I pray that God continue to richly bless you and Walk Worthy Press.

Thank you, Jamie Raab, senior vice president and publisher of Warner Books, for believing in *I Say A Prayer for Me*. I appreciate you and Warner Books.

How blessed I am that God provided a cadre of editors including Warner Books' senior editor, Karen Kosztolnyik. Thank you, Karen, for your thoroughness, professionalism, and kindness. Production editor, Eric Wechter and copyeditor, Fred Chase left no word, sentence, paragraph, or page unturned. I learned early in my writing experience that editors make me look good; so I embrace your expertise and thank God for each of you!

Irene Prokop is another editor who worked diligently on this book. Thank you, Irene. Your experience, insight, and love for the Lord showed through your work right down to the green editing pencil, which was gentle on the eyes and my sensitive writer's spirit. Irene, you must have sent Fred Chase an e-mail suggesting a green pencil! Or am I just so new to the ways of publishing?

Definitely having an impact on this and all writing and breathing projects is my mother, Virginia Ingram Anderson. Thank you for giving birth to me, raising me, loving me, and praying me back home into the welcoming arms of Jesus Christ. I love you, Momma—always have—always will.

Daddy, I know you are with Jesus now; and that gives me comfort beyond earthly belief. Although you left before any of my books were published, I believe that because God loves me and promised in His Word to give me the desires of my heart, you have—in the spiritual realm—seen and touched them both. Thank you for everything you did and didn't do. I understand now that because you were as you were, I am becoming who I am.

Father God, thank you for my brother, Stan Anderson, Jr. Stan, you believed in me from the beginning. You have loved me through it all. I pray that I am the kind of "big sister" that every "little brother" deserves.

To each of my nieces and nephews from the oldest to the youngest, thank you from your loving Aunt Stanice. Know this: Jesus is real! Alive! And has a unique and wonderful plan for your life. The legacy that I pray to pass on is love for the Lord Jesus Christ.

The Andersons: Thank you to my aunts who encouraged me and assured me that I could make it, God being my Helper.

I am totally grateful for my son's paternal grandparents, Katherine Dean and the late Douglas Dean. Thank you for raising Michael, Jr., when my addiction prevented me from being a consistent, dependable, and sacrificial mother. In spite of everything, you loved me like a daughter and taught my son to love me unconditionally.

Michael Tucker, Sr., thanks for teaching our son about manhood, loyalty, and sacrifice. You are an awesome father and a wonderful lifetime friend. Thank you for your unconditional love and support through these many years.

A special thank you to my son, Michael Tucker, Jr. Having you in my life has taught me that all men are not to be blamed for the harm done by a few. You are my cheering section, and what makes my being here on earth not in vain. I didn't do much right in the beginning; but you never stopped loving me or believing in me. When there was no one else on the planet that I felt loved me, I knew that you did—and thus, I persevered. May the way I live my life with the help of the Holy Spirit show you that through Christ all things are possible.

And to all the readers who are giving me the opportunity to speak my stories into your lives, I thank you. My prayer is that God meets you within the pages of this book and breathes hope, love, healing, and peace into your hearts. I look forward to meeting you and thanking you in person on some God-assigned day.

Praise God from whom all blessings forever flow!

Contents

Contents

CONTENTS

Tell Me

Tell Me
A Story that I have not heard
Lead me to prayer
Give me an encouraging Word
Tell Me
A Story that will teach me how to see
That God loves and cherishes even me
Tell Me
A Story of God's Goodness and Power
So I won't give up in this next hour
Tell Me
A Story of what He's done for you
Then maybe I'll believe that
He can do the same for me too
Sometimes I get weary
I get weak, I feel worn
Tell Me
A Story so I'll know it was not by mistake
That I was born
Tell Me
A Story of how God leads the way

Tell Me
A Story so that I can get through one more day
Tell Me
A Story so I won't feel alone
Tell Me
A Story of how faith is grown
Does God really work in mysterious ways?
Does God care how I spend the hours of my days?
Does He love me? Does He care?
Will He always be there?
Tell Me
A Story because sometimes life just ain't fair
Sometimes I feel like I'm living in a lion's lair
Tell Me
A Story and please make it true
I need to know God loves me
As much as He loves you.
Please Tell Me.

Introduction

I am honored that the book God gave me to write is in your hands.

First, allow me to introduce myself. I was that family member, co-worker, stranger on the street, or friend of a friend that once was the epitome of love, promise, and joy who slowly, over time, began to get lost in the degrading world of drug addiction and alcoholism. I was the person whose family, friends, and employers cried at the thought of the person I had been and the unrecognizable person I became—an addict hopelessly lost to heroin. A lonely, desperate, moralless, and bitter woman hell-bent on self-destruction.

And you were the person who took a moment out of your precious day to pray for me, say a kind word, or encourage me to lift myself out of the pit and press forward. You were the person who gave me the money to buy a cup of coffee to get the chill off my life. You donated the clothes, furniture, and food that found their way to my first apartment after I got out of the addiction treatment center. You helped me find a job and take my first steps on the path of my brand-new independent life.

You sent a donation to one of the many charities that helped me get up on my feet. You could even have sent a donation to the television program I watched eighteen years ago that changed my physical life and eternal destiny. You could even be one of the countless people who told me that God had a plan for my life and that I mattered.

You shared with me the story about the Jewish boy who, although he had used up his inheritance and ended up eating with the pigs, went home to ask his father's forgiveness. His father saw him coming up the road toward the house, dropped everything, and ran to meet him. He threw his arms around his son, welcomed him home, prepared the finest meal, gave him his finest robe and ring, and thanked God for his son's return.

I am that family member, co-worker, stranger on the street, or friend of a friend who finally came home.

This book is my small attempt to say thank you for myself and others like me. It is also about sharing what I have learned during the past eighteen years since I have come home. I truly don't believe that it has been all about me or just for me that I have had the experiences that are rebuilding my life. It's said that "to whom much is given, much is expected." I have been given so much, I feel I have a responsibility to share the wealth that God and others have shared with me along the way.

This book is a way of walking out my faith that God will give me everything I need to live my daily life in victory. Allowing me to write and send this book out into the world is God's gift to me and you. I believe He wants to remind us that what He does for one He will do for another and that He is the same yesterday, today, and forever.

*

INVITE GOD
INTO
YOUR LIFE

*

I Only Meant to Wet My Feet

"Beware of guys with matchbook covers torn off at the end," my father warned me as he walked away.

"What exactly does that mean, Daddy?"

He turned and, with a smirk that seemed to question my intelligence, said, "It means that they use drugs!"

"Use drugs! With a matchbook cover?"

"Yes!" Offering no more as he went to his next task.

Our "talk" about drugs was apparently over. I shrugged it off and thought, *How stupid does he think I am? Does he think that even at seventeen years old, I don't know anything? After all, I knew drugs were injected. I had seen the movie,* The Man with the Golden Arm. *Plus, I had seen junkies on the corner in front of the poolroom. They shoot dope into their veins. Boy, to be considered such a smart man, he sure is dumb about the things of life.*

It was clear to me that I was going to have to learn things on my own—just like I had learned through being raped three years earlier that men were not to be trusted; not even fathers. After all, they were men first, and fathers second— only out of a sense of duty.

Of course, neither my father nor mother knew about my being raped; but then there was a lot about me they didn't know. I never got the sense that they wanted to know anything about my inner reality. I was their dream-daughter and I lived my nightmares in private, like a "good" Anderson was taught.

After graduation from high school, I started going out almost nightly to what we called the Go-Go's: dances with live bands in rented halls. Usually beginning at 10:00 P.M. and lasting at least until 2:00 A.M., the dances were an all-consuming lifestyle that consisted of fabulous outfits, everyone trying to outdo the other, luxury cars, dancing to the point of near-exhaustion, and trying to "pull" the guys with the nicest cars and sharpest clothes. It didn't matter that they weren't about anything progressive and wholesome. Most of us had petty jobs that afforded credit cards to accumulate the clothes and most of the guys sold drugs or were involved with some other criminal activity. It was living life on the edge, which, for reasons I didn't understand then, appealed to me.

After the Go-Go's, I went to after-hours joints where the guys gambled and the girls watched, ordered bootlegged drinks, and shopped through the various "hot"—as in stolen—wares, especially the clothes that were needed to maintain the lifestyle.

By sunup it was time to go home and since I worked a day job, it would mean taking an hour or so nap, showering, and then heading off to work. By the afternoon break, I would be so sleepy I could barely stay awake. That is until I was introduced to NoDoz, a stimulant that warded off sleep. A few of those and I could get through the rest of the workday and then go home and get ready for the Go-Go again.

Soon I was taking NoDoz like it was candy and using credit cards to charge clothes like I never had to pay for them.

I felt discombobulated most of my life—long before my teen years, so I was ripe for what happened when I was twenty years old.

Early one weekday morning after the Go-Go, a group of friends and I went to another friend's house for breakfast. There was a guy that interested me in the kitchen. I walked toward him and asked him to light my cigarette. He pulled out a book of matches. As he opened the cover and struck the match, I noticed that the cover was torn off on the end.

"What's that?" I pointed to the matchbook.

"What?"

"Let me see those matches."

As he handed them to me, I recalled my father's words from a few years earlier and my curiosity was piqued. While, I must admit, *danger!* was my first thought, my inquisitive spirit overwhelmed all good judgment.

"Why is this matchbook cover torn off like this?"

"You don't know?"

"No."

"Come on! As fly a girl as you are, you really don't know?" With a slimy smile, he proceeded to reach into his jacket pocket and pull out a clear capsule with white powder inside. He then pulled out the missing strip of the matchbook cover, which was folded in half like a paper airplane without the cockpit torn out of the middle. He turned the strip over, carefully twisted the capsule open, and poured the white powder onto the furrowed strip. It was much like he was putting toothpaste onto a brush.

In the next instant, he directed the strip to his nostril and inhaled deeply. The white powder jetted up his nostril and disappeared. He smiled and shook his head as if to scatter the powder through his skull or something. He proceeded to line the remaining powder on the strip and like a vacuum cleaner his other nostril sucked it up. He made a snorting sound like a hungry pig and then handed the matchbook strip to me. School was in. He was the teacher. I was the willing student.

Lesson 1: "The strip is called a 'quill.' And what you are about to experience is 'boy,' also known as 'dugee,' also known as heroin. But it won't hurt you, as long as you put it up your nose, which is called 'snorting.'"

"Are you sure?"

"Yep! Just don't ever shoot up and you'll be all right."

I snorted the next white-lined quill of boy that he poured.

"It burns!"

"Oh, you'll get used to that. It just means that it's good."

Again, I snorted. My head seemed to take flight. A euphoric trance took control of my brain. I felt light-headed; but what I remember most is I felt memory-light. No thoughts other than those of the moment. A powerful feeling surged through my body. It was like I could conquer anything and anybody.

His next move was toward me—to kiss me, I suppose. But he was in for a rude surprise. I pushed him away so hard against the refrigerator that the bottles inside clanked. I knew then that no man would ever hurt me again. Finally, I had control of what happened to me.

While the rape had turned my young world upside down, I thought that maybe this boy also known as dugee also known as heroin would give me the power to turn it right-side up. So, my love affair with drugs began.

As I look back it reminds me of the song by the Whispers that goes, "I only meant to wet my feet; but you pulled me in . . . oh, the waters of love run deep." The song speaks of falling in love; however, many of us only mean to wet our feet but are pulled into some harmful behavior that drenches and quenches the fires of our spirits. Well, I found out that the waters of addiction run even deeper.

While I went from NoDoz to snorting heroin, left unad-dressed, my inner reality of pain and despair would always show up between highs. I was in denial about my problem for many years, thinking that I wasn't that bad. I would trade seats on the *Titanic* by changing the kind of drugs from pills, to dropping acid, to smoking reefer, to drinking liquor—but my ship was sinking nonetheless. And I was the last to know.

When I went off to college—only to avoid paying the credit card bills I had accumulated—I still used some form of drug and alcohol. Because I was in school, or kept a job, was not homeless or on some corner begging or on some stroll prostituting, I felt that I could not possibly be a junkie or drug addict. I still looked good—or so I thought. But my life was starting to become more and more controlled by drugs—the getting and using. But I only meant to wet my feet.

One thing about addiction though—it progresses! It's a downward spiral that leads to jail, and sometimes death.

I would always try to be around people who I thought were worse off than me. When I snorted, I befriended people that were injecting drugs. Then I could say, "I'm not that bad." However, at the age of thirty—ten years after my first snort of heroin, I injected it for the first time.

It's said that addiction is a "feeling disease." Being a lover of words, I broke the word "dis-ease" down. To me, it has come to mean that I am not at ease in whatever my reality is—I have a problem with my feelings and understanding that feelings are not facts. I was not at ease with the feelings associated with my rape, abortions, my squandered life, being a mother, a wife abandoned by her husband, a daugh-ter abandoned by her father, and even being in my own skin—I never felt comfortable with being who I was and all that it meant or didn't mean. I used drugs to forget—to stay numb—to not have to deal with reality!

The night before I shot heroin for the first time, I was arrested for assault with a dangerous weapon, unauthorized use of a vehicle, and breaking and entering. With drugs comes an unspoken responsibility to maintain the lifestyle. I had become a dealer of the pettiest sort. "Hustling backward" it's called. I made money and spent it faster than I made it. I had recruited young boys to help me in my life of crime since I was a woman alone. As a result of trying to get some money owed to me, I accumulated these charges. I spent the night in jail, which had never happened before. The next day when I got out, a girlfriend of mine came over with some heroin.

While she was known to use drugs intravenously, I was known as a snorter. However, the possibility of facing twenty years to life in jail was very disturbing. I recall thinking about how useless my life had become—me—having had so much potential (as I was always told—until it became a curse rather than a blessing, because I knew that I was not living up to that potential). Now I faced the possibility of prison.

My friend passed me my half of the heroin so that I could snort it. I watched her as she prepared the heroin mixture for the syringe. I just wanted to turn my life off—if only for a few minutes.

"What's wrong, Stacey? Why you savin' yours?" She had taken her eyes off her mixture as she prepared to tie her arm up to locate a vein.

"No. Put it all in the cooker!" I pushed my portion toward her.

"All of it?"

For a few brief seconds, with pleading eyes she said, "Are you sure?"

"Yeah! Come on, hurry up before I change my mind!"

She did as she was instructed. "Well let me go first, and then I'll do you."

I watched as she plunged the mixture into her arm. I could see only the whites of her eyes, as they rolled back into her head. Her neck pivoted back and bobbed back and forth as she fought for control. She was in a place that I wanted to go—that I felt like I needed to go.

I went to that peaceful, quiet, and carefree place; but another thing I found out about drugs: They turn on you— you always have to come back to reality. When the high wore off, I was still facing prison time and my life was still out of control.

You see, I only meant to wet my feet—but it pulled me in—the waters of addiction run deep!

Within three years, I overdosed and had to be revived three times, spent three months in the hospital as a direct result of the overdose, got in and out of a physically abusive relationship, lost my job, slept on a mattress on the floor of an apartment that I eventually got thrown out of for nonpayment of rent, did things with men that I never dreamed I was even capable of doing, stole food to eat, was blessed to get charges reduced to attempted unauthorized use of a vehicle and thirty days' probation with a year's suspended sentence, and, thank God, ended up in a treatment center with the help of a pastor of the church across the street from the methadone clinic that I went to.

Oh, but I only meant to wet my feet.

After I came out of treatment, I desperately wanted to get on with my life. No, I couldn't change the past; but I found out with the help of people in the twelve-step programs that I had to deal with my past—if I wanted to stay drug-free. I had to deal with the roots of what caused me to use in the first place.

And so began my journey—as painful as it has been sometimes—to deal with scars and open wounds left by rape, abortions, a failed marriage, an abandoned son, and the life-style. I had to go to God because it was too much for me to handle on my own. The wounds were too deep and the inner pain was too great. The twelve-step meetings I attended were only an hour a day. Even if I went to two meetings a day that was only two hours; but I had to learn how to live with myself for the remaining twenty-two hours, what I had done in my past, and my hopes of the woman that I had wanted to become.

I started praying constantly, reading all I could about God, asking questions, watching other people who walked in faith, and trying to emulate them. Even in my new faith-walk, I only meant to wet my feet—but it pulled me in—the waters of God's love for me ran deep—even deeper than drugs. I began to feel comfort when I prayed. I began to see God answering my prayers, making a way for me, leading me to jobs, people, apartments, and a healthier lifestyle. I saw God bring my son and other family members back into my life. The cravings for drugs started to leave. The desire to use drugs left me. As I witnessed my life change and the lives of my new drug-free friends, my relationship with God became even more personal. It was no longer a God out there in the sky anymore who had little time for the likes of me. He became *my* God and I was His daughter and even though my own earthly father rejected me, I began to trust and know that God never would.

Yes, I only meant to wet my feet!

"Fools rush in where angels fear to tread." We can hear the train coming and still insist that we can get over the track before the train arrives. Our first thoughts warn us of the danger ahead on the road but we head down the road anyway.

Whether it be credit cards, drugs, alcohol, chocolate, working, playing numbers, trying to keep up an image that is killing us from the inside out, we have a tendency to think that becoming out of control can't happen to us. We also have the tendency to think that the past is the past—let it be—out of sight, out of mind. However, what happens to the old baggage that follows us to the present and attaches itself to the journey to the future—if we don't do anything about it? We wonder why our relationships sour so quickly, why we can't let go enough to love and be loved, why we can't let anyone close to us, why we worry so much about everything, why we feel so useless, unloved, and unwanted. Why we feel that we are better than, or less than, other people. Why we procrastinate, or get so angry, or so depressed. We need to address that old baggage by offering it to God through prayer, asking for healing and guidance on the steps we can take to do our part in becoming all that God birthed us to be. It can begin when we invite God into our lives.

Dear Heavenly Father: When we veer off the righteous path that you prepared for us even before we were born, steer us back—love us back onto your way. We know we have free will and sometimes that seems to be a curse more than a blessing because we sure know how to mess up these precious lives that you gave us. Help us to say "No" to anything that is not of You. Help us believe that as long as there is breath there is hope and that you can change a life as sure as the sun will set and the moon will rise. Nothing is impossible for You. Hear our prayers for our loved ones and acquaintances who are saying "Yes" to the wrong things. Show us your reality and help us to stay focused on your love that can heal any wound, bind up any broken heart, pull up and destroy the roots of any pain left from our pasts so that we can live up to our potential in You. Amen. So be it!

My frame was not hidden from You,
When I was made in secret,
And skillfully wrought in the
Lowest parts of the earth.
Your eyes saw my substance,
Being yet unformed.
And in Your book they all
Were written,
The days fashioned for me,
When as yet there were none
of them.

PSALM 139:15–16 (New King James Version)

In the
Lion's Den

I always thought of a bathroom as a safe place until the day it became my prison. As my T-shirt clung to my body with sweat, I gasped to find enough of the hot air in the tiny windowless bathroom to fill my lungs. I sat on the toilet lid and strained to hear John's movements in the other room. He was my dealer, my lover, and later became my husband. My stomach cramped. My head throbbed. My bones ached from the inside out reminding me that it was time for my next shot of heroin. I had to figure out a way to get past John and make my buy since he was determined not to give me any more dope. Holding me hostage in the bathroom was John's idea of an addiction treatment program.

For hours, I banged on the walls and door until my hands were red and sore. "Let me out, John, please. I can't stand it any longer. I'm so ill, John, please let me out."

From the other room, he yelled, "I'm not letting you out. So just shut up."

Every time I opened the door and attempted to walk out, he would beat me with his fists back into the bathroom.

I felt humiliated and degraded. I didn't know what I hated more—my addicted reality or John's diabolical plan to "help" me get off drugs. However, desperation got my creative juices flowing.

I surveyed the tiny tiled bathroom like a soldier on reconnaissance. On the shower rod, John's lush maroon robe with matching belt hung on a wire coat hanger. I opened the wood cabinet under the sink and found a can of hair spray. A red cigarette lighter was on the floor next to the tub.

As a diversionary tactic, I started talking: "I know you're right, John. I can kick this habit. You won't have to hit me anymore. I'll be good. John, please let me out!"

"You must think I'm crazy. I'm not letting you out, I don't care what you say."

I gently pulled his robe off the hanger, then unraveled the black wire hanger, pulled the wire straight, and folded it in half. I wrapped John's robe around the hanger and tied it securely to the hanger with the belt. "Please, John, I can't stand it anymore. It's hot, please let me out."

"If you don't shut up all that noise," he continued, "I'm gonna come in there and make sure you *can't* say another word."

I wet a washcloth and wrapped it around the exposed bottom half of the wire hanger. I turned on the water in the sink full force and made a few splashing sounds.

"That's better, wash your face or something." John's voice calmed as he continued. "Get yourself together."

While he talked, I doused the robe with hair spray. My hands trembled as I picked up my new makeshift torch in one hand. I took a deep breath and flicked the lighter. Nothing. Again. A few sparks. *"Come on, lighter, you've got to work,"* I urged. *Calm down. You're just nervous. Your hands are sweaty.* I wiped my hands on my denim shorts. I flicked the lighter again. The pure blue yellow flame leapt from the lighter and seemed to, on its own, strain toward the makeshift torch. I held the torch away from my body. Whoosh! The robe ignited. The flame grew.

Slowly, I opened the bathroom door and stepped over the threshold. Out of nowhere John pounced like a lion after its helpless prey. But this time, I wasn't so helpless. With torch flaring, I held it out as a shield. Flabbergasted, John took a few steps back away from the growing flame. I wielded that torch like Zorro wields his sword.

I walked backward toward the door of the apartment. I could almost hear John's devious mind ticking. His nostrils flared. He cursed and ranted; but he dared not come close. Never taking my eyes off him, I opened the door. When I saw I could clear the door, I stepped out into the dim corridor and hurled the torch at John. I didn't wait to see where it landed. I broke into a run like a sprinter at the sound of the starter gun.

"Help! Someone, please help me," I shouted as I ran down the corridor of the apartment building.

A man came out. "What's going on?"

"Help me." A woman and a few kids were out in the hall. I dodged to keep from running into them. "Help me, he's coming after me."

But no one helped me. As I was about to negotiate the turn into the lobby, my legs got tangled up in something. My knees hit the carpet and I felt the burn of the slide. That something I was tangled up in was John. He sacked me like I was a quarterback inches from the goal line. I felt my lips explode and tasted warm blood in my mouth. There was no Good Samaritan in this crowd, it was clear; I was on my own.

I struggled to get free from John. He jerked me over onto my back, straddled me, and slid his rough, heavy hands around my throat and tightened his grip. I kicked and tried to scream but he was choking me. The light panel on the ceiling seemed to flicker out.

From a distance, I heard a loud piercing sound. I was sure that it was the smoke detector in my apartment. Immediately, John released his grip on my neck and turned to look toward the apartment. I shoved him off me and attempted to get up. He grabbed me at the waist and slammed me back down to the floor. He punched my already bruised body. Pain shot through my arms and chest. He finally got his choke hold on my neck again. I couldn't breathe. The alarm kept sounding but grew fainter. I prepared myself for death. In that moment, he released his grip, got up, and ran toward the apartment. I gasped for air, struggled to my feet, and ran out of the building. I jumped into the first taxicab that stopped. I went to a friend's house and stayed there for two days. I was afraid to go back to my apartment.

Finally, I decided to go home. I prayed that John would be gone. *Anyway, that's my apartment,* I thought. *I can't let that man run me out of my own place.* As I got out of the taxicab and walked toward my apartment building, it seemed to swell in front of my eyes, transforming itself into an ominous, tall, looming giant that was about to swallow me up. I paid the driver and slowly walked into the mouth of the giant.

As I walked through the lobby, I heard my neighbors whisper to each other, "That's her. That's the one." My legs became heavy. Each step toward my apartment became harder to take. My heart picked up a staccato beat and it got harder to breathe the closer I got. I fumbled in my purse for my keys but without taking my eyes off the door.

As I raised the key, I felt an electrical shock that prevented me from putting the key into the lock. Thoughts flashed through my mind: *Suppose John was in the apartment. What would I do?* The thoughts that came after that startled me a bit— *"No, don't go in he apartment. Danger!"* The thoughts were so strong and took over everything that I was trying to think about that I figured it may have been God that planted the thoughts as a warning to me. I could offer myself no other explanation. Still, I shook my head as if to obliterate the thoughts. This was my apartment and if there was danger waiting on the other side of the door, I felt like I would be able to handle it. I pressed my ear to the door. I heard no movement or any other sounds.

I opened my stance as if to brace myself for whatever was on the other side of the door. Ready to turn the key, I grabbed the doorknob but its heat demanded its release. I jumped back. Again, urgent thoughts: *"Danger! Danger! Get help. Call the police."*

Again, I cautiously pressed my ear to the door. Silence. I touched the doorknob. An electrical shock that felt like the points of a handful of straight pins plunged into my hand. It knocked me back away from the door. There was the thought again—*"Danger!"*

I ran down the corridor to the rental office and called the police. They assured me that officers would be dispatched immediately. After a half hour, still no police. I went back down the corridor toward my apartment. I reached for the door-knob only to be met again with the inexplicable heat.

I went back up the corridor and sat in the lobby. One hour after my initial call, two police officers walked through the lobby door. "Did someone here call the police?"

"I called."

"What seems to be the problem?"

I explained that I sensed danger and that I was afraid to go into my apartment. They walked with me down the corridor toward my apartment. One of the officers told me to hand him my key and said in a protective voice, "Step aside, miss."

I positioned myself behind both officers. The first officer slowly unlocked the door, turned the doorknob, and opened the door. I heard the thud as the door swung open and hit the wall. The lights in the apartment were off and there was only silence. The officer hit the light switch directly inside the door. Light flooded the hallway of my apartment.

"This is the police. Is anyone in here?" Nothing. Both officers loosened the strap on their holsters and crossed the threshold with their hands on their guns. They walked cautiously down the hall.

"You stay out there, miss," the officer commanded. He flipped the switch and light flooded the living room, revealing John sitting in the middle of the floor on the black vinyl recliner. The rest of the furniture was gone. The blinds were drawn closed. The walls were bare.

The police asked John for identification and an explanation of his presence in the apartment. He claimed he was napping and heard nothing. I assured the officer that his name was not on the lease. They escorted him out and told me to have the locks changed.

I collapsed onto the lone chair. I felt a hard object stuffed down the side of the vinyl chair cushion. It was John's switchblade. All of my emotions rushed through my body like a swollen river ready to burst through a cracked dam. I sobbed and thanked God for the warning through the heated doorknob.

Is there something trying to hold you hostage today? Even subtle things like resentments, an unforgiving spirit, negative thoughts, unhealthy relationships, food, low self-esteem, fear, chocolate, procrastination, anger, loneliness, the past, anxieties, and inertia can be hostage-takers.

Often we know the "what," it is just the "how" to grow past it that eludes us sometimes. For so long, I sought so many man-made remedies that never did what the labels promised. It was not until I made a decision to change and acted on that decision by taking the first step toward healing and help that my desperate reality changed.

For many of us, it will take different levels of awareness, sometimes even pain and despair, to get us to the point of surrendering our particular hostage-takers to God. I equate my point of surrender to a person that is drowning in the ocean. The lifeguard dives in to get the person but she's flailing her arms in panic so that the lifeguard cannot get a grip on her to take her to the safety of shore. However, lifeguards are trained to use whatever is necessary to get their victim to safety—even if it means knocking them out. I was one of the ones that had to be knocked out. I was sprawled out on the ocean of life like a knocked-out boxer on the canvas of the ring. That's what it took for me to surrender my self-destructive behaviors.

We don't have to be knocked out to surrender, if we allow God to guard our lives. We can practice daily surrendering our lives, cares, and worries to God. We can welcome Him to provide the guidance and care that we don't have to be without. This daily surrender is what gives us the strength and the power to stay on the path of spiritual health and wholeness that we choose to remain on.

There is an old adage that we can put to rest: "God only helps those who help themselves." I believe that to be false. I was not trying to help myself; but God, with His mercy and grace, rescued me. And He is willing and able to rescue anyone willing to be rescued.

I imagine God looks at us and says: "Let me spare this helpless child of mine. Some of my children don't know it yet but I have a marvelous plan for their lives. No matter how hard and fast they try to run in the opposite direction of my plan, I am still with them. Poor babies, they don't know yet that there is no place that they can go that I am not present. I

19

love them so much that I'm going to get them out of their situations, just like so many of the other times that they're not aware of—yet. Let me alert them by planting thoughts into their precious minds of the impending danger and the safety that can be found only in and with Me."

Most of us have felt at some time or another something deep inside our spirit that alerted us to impending danger. Sometimes we ignored it—sometimes we heeded the spiritual warning and got out of harm's way—just in the nick of time. I have come to believe that it is the love and protection of an all-knowing, all-seeing God who stands watch over my life. All you need to do is ask Him in.

Dear Heavenly Father: Your goodness and mercy continuously astonish us. When we think about the inexhaustible and unexplainable ways that you have shown Your love for us, we are in awe of You. You protect, guide, and make provisions for us even before we know that we are in need. You rescue us from danger unseen and from danger seen. Thank you for showing us that you are a real personal God who so loved the thought of us and so created us to know you, trust you, walk with you, and enjoy fellowship with you—daily. Help us to see and feel Your love that is woven throughout the fabric of our lives. Amen. So be it!

O people of Zion . . . you will weep no more. How gracious he will be when you cry for help! As soon as he hears, he will answer you. Although the Lord gives you the bread of adversity and the water of affliction, your teachers will be hidden no more; with your own eyes you will see them. Whether you turn to the right or to the left, your ears will hear a voice behind you saying, "This is the way; walk in it."

ISAIAH 30:19–21 (New International Version)

God Has the
Last Word

I never will forget that yellow-bodied Schwinn English Racer with the white rims nor what happened that very last time I rode it. The hot summer breeze swept across my sweaty face and arms as my bike glided downhill on Connecticut Avenue. I saw tourists posed for photographs that they would later show back home of their trip to the nation's capital. A young couple with two children in tow instructed them to "lick faster" as the ice cream on their sugar cones melted and trailed down their little arms in the mid-July heat. Lovers meandered arm-on-waist and looked at shop window displays. I stopped the bike at a red light and decided to go into a store to buy a Sunday paper and a grape soda to take to work.

I had been hired to work eight hours a day—Monday through Friday. However, I worked twelve to sixteen hours a day and sometimes even spent the night at work—but that was my secret. I never reported the extra hours. My motive? It was a whole lot easier to work than to think about what was going on—and not going on—in my life. My life became more painful as the years stole by. I was a walking festering wound. My life was a contradiction of terms. Life, I breathed; but Death, I felt, was closing in on me.

I patted my pocket to make sure my little package was still there. *Good*, I thought. *I'll numb the pain in a little while.* I got off my bike, pulled it up the curb, and rolled it into the high-rise office building.

"Good afternoon, Stanice," the security guard greeted me. "Pretty hot today, huh?"

"You got that right."

"So, how you doing today?"

"I'm all right," I said, offering my usual lie.

"Don't work too hard."

I managed a smile and entered the waiting elevator. Once upstairs, I unlocked the double glass doors, turned on a few lights, relocked the door from the inside, and left my keys in the lock. That way, if someone came in, I would hear the keys rattle.

I walked through the suite's corridors, checked offices, and listened for sounds other than my own footsteps. It was confirmed—I was alone.

I went to the kitchen area and with a paper towel wiped the sweat off my body. I filled a cup with tap water and went into my small office. I turned on the radio and locked my office door. I walked behind my wooden desk and reached into my pocket and pulled out my little plastic package and sat down. I slid open the desk's bottom drawer and took out the old pair of panty hose that I kept there. I opened the bottle of soda, took a few sips, and with the point of a pen pried out the plastic cap liner. I poured the heroin powder out of the plastic package into the soda cap, added water, and bent one of the outer rim sections of the cap for a makeshift handle.

With a lit match in one hand and the cap filled with the heroin mixture in the other, I soon heard the slight bubbling sound, smelled the medicinal odor, and drew up the warmed mixture into the syringe. I tightly tied my arm with the panty hose and held it between my teeth. After about ten minutes, I finally found a vein that would welcome the heroin that would take the cramping of my stomach and the ache in my soul away simultaneously. Then I could get to work.

Instead, after seconds of euphoria, everything faded to black. Time no longer existed.

BAM! BAM! I felt the sensation of somebody or something beating me in my chest. My eyes popped open. I saw flickers of bright light. I felt extraordinary heat surging through my body. Sweat poured off me in rivers. My red spandex top felt like it was squeezing me so hard that it would turn my body inside out. *Who are these people moving all around me?* I thought. I heard loud noises, then the muffled voices of men. There was urgency in their cut-off sentences, but I could not decipher the language or the rhythm. *"Somebody help me, I'm being violated,"* I thought. The blackness overwhelmed me again.

The next thing I remember was the sun shining in my eyes through the tops of what looked like trees. I heard cars. I felt like I was floating. Still I heard people's voices but I couldn't make out what they were saying. I even saw a few lips move but no sound came out of them. *Where was I?* I just couldn't get my brain to work.

A siren. I remember knowing that I heard a siren. It was loud; then barely audible. Light. A bright light flooded my vision. I felt hot tears on my face. *Or was I sweating? Why was I crying? Where were they taking me?* I couldn't put anything together. Nothing made sense. Blackness. Then, light. My name. Someone was calling my name. "Stanice. Breathe. Breathe. Stanice, breathe." *Who was telling me this? Who was calling my name?* Blackness.

In what could have possibly been the next moment, I knew that I was in a hospital examination room. One of the many faces I saw was familiar to me. "Neicy, Neicy," she said. *Who is she? And why is she crying?* I saw the glint of a long, thick needle in the air above me. I felt something stabbing in my chest. I raised the top half of my body up off the table. I felt something that was beyond mere pain. It was so much bigger than I was and it overtook me. I heard a piercing scream. It was me screaming and I knew it. Blackness.

I woke up in a bright room with a maze of monitors around me that binged and pinged with a mysterious beat. I couldn't swallow. My throat hurt. Something was in my mouth and down inside my throat. Nurses with white pants, skirts, and brightly colored smocks were busying themselves all around the large room. I tried to talk. I couldn't. It became apparent by the snatches of what I saw and heard that I had overdosed. In the painful reality of that moment, I looked straight ahead.

There at the foot of my bed stood my boss, a petite Italian woman with a perm that gently framed her face. She held a beautiful bouquet of flowers; but she couldn't hold back the streams of tears flowing from her eyes. She dabbed her eyes and nose with a wad of white tissue stained tan with makeup. I would have rather faced a death squad of soldiers with loaded rifles aimed at me than see my boss standing there with her heart breaking right before my eyes. I cried. I struggled to speak but I couldn't.

The nurse laid a small picture-frame-sized blackboard and a piece of chalk on my bed. She untangled the many wires linked from my body to their respective machines—which I assumed were keeping me alive. I heard the heaving sounds of the respirator.

I motioned with the hand that was not connected to any apparatus for my boss to come nearer. I took the chalk and she steadied the board. Slowly and painfully, I wrote, "I AM SORRY."

I later found out that because the doctors could not find a vein to start an IV, in order to save my life they had to go in to start a line in my chest. However, air entered the line, and one of my lungs collapsed. Breathing only seven times a minute, I had been attached to the respirator three days before I became conscious enough to recognize my boss. I also later discovered that my cousin, an employee of the hospital, had been on duty in the emergency room the day they brought me in. She recognized me, gave the doctors some family history, and called my mother.

When I finally did get out of intensive care, three men that I didn't know came to see me. They introduced themselves as the paramedics from the ambulance that found me and brought me to the hospital. Two of them pulled up chairs around my bed, and the one who chose not to sit said, "We had to meet the woman who actually died three times on the way to the hospital but kept coming back. You would flat-line, and we struggled to bring you back. And when you did come back you whispered, 'I want to live.' Each time you died, you'd come back to life and whisper, 'I want to live.' So we had to meet you."

I asked them, "How did you find me in my office that day? I know I was alone."

"One of your co-workers stopped at the office later in the day on her way to the airport. She had forgotten her attaché case. When she got to the office, she saw your keys in the door and called out your name. When you didn't answer, she went to your office. The door was locked but she heard the music and knew you had to be in there. She called the building security guard, who verified that you had gone up to the office earlier. The guard came up and kicked in the door. They found you sprawled over your desk with the needle still in your wrist. One of them called 911. We found you very close to death."

Through the tears, I thanked them and hugged each one. "You take care of yourself. You're a very lucky woman," one of them said as they left the room.

I was released from the hospital in late October. I know beyond a shadow of a doubt that luck had absolutely nothing to do with the fact that I was breathing! It has become clearer to me through the years that God had the final word—LIVE!

Some of us have been close to death; but God had the final word. Perhaps somebody prayed for us, perhaps there was an unspoken prayer in our own hearts that God heard and answered. When I think back over my life and recognize all the precarious situations that I have put myself in, wrong choices I have made, chances I took with my life and yet here I am—alive—in my right mind (most of the time)—I get overwhelmed with the feeling of gratitude for a God who loved me so much that He took the time to hear a prayer and save my life. No matter what is going on in my life, as I look back and see how far God has brought me, it ALWAYS brings me joy!

Most of us know the words to the great hymn, "Amazing Grace, how sweet the sound that saved a wretch like me." I don't know about you; but I can relate. That is my story—that is my song.

Dear Heavenly Father: You are All-powerful, All-knowing, an Ever-Present help, and oh, so full of mercy. Thank you, God, for the gift of life and may we never, ever take that glorious gift for granted. May all that we do, say, and even think be to Your glory and for Your glory. Thank you that in Your kingdom there are no coincidences, that You are an On-Purpose God who has a plan for each of us that far exceeds what we could ever think, ask, or imagine. Help us to believe more each day that you have a plan for each of our lives or we wouldn't be breathing today. Amen. So be it!

They took away the stone from the place where the dead
man was lying.
And Jesus lifted up His eyes and said,
"Father, I thank You that You have heard Me.
And I know You always hear Me,
But because of the people standing by I said this,
That they may believe that You sent Me."
Now when He said these things, He cried with a loud voice,
"Lazarus, come forth!"
And he who had died came out bound hand and foot with
graveclothes,
And his face was wrapped with a cloth,
Jesus said to them, "Loose him, and let him go."

JOHN 11:41–44 (New King James Version)

The Awakening

After the heroin overdose and once my left lung was reinflated, I would sneak out of the hospital to get drugs. Once
my medical condition improved, I voluntarily signed myself
into the psychiatric ward in an attempt to stop using. No matter how hard I tried, the compulsion and obsession was so
overwhelming that I would give in *every* time. God knew my
heart's desire to stop injecting heroin but I couldn't stop. My
lack of control revolted me.

I had been taken by ambulance to the hospital in the heat
of summer and released in the cool of fall—addiction to
heroin still intact. Within months, fired from my job because
of my erratic behavior, on the brink of eviction from my
apartment, without a man to take care of me, and unable to
take care of myself, something happened.

By accident, I glanced at my own eyes in the bathroom
mirror and got a glimpse of the horror in my soul. The heroin-
filled syringe fell from my hand into the sink. I stared at it,
knowing that in a few minutes it would be filled with my
blood. I reached down into the sink for what had come to
represent the sum total of who I was—what I was. For a brief

moment, I wondered, *When did I turn down this road? When did my hair start turning silver? Exactly when did the music stop and everyone else go home? When did I cross the line from recreational drug use to this ugly side of addiction?* I remembered the previous week's stay in a jail cell—the third person in a cell made for two—I envied the roaches that crawled in and out of the bars. They had more freedom than I did. My eyes, filled with tears, looked like deep, dark pools of death. I wondered if death would be my only way out.

My mind was deluged with thoughts; but there was no time to think. *There was work to do. I had to get the heroin in me. My stomach cramped. My bones were cold.* I poked and threaded the syringe in a slightly rolling vein in my neck. The blood cascaded into the clear, notched cylinder. I pushed the plunger and watched the mixture disappear from view, leaving only the warmth exploding a hundred times in my body. My agonized thoughts died an unnatural death.

I looked around my efficiency apartment. There was a dingy white sheet strewn on the mattress on the floor. A faded blue understuffed chair in a corner. A thirteen-inch black and white TV with a wire hanger antenna perched atop a scuffed white plastic table. Furniture was not a priority.

I went to the kitchen to get something to drink. I opened the refrigerator. There was only a stick of butter and a plastic container of purple punch. I drank a cup of punch and hoped it would satisfy the hunger pains. There was no time to go steal a meal. My only priority was enjoying the heroin I had sold my body to get.

The man's voice on the television grew louder: "I lived my life to use drugs. I hated to see the beginning of each new day because I knew the vicious cycle of addiction would start all over again."

I turned to see this man that seemed to be telling my own story. He was handsome and clean-shaven, with incredibly peaceful eyes. What I saw and heard him say contradicted one another.

He continued. "I lived like an animal. I had no friends and I felt shame whenever I went around my family. I was lonely and most of all tired of existing in the binding grip of drug addiction."

Thoughts crept into my mind like thieves in the night. *An addict? Me? I could stop if I wanted. I stopped for a whole week a few times. With my family heritage, I just couldn't be a common garden-variety junkie.* I was drawn to that man's voice as he dared to express things that I didn't want to think about.

Then there was a dramatic, reenacted scene depicting him standing in front of a window with the blinds opened. With one hand, he held a mirror up to his neck with his head slightly tilted back. In his other hand, he held a syringe that probed his neck for a willing vein. It was like a dream; I watched this man's form change into mine. I saw myself on that TV screen. For the first time, I knew, beyond the shadow of denial, that I was an addict.

I spoke to the man on the screen like he was sitting across from me in my apartment. "If you were like me, what did you do? How did you stop?"

He said to the interviewer, "I got on my knees and prayed. I asked God to forgive me for my sins, come into my heart, and live his life through me."

I figured I had tried everything else. *I might as well try this,* I thought. I was already on the floor, so I rolled off the mattress onto my knees. I prayed, "God, do for me what you did for that man on the TV. Change my life. Please forgive me." I continued the prayer with the words I'd heard that seemed etched in my heart.

With my eyes still closed, a feeling came over me like I was cradled in unseen arms. The feeling overwhelmed me as the heavy burden of guilt seemed to be lifted off my shoulders. It was as if it were God reassuring me that He heard my prayer and that He forgave me.

My imagination—for what else could it have been?—took over and the door to my apartment seemed to open and the room was draped in a shimmer of light. Confessions of things I had done poured from mouth—things I had never uttered to anyone. I told God all about the places I had been, the degrading things I had done, as well as the things I had left undone.

To this day, I cannot explain all that happened that night but as tears streamed down my face, I sensed I was in God's presence. In an awe-inspiring moment, I realized that He saw me when I wallowed in the pigs' sty. He was now my way out. It was because of His grace that I made it out alive. In those moments more than seventeen years ago, I finally believed that I was God's creation and He really loved me.

It would be dishonest for me to say that I stopped using drugs that same night. I didn't. But hope that a new way of life was possible for me was born inside of me that night—and is with me still.

Months later, I entered an addiction treatment program with the help of Reverend John Kinard, the assistant pastor of the church across the street from the methadone clinic. I did not have health insurance or money but God made a way out of no way.

Still, I prayed and asked God to take away all traces of my addiction, including the strong cravings. The answer to my prayer came when I was reading the Bible one day and came across the words of 2 Corinthians 12:9 (New King James Version), "And He said to me, 'My grace is sufficient for you, for my strength is made perfect in weakness.' Therefore most gladly I will rather boast in my infirmities, that the power of Christ may rest upon me."

As part of the treatment plan, the counselors introduced us to twelve-step program meetings. I guess that was part of God's plan for me. At the meetings, I stayed surrounded by people just like me who were learning how to support each other in staying drug- and alcohol-free—one day at a time.

Over the past seventeen years that I have been clean and sober, I learned to crawl, walk, run—determined to embrace change—destined to live God's plan for my life—dedicated to sharing with others what God has done in and with my life.

Now, when I look in the mirror, I no longer see eyes that look like deep, dark pools of death. Instead, I see eyes sparkling with the possibilities of life because of the grace, mercy, and love of the Living God.

Perhaps you would like a new beginning? I have learned that new beginnings are possible and not just of an entire life, but I can even start my day over. When I'm at the office feeling the stress of too many decisions, feeling that I'm not appreciated, or just overwhelmed by the magnitude of the day's task—I can slip away to a quiet bathroom stall, or outside (weather permitting), or the garage. With practice, I have learned to take all my concerns, worries, and frustrations with me, and when I get to that quiet place, I give them all to God as I pray. Sometimes, I hum a song that brings me comfort, like, "It's me, it's me oh Lord, standing in the need of prayer, not my mother or my father, but it's me oh Lord, standing in the need of prayer." It works! By the time I get back to my office, the negative is drained off and away from me. Refreshed, I begin my day again. Prayer and spending time alone with God in my mind and heart always gives me access to a new beginning.

Do you need a new beginning? Have you prayed for the way to be shown to you? Have you invited God into your life? What better day than today to go to the Throne of Grace to lay your burdens down. You can have the *peace* in your life that only God can give.

Dear Heavenly Father: Thank you for your incredible patience with us. With your kind of power, You could say "poof" and we would be no more. But instead, you choose us, forgive us, wrap your loving arms around us, cradle us, and assure us that we are not alone. Thank you that you are the same, yesterday, today, and forever, and because of that you can do for anyone what you have done and continue to do for us. Thank you for the personal relationship that we are developing with You. Amen. So be it!

There is therefore now no condemnation to those who are in Christ Jesus, who do not walk according to the flesh, but according to the spirit. For the law of the Spirit of life in Christ Jesus has made me free from the law of sin and death.

ROMANS 8:1–2 (New King James Version)

New Beginnings

I was thirty-four years old when I called Reverend John Kinard and asked for help to get out of my drug-addicted life. At the time, he was the director of the Anacostia Museum, as well as assistant pastor at John Wesley A.M.E. Zion Church in Washington, D.C. I heard him say to his secretary, "Clear my calendar, Stanice is on her way." By the time I got to his office at the Anacostia Museum, he had already arranged a bed for me in an addiction treatment center.

"They are expecting you at 3:00 P.M., do you need money?"

I had enough money for a one-way bus ride so I said, "No, I have money."

I arrived early so I sat across the street at a McDonald's and asked a man for change so that I could buy a cup of coffee. While I sipped my coffee I thought a hundred times, *I can't go through with this. I can just come back tomorrow.* I was so afraid that if I left there I would not make it back. Death was getting closer to my door. My girlfriend, Sister, who I used with, had died only days before from an overdose. I knew that had I not been on a temp assignment that day, I would have been dead because it was always understood between us that I got the first shot of dope. A prayer filled my mind, *"Thank you, Lord, for sparing me. Help me sit still until it's time to go across the street and into the new life that you promised me."*

I walked through the treatment center door at 2:55 P.M. with only the clothes I wore—a pair of dirty jeans, a tight beige turtleneck sweater, a jacket, and a pair of brown suede hush puppies on my feet. They had protected me from most of the bitter cold—as long as I kept moving.

The first few days' sleep came hard. My body ached for heroin, my bowels locked, and my mind tried to convince me to leave. *"You can do this another time."* But somehow, I knew it lied. I prayed for the strength and courage to stay.

While in a group session one day, the counselor facilitated a meditation exercise. We were to close our eyes, listen to the taped music, relax, and go to a place, in our minds, that was peaceful. Once in this place, we were to visualize a person that we would really like to see and talk to.

So I surrendered to the music and traveled in my mind to that place. There in a tranquil garden surrounded by vibrant red and yellow roses a figure of a man whose features I could not make out stood at a distance with his arms opened wide. I focused on his opened arms. It was reminiscent of the photographs that I grew up with of artists' depictions of Jesus. I thought that he waited for me so I ran into his opened arms. I cried and told him all about my cramping stomach and pounding headache. I told him that I had difficulty sleeping ever since I stopped using drugs and that I needed to know that He was with me in the treatment center. I imagined feeling the warmth of His embrace. It was strange but I felt my fears and the weight of my problems lifted and carried off into the wind like feathers blown off an outstretched hand.

Still in the visualization exercise, I strained to hear a bird chirping an angelic melody. I looked into an imaginary tree and on the topmost branch was the bluest bluebird I had ever seen. I felt my arm raise up; but I wasn't sure if it was a part of the exercise or the reality that awaited me once I opened my eyes. I opted to keep my eyes closed, concentrate, and not leave that place.

A loud voice interrupted the calm of the garden. "Okay. Come back, people. The exercise is over." I opened my eyes, and looked around at my fellow patients sitting in the circle of green vinyl chairs. A heavy dark-skinned man with his arms folded across his heaving chest snored loudly. The young woman that sat beside him jabbed him with her elbow and he awoke with a jolt.

As I squinted to focus in the brightly lit room, I felt a soft wad under my right arm. When I moved my arm, a brown bundle fell to the floor. It looked like a wool sweater and a pair of slacks. *My God,* I thought, *a change of clothes.* Before the visualization exercise all I had was the clothes on my back.

"Where did these come from?"

As I looked around the room, I saw that I wasn't the only one with a bundle of clothes. There were two others just as surprised.

The counselor announced, "Now that we all are awake, I want to introduce you to Reverend Byrd. He has worship services here on Sundays for anyone who wants to attend. But today he stopped by to bring clothes for those of you that had a need."

"Thank you, Reverend Byrd. This is great." I thought, *This is more than a coincidence to see a bird during the exercise and then be introduced . . .* "The Lord really does work in mysterious ways, Reverend Byrd."

He nodded his graying head in agreement.

Then one of the counselors asked, "Does anyone want to share with the group their experience during the exercise?"

I raised my hand high like a kid in kindergarten, "Yes, I do!" I didn't wait to be called on, I just blurted out, "I saw Jesus!"

The group of my peers broke out in laughter.

A woman with a scar on her face like someone had thrown acid on her laughed above the others. "Yeah. Sure, you right."

Neither their laughter nor the comment deterred me. I continued. "It was like the song. You know. 'In the Garden.'" I could hear the melody in my mind so I started singing, "I come to the garden alone while the dew is still on the roses . . ." I didn't remember some of the words so I just went on to the chorus, "And he walked with me and he talked with me and he told me I was his own."

"We got us a live one here y'all," one of the men in the group said as he gave the guy beside him a high-five.

"Okay. Settle down. Anyone else?" Ms. King, one of the addiction counselors, graciously took the focus off of me.

From that point on, my peers ridiculed me. Especially when I asked to have church. Outside of scheduled group activities, I kept to myself and read my Bible. I wanted to learn a new way of living without the use of drugs. In order to effect that change, I knew I needed a lot of help and I had no problem asking for it. My purpose for being there was not to find a man or to sabotage myself. Most of my peers thought that I was crazy and in no uncertain terms told me so. One woman even threatened me in hopes that I would stop asking for group therapy and church, and that I would stop participating in my recovery as much as I was. *Why?* I wondered. As if she read my mind, she offered, "It just makes the rest of us look bad . . . You asking for all that stuff you be askin' for. Relax, just enjoy the three hots and a cot. You ain't gonna be able to stay off drugs no way."

Eventually, one of my fellow patients set me up by planting somebody's item of clothing in my drawer. Of course, one of the women "just happened" to find it in my drawer and told the counselors that I had stolen it. I felt alone, betrayed, and once again—different. Like a lone salmon straining to swim upstream when every other fish in the river is carried along by the strong undercurrent downstream.

I stayed in that environment as long as I could. However, thirty-two days into the six-month program on January 1, 1985, I signed myself out of the treatment center against medical advice. As I headed for the door, Ms. King said, "Stanice, remember, don't pick up the drug and you won't use it. And, please, whatever you do, continue to go to the twelve-step meetings."

"I will, Ms. King. I can't go back to the old life now."

I slowly walked out of the gray metal front double doors of the treatment center. Hearing the clank of the cold metal on the door frame as the doors closed, I thought of my life closing shut to the old way of living. Even though the briskly cold wind howled all around me, I felt a sense of wonder and expectation that I could make it. Each step I took brought me closer to my new reality—life without the use of drugs.

However, the closer I got to the gates of the institution that emptied into the uncontrolled world, I felt my heart picking up pace as if fear was knocking at my chest begging entry. I stopped. I looked back at the treatment center and then forward toward the gate. I wondered, *How will I make it outside of a controlled environment? Maybe that woman in the treatment center was right. Maybe I won't be able to stay drug-free. Maybe it's too late for me. What do I do now? Where do I go?* My father had disowned me a long time ago. My mother? I just couldn't go to her. Plus, I was too ashamed of what I had not done with my life to go to any of my family.

I pulled the collar of my new sweater up around my neck, held my jacket closely around my body, and again headed for the gate. I was not sure if I shivered as a result of the cold or the fear. But one thing I had learned while I was in that treatment center was how to pray. So I walked and prayed, "God, show me what to do and where to go. I need to know that you're with me even though I am leaving treatment early. And whatever happens or however you feel about me, please don't let me pick up a drink or a drug. 'Cause like the counselor said, 'If you don't pick it up you can't use.'"

Once off the institution grounds, I crossed the street and headed to the phone booth. I called a guy who had been a paid date more than anything else; but I also thought of him as a friend. *God, please let him be home.*

"Tommy, is that you?"

"Where you been, girl? I've been worried about you. Are you okay?"

"Yeah, I'm fine. I'm just leaving a treatment center. I got me some help. I don't drink or use any other drugs now."

"That's all right! I knew you could stop once you put your mind to it."

"Believe me, Tommy, I put more than my mind to it. I know that it was God that set me free from the bondage of addiction!"

"God?"

"Yeah. I'll tell you about that later. Right now, I need a place to stay for a while. Can I stay at your apartment with you?"

"Sure. Come on. Catch a taxicab. I'll wait outside to pay for it."

I hailed a cab and got in. As we pulled out into the traffic, I looked out the back window at the treatment center until it was out of sight. *Oh well,* I thought. *No turning back now.* A strange mixture of fear and hope filled my mouth with the salty taste of tears. When I get scared, I talk. "How are you today, sir?" I asked the cab driver.

A pair of soft hazel eyes peered at me from the rearview mirror and with a thick Jamaican accent he said, "I be doing okay today. A little slow for a New Year's Day, though. And you? How you be doing?"

"Well, I'm a bit scared." I couldn't believe my ears. I confessed to this total stranger that I was afraid. And I dared to go on. "I just walked out of the treatment center back there and I'm feeling real shaky right about now, but I know I'm going to be all right."

"Indeed you are. I know Bill W. myself, you know."

"Bill W.?"

"Oh yeah, that's right, you're fresh out of treatment and all. You probably don't know about me friend Bill W. AA, girl! He was one of the men who started the Alcoholics Anonymous meetings, you know?"

"Oh! No. Didn't know that."

"Yeah. Got me a meeting list right here." With one hand on the steering wheel he leaned over and popped open the glove compartment, reached in, pulled out the list. His eyes still on the road ahead, he reached over the back seat and handed me the blue and white brochure. "Just in case you want to know where AA meetings be held."

"Oh. Yes. Thank you."

"I'll show you, as we go along the roads here, where the meeting places are."

By the time we got to my friend's apartment, I believe I knew where every meeting in the city was.

As we pulled up to the red-brick apartment building, there was Tommy standing inside the glass front doors. That was one of the things I really liked about Tommy. He always kept his word. With a gigantic smile and breath smelling of beer, he reached over me and paid the driver.

As I got out of the cab, I reached up front to shake the driver's hand. "Thank you so much."

"Not a problem. Not a problem. You just don't use drugs no matter what and get to a AA meeting tonight."

I waved goodbye to this cab driver who had been my guardian angel.

As we walked up the stairs to Tommy's apartment, I said, "I just need to stay with you until I can get a job and figure out what to do next."

"Sure, baby, that's fine."

I sent up a silent prayer, *"Lord, please let him say okay to this part, too."* With my next breath, I laid out the conditions of my staying with him.

"Remember on the phone when I told you that God helped me stop using?"

"Yes."

"Well, I am trying everything a new way now. I got a whole new life and I'm determined to live now the right way—God's way. So for me, this new life means that I cannot have sex with you anymore—us not being married and all. So I can't stay with you unless you understand that I will be sleeping on the couch and not available for your fleshly pleasure."

He looked at me like I had lost my mind. "Say what?"

"Yes, I didn't stutter, you heard me right. And since I don't drink or drug anymore, you got to help me by not having any drugs or alcohol in your apartment. Okay?"

"Now, let's just hold up a minute here. You carrying me a bit too fast. I got to think about all that."

I stopped walking, determined to stand my ground, even if it meant having to go to a homeless shelter.

He walked on. Realizing I was not beside him, he stopped and looked back for me, and barely over a whisper he nodded his head and said, "Okay. If that's the way you want it."

All of us need help at some point in our lives. I believe that the hardest part for us, sometimes, is admitting that we need help. We live in a society that tells us only the strong survive—that we have the power to create our own reality—

to pull ourselves up and out of any muck and mire—if we but put our minds to it. But some situations all the willpower and positive thinking in the world will not and cannot change. Sometimes, we have to have our backs against the wall, be at the end of our road, at the edge of some death-defying cliff with nowhere else to go but over into the rocks and certain death below. I was emotionally and spiritually at that point in my life before I was able to cry out to God to help me. The God of my youth—the God I had heard about but was not sure existed. However, at that point I figured if I cried out and there really was no God, I would be totally screwed! Oh, but I'm here to share with you that God heard my cry and came to my rescue.

Another misconception I had was that I had to clean myself up and then go to God. I actually believed that he would not even consider my prayers if I wasn't living right—if my life was a mess. I found that no matter how I tried to get it together nothing worked and it was while at this crossroads in my life that I admitted I was powerless and that my life had become unmanageable. As best I could—I surrendered. I cried out, "I can't, but maybe like they say—you can." God heard and set me on a new path—gave me a new beginning.

What He has done for me, He is willing to do for you, or a loved one, or a stranger on the street. Perhaps you feel like you are at the edge of cliff, thinking that there is no way out. Perhaps you are saying to yourself, "Once I clean myself up, I'll go to God" or "When I'm older" or "Things are not that bad for me." But let me ask you: "Do you have peace in and with your life?" Do you have an intimate relationship with the Living God who promises to give you life more abundantly? Do you know God's wonderful purpose and plan for your life? God wants to give you a new beginning at whatever crossroads you may find yourself right now.

Once we start walking out our lives on God's tailored path, I found that there must be daily surrender. I dare not mislead you, surrender doesn't come easy for people who have ingrained in them the faulty philosophy of William Ernest Henley's poem "Invictus": "I am the master of my fate: I am the captain of my soul."

However, once we see the fruit of surrender—love, joy, peace, patience, and changed lives—it becomes easier to surrender that which is just too much for us to handle—namely, living and all that comes with it.

God is able and will, if we ask, pick us up, dust us off, and set us on a new path that will produce maximum fruit in our lives.

Dear Heavenly Father: We are so glad that what you do for one, you will do for another. Someone right now is in need of the kind of help that only you can give. They may have a loved one caught in the grip of addiction, they may even be caught up themselves; they may not even have a drug or alcohol problem, but they just need to know that you hear their prayers and that help is on the way. You know all things, Father, and we are just trusting that you will take care of whatever it is that is weighing heavy on their hearts. You are the Weight Lifter and the Way Maker. Thank you for the people that you bring into our lives to help us on our way and the Guardian Angels that are camped all around us—standing ready to protect and remind us that you will never leave nor forsake us. You alone are worthy to be praised! Amen. So be it!

"Behold, I am with you and will keep you wherever you go,
And will bring you back to this land;
For I will not leave you until I have done what I have spoken
to you."

GENESIS 28:15 (New King James Version)

I AM WHO I AM

Although I asked God to forgive me for all the wrongs I had done, the good that I had left undone, and to change my life from the inside out, it was not easy for me to embrace God as my Heavenly Father. Even though I had read in the Bible, "Therefore, if anyone is in Christ, he is a new creation; old things have passed away; behold, all things have become new" (2 Corinthians 5:17, New King James Version), being new to my faith-walk, it seemed that the old me was dying hard! I had so much old baggage that I was dragging into this new relationship with God.

I felt alone in my struggle. How could I tell people just what was going on in my mind? I knew that it was not holy and yet the Bible said, "But just as he who called you is holy, so be holy in all you do."

I wondered, *Why wasn't I getting it? Why was this not a reality in my life yet?* I dared not admit this to others because what would people think? That's the way I was brought up: "Don't do this. Don't do that. After all is said and done, what will the neighbors think?" That was my family's creed. I still carried around with me those old attitudes.

I had to struggle at night when I got down on my knees and tried to sincerely pray, "Our Father who art in heaven." I started to be honest with God in my prayers and tell Him exactly where I was and where I was not in my faith. I realized that I was using my earthly references to try to refer to the heavenly omnipotent God. I had to learn how to surrender the old baggage to God before God could take me through to the next level in Him.

I realized that I was transferring my past experiences with men onto the personage of God the Father. Just the word "Father" brought back a flood of memories that were so dark I could not find my way through to get ahold of the reality of God as my Heavenly Father. Whenever I heard, read, saw, or said the word "father," I immediately thought of my own earthbound father.

"Father" to me meant "absent." Absent emotionally and physically. "Father" to me meant the pain and suffering of being abandoned, ridiculed, and belittled for most of my life.

"Father" meant "critical." I thought of the letters that I wrote home while I was in college. My dad would edit them and send them back to me with comments written in the margins. One read, "Did you notice that you wrote Daddy with a capital D and Momma with a small m?" I'd think, *No I didn't notice nor do I care. I just want you to write me back and sign it "Love, Dad."*

"Father" meant "threats." I thought about the days that my dad drove me to the door of the women's detention center and threatened to take me in to be locked up in one of the jail cells unless I promised not to run away again. I wondered, *Why doesn't he ask me why I run away?*

"Father" meant "comparisons." I could hear my dad's harsh voice bragging on other folks' children saying, "So-and-so's daughter is doing thus and so. Why can't you do that or be like her, him, or them?"

"Father" meant "unprotected." I remembered the look of disgust on my father's face as he looked down at me on the floor, after my mother, in one of her fits of rage, had beat me and threw a spray starch can at my head. Exasperated, he pointed to my mother, who lay sprawled on the chair from the exhaustion of beating me, and offered his summation: "Look what you've done to your mother."

"Father" meant "perform." I thought of my dad putting me on display. "Go get your tap shoes, baby, and dance for us." Or when I got older, taking me to politically inspired events because my mother didn't want to go and he needed to show his constituents that he was indeed a "family man."

The word "father" also meant "men." Men like my first husband, who packed and left me at the first sign of trouble three months into the marriage. The man who eventually became my second husband, who raped me at will and slapped me so hard that I heard lights and saw bells. The three men who beat and raped me when I was fourteen years old who promised to kill me if I told anybody what happened. My first boyfriend, who at sixteen years old broke into my parents' home while they were out of town, held me down and sodomized me.

I recalled my brother banging on my window on a cold early morning, coked up out of his mind and begging for money. I was so afraid of what he would do and what someone would do to him, as I didn't live in the best of neighborhoods at the time, that I called the police and had them take him away.

I recalled the day just as I had fed my two-week-old son and put him in his crib for an afternoon nap. I relaxed and looked forward to his father coming home. However, at the exact moment that the telephone rang, our son cried out at the top of his little lungs. I ran to his bedroom, picked him up, and answered the telephone. As I stood there, trying to comfort little Michael, I listened to the soft masculine voice on the other end of the line as he informed me that my son's father had been arrested and would not be coming home. My son's father was sentenced to years in prison, leaving our new baby and me alone.

So you see, if God was a man how could I trust him? It was hard for me even to believe that he could love a "damaged" woman like me. These were my thoughts. This was my dilemma. We did not go over stuff like this in the Bible study group and I sure couldn't raise my hand in church and let somebody know what was on my mind and expect empathy. I felt alone. I was also afraid because if God couldn't or wouldn't love me—nor I Him—then what?

Then one day I was reading my Bible seeking the answers to my questions. I read the story about Moses, of how having seen the burning bush and given his assignment to deliver God's people, Moses said to God,

> *"Indeed, when I come to the children of Israel and say to them, 'The God of your fathers has sent me to you,' and they say to me, 'What is His name?' what shall I say to them." And God said to Moses, "I AM WHO I AM." And He said, "Thus you shall say to the children of Israel. I AM has sent me to you." (Exodus 3:13–14, New King James Version)*

I reread the verses and pondered them and asked God, "Let me not lean on my own understanding, what are you saying to me in these verses?" My eyes locked in on the capital letters printed on the page, "I AM." I thought, *I am what?* My need to know was great and I was not letting God loose until I had understanding that would help me.

For days I meditated on these verses and then, in the stillness of the night, thoughts so clear and perfect came into my mind that I knew they had to be coming from God in answer to my prayer. *"I AM. I AM WHO I AM. Whatever you need me to be—I AM. You need me to be Black? I AM. You need me to be white, yellow, Indian? I AM. You need me to be loving, kind, merciful, forgiving? I AM. You need me to be a woman? I AM. You need me to be whatever you need me to be? I AM. I AM all things and no one thing. I AM mineral, water, solid, vegetable, transparent, air. Whatever and whoever you need me to be, Stanice—I AM WHO I AM."*

I wept as I whispered a prayer, "I need you to be something totally different than anything or anyone I've ever known. I need you to be greater and more powerful than anything or anyone I've ever even heard about."

Again, a thought was laid in my mind like a soft comfortable pillow: *"I AM WHO I AM."*

The concept was far beyond my limited understanding; but I found comfort in the simple words to Moses. So much so that my heart seemed to leap in my chest as I felt my deepest need and spiritual hunger finally being met.

Slowly, I embraced the concept of God as my Heavenly Father. As I lifted up my wounded heart and emotions to God in prayer, the healing process began. Through years of seeking to build a very personal and intimate relationship with God, I have found Him to be a father to the fatherless, a husband to the husbandless, and brother to the brotherless. God became to me the father I never had but always needed and the husband I always wished for but didn't get. No man, woman, or child could ever have filled that void. Only God could fill it because He created the void that could only be filled by Him. I realize that all my life I looked for love in all the loveless places. The love that I yearned for all my life, God alone has supplied.

Now, "Father" means "forgiveness." The forgiveness I've received is the forgiveness I freely give. Don't weep for me but rejoice with me—Because I am not a victim. My name is Stanice. I am a survivor and a grateful daughter of I AM WHO I AM.

Perhaps you struggle with the same thing. Perhaps the same sorts of pictures plague your mind when you hear certain words. Know this—you are not alone! Many of us have had at some time in our lives words, sights, sounds, smells, tastes that would conjure up all kinds of menacing ghosts in our closets. Ghosts that we would really rather not deal with but we come to know that if we don't, one day the ghosts will come out of the closets and never go back in.

Sure, we can deny that the baggage exists; but we can also dare to believe that God loves us as much with the baggage as he does without it. We can choose to surrender our baggage to God and let Him fix it because we can never do so on our own. You have nothing to lose but the past, which cannot be changed, but the baggage can keep you from living in the present and hoping for the future.

We can get down on our knees and recognize our need for God to do for us what we cannot do for ourselves. This is the beginning of purging the ghosts in the closet. We can refuse to be held captive anymore.

How about you? What baggage are you lugging around? What ghosts in your closet need purging? Darkness flees in the Presence of God.

Dear Heavenly Father: Thank you that you meet us at the place of our need. Thank you that you know the old baggage that we may be carrying now or have carried in the past. We thank you right now that darkness and light cannot coexist. We seek your face, right now, Daddy God. Show us who we are in You. Remind us of your unchanging love, protection, and care. Wrap your invisible arms around us, whisper in our thoughts, in the stillness of the night or in the day's activities, "(<u>say your name here</u>), I love you. You are mine and I have called you by name." Amen. So be it!

For you were once darkness, but now you are light in the
Lord.
Walk as children of light
(For the fruit of the Spirit is in all goodness, righteousness,
and truth),
Finding out what is acceptable to the Lord.
And have no fellowship with the unfruitful works of darkness
But rather expose them.

EPHESIANS 5:8–11 (New King James Version)

Whispers of Doubt

Have you ever listened to the Whispers of Doubt? I have. I was writing inspirational stories that I e-mailed daily to people around the world. To be honest with you, I thought about not writing them anymore because maybe I had misunderstood God's direction to write the stories. I felt that God reassured me at each sitting that I was in His will because the words flowed so easily and I felt so at home whether on the computer keyboard or with a pen and piece of paper. Even under these favorable conditions, I started to doubt God's ability to see me through this. I started listening to the Whispers of Doubt.

One friend called me and said that I had misspelled words in my story. Another friend called and said that my stories delved into issues that were just too deep for human consumption. Slowly but surely the whispers grew louder. I allowed those comments to negate everything positive that I felt about my stories as well as the wonderful comments I'd received from strangers.

Questions and remarks swirled around in my brain like, *"What makes you think that God would give you such an assign-*

ment? You're misspelling words, your words are not communicating God's truths clearly."

The Whispers of Doubt gathered such velocity and punch that I felt like a nearly defeated fighter in the ring, so at the imaginary bell's sounding, I limped back to my corner drained and tired, feeling like I couldn't possibly go another round with Doubt. I was out of my league. Doubt was a heavyweight champion and I was only a featherweight contender—a wannabe. Back in my corner of the ring in a semiconscious state from the direct blows to my head and heart, I sent up a silent prayer.

It appeared that my prayer was heard and God sent my readers, guided by ministering angels, ringside.

In the next moment, the telephone rang. It was my dear friend Traci. Excitement filled her voice as she told me that she had gotten phone calls from people from across the country, asking her one basic question: "Where is the *Food for the Spirit* e-mail?"

I told her about my bout with Doubt.

"Doubt lies," she hurled at me and then continued without taking a breath, "I told you that there would be those who would come at you with negative stuff. But don't listen. Stanice, you've got to keep writing. Don't stop. I'm telling you, these people, half of whom we don't even know, are telling you they want to read more of your stories. How much confirmation from God do you need?"

Her words, harshly spoken as they were, hit my heart like a doctor armed with a defibrillator, shocking me back to life. "Clear? Clear!" Then ZAP. "I got a pulse!" the nurse watching the monitor exclaims.

You know how sometimes people can say something to you and you just know God is breathing every word? Every word they utter bypasses the head and goes straight to the heart. Well, I knew that God was in the midst of answering my prayer. The tears welled in my eyes and with the next blink they escaped and ran down my cheeks toward the telephone receiver. It was my Heavenly Father speaking through Traci. I felt the kiss of a personal God who knew my thoughts and hushed the Whispers of Doubt.

Coincidence that my telephone had rung at the moment it did? That my soul thirsted for a Word from God and, whoops, there it was? That my readers took the time to call her? No. Not coincidence at all. And so today, accept this salve for your soul—the same God who hears my feeble prayers, hears yours. And *He will answer.*

Dear Heavenly Father: Thank you for hearing and answering our prayers. Thank you that greater are You than the doubts that fill our inner world. As we limp back into our corners at the sounding of life's bell, we ask that you continue to strengthen, refresh, and hush the whispers of doubt so that we may fight the good fight and finish the race set before us. Continue to surround us with godly counsel that will tell us not what we may want to hear but what we need to hear. Surround us with people who will encourage and uplift us especially in these last days. With and because of You, we already have the victory. Amen. So be it!

Blessed is the man who endures temptation;
For when he has been approved,
He will receive the crown of life which the Lord has promised
to those who love him.
Let no man say when he is tempted, "I am tempted by God";
for God cannot be
Tempted by evil, nor does He Himself tempt anyone.

JAMES 1:12–13 (New King James Version)

✳

FAITH

✳

Start Packing

"Dorine, no one is going to rent me an apartment."

"Baby, you don't know that."

"But Dorine, my credit is bad. Plus, I only make $5 an hour."

"You just act like you gonna move and start packing."

"But Dorine—"

She cut me off. "Where is your faith? Start packing. God will take care of the rest."

As I hung up the telephone, I wondered, *What kind of philosophy is that? Just start packing?* I was only thirty-seven days clean and sober. I had a job, but it was ten miles outside the city and I didn't have a car. It took most of my salary for transportation to work and to recovery support groups. However, I knew I had to get out of my living situation. I was living with Tommy, a man I knew when I was using. Although he allowed me to sleep on his couch and didn't bother me, he did have women who came in and out all times of the night to shoot heroin and smoke marijuana.

Me in my own apartment? The thought entered my mind again and tickled my heart. I smiled and walked to the hall closet to get my pillow and sheets to lay across the musty black sectional sofa in the living room where I slept. As was my custom in his apartment before sitting, lying, or kneeling, I checked to make sure there were no roaches crawling in the immediate area. I thought it strange that while I was using drugs, I didn't mind the roaches. As long as they didn't get in my dope, we could coexist.

Before I lay down for the night, I knelt to pray. "Lord, thank you for yet another day clean and sober. With what little faith I have, can you please make a way for me to move into my own place?"

In the background I heard knocking on the door and then I felt the vibration of footsteps as someone walked through the living room. A woman laughed. "Is that who I think that is on her knees?"

"Leave her alone," someone whispered, coming to my defense.

"Lord, help me say no to whatever is about to happen here. Help me get through this night without using any drugs."

The next morning I awoke feeling refreshed and well rested for the first time since I had stopped using. With a new resolve and a bit of hope, I went to work. While on a break, I telephoned the senior pastor of the church I had joined while I was still on methadone. While I waited for him to come to the phone, I thought about his assistant pastor, Reverend John Kinard, who a few months prior had arranged for me to get into a residential treatment center. *God made a way then*, I thought.

Once he was on the phone, I assured him that I was still drug-free. I then went on to explain my living situation and asked if he knew anyone in the church who might have a room I could rent.

"Well, I don't know anyone with rooms but there are a few people that own or manage apartment buildings."

I wrote down the information, thanked him, and promised to call back with an update. I left work that day with an empty box under my arm. When I got back to Tommy's apartment, I started packing.

"You're moving?"

"Yep. I'm moving."

"You got your own place? That's great!"

"Well, not exactly. Not yet, but, it's coming. I just want to be ready when it does."

His eyebrows furrowed. With slightly squinted eyes, he looked at me for further explanation. But when he saw that I had none to offer, he walked back to his bedroom.

I sat on the end of the sofa and looked down at my box. It saddened me that I had no household items.

"Stacey, for your box."

I looked up. Tommy's outstretched arms held two powder blue bath towels with matching washcloths and a Big Ben–type alarm clock, new in a box, balanced on the top of the pile. "I was saving these for a special occasion. I think this qualifies."

Whether we are in a homeless shelter or a palace, there is a step that we need to take to get to that next rung on the ladder to our dreams and desires. We must come to believe that God will give us the faith to take that next step. All we have to do is ask. We have not because we ask not. In taking that next step, we will find that God will meet us there in that next step. We need to move past talking about all the things we want to do and couple the words with some action. Thereby, we move from lip service to stepping-out-on-faith service.

If we want to write a novel that we say we want to write, just start writing. If we say we want to leave an abusive relationship, just start leaving. If we want to be in the next television commercial, just start auditioning. If we want to go on that vacation of a lifetime, just start saving. If we want to ace that test, just start studying. If we want the job we've desired for a long time, just start getting together our résumé.

The variables are as many as the grains of sand on the oceans' shores. We must fill in our own blanks with the desires of our hearts and "just start packing." Just like a muscle atrophies if not used, so will our faith if we don't use it. Little faith becomes much faith when we exercise it. It's as simple as this—we won't get to Step Two in God's wonderful plan for our lives until we've taken Step One.

Dear Heavenly Father: We seize this moment to acknowledge, as did Abraham before us, that You alone are Jehovah-Jireh, God the Provider. Thank you for supplying all our needs, including the helpers that you plant along our path. It's amazing to us how You give us such favor with yourself and with people. Thank you that when we ask, you graciously give us the courage and faith to take the next step. Our faith may sometimes be as tiny as a mustard seed—but because of You—it can still move mountains. Amen. So be it!

You, who have shown me great and severe troubles,
Shall revive me again,
And bring me up again from the depths of the earth.
You shall increase my greatness,
And comfort me on every side.

PSALM 71:20–21 (New King James Version)

Press Your Way

I stepped off the bus, pulled my hat down over my ears, and put on my wool gloves. A group of men stood around the liquor store passing a bottle wrapped tightly with a brown paper bag. One of the men, with tattered pieces of his flimsy trench coat flapping in the wind, checked his fistful of lottery tickets. Children played tag, darting between the parked cars and over the debris-strewn street. Shards of glass sparkled under the streetlights like a garden of clustered diamonds.

I reached in my coat pocket and pulled out the piece of paper with the address of the apartment that I came to view. I held my purse strap tightly to my side and walked briskly down the street. Finally, I saw the address I was looking for. As I climbed the steps, I felt something hard under my shoe. I looked down and could not believe my eyes. It was a bloodied syringe. *This has to be a sign*, I thought. I turned and ran back to the bus stop. This was the fourth apartment in my search to find a place that I could call my own—and again—disappointment.

Maybe Dorine was wrong. Maybe I'll have to live on my friend's sofa until I can at least get a better-paying job. These thoughts made tears well in my eyes but the bus came before the tears escaped. *I'll cry later.*

A week passed and the senior pastor, Dr. G. Ray Coleman of John Wesley A.M.E. Zion Church, telephoned me.

"Did you find an apartment yet?"

"No. I've looked at four. One was rented by the time I got there, one a rat ran from behind the stove, and another I just couldn't afford. And the one I went to see last night? I don't even want to discuss it."

"Well, you just hang in there. It's going to all work out. Don't give up."

Later on that night, I called *The 700 Club* twenty-four-hour prayer line. A woman with a Southern accent answered. I told her what I was going through.

"Please, ask God to give me more faith. I need more faith."

She prayed right over the telephone for me.

While I was at work the next day, I got a phone call from one of the church members, who told me about a vacancy in an apartment building that she managed. She gave me the address and told me where to go to pick up the keys.

After work, I went to look at the apartment. The bus let me off at the corner in front of a liquor store. However, I noticed that it was well kept and no one was hanging around. I headed in the direction of the doctor's office building, adjacent to which was the address I was looking for.

It was a neatly shingled two-story house with the door and windows painted money green. Inside the main door, there were two doors side by side, with black metal numbers, 1 and 2. I unlocked Apartment Number 1 and stepped inside. It had a rather large combination living room and eating area, a small windowless bathroom, one bedroom, and a kitchen. The back door led to a large gray-painted wooden-slat porch with steps leading down to a long and narrow chain-link-fenced yard. I looked to the sky and shouted, *"Lord, I love it. It's perfect."*

And so was the rent: $300 a month with all utilities included plus a $300 deposit. I had about $75 in my savings account. *Where will I get the rest of the money?* I wondered, but I called the manager anyway.

"I would like to rent the apartment."

"Just come down and fill out the application. You pay the money after we run a credit check and your application is approved."

My mind filled with one thought: *With my credit history, I'm dead and stinking in the water.* I went to the office and filled out the application—anyway.

All the way home, negative thoughts bombarded my mind: *You know your credit is bad. You're not getting that apartment.* I continued to pack boxes for the move—anyway.

A couple of days later, the manager called, "The apartment is yours. Just bring the $600."

I called Dr. Coleman. I told him that I had found an apartment but I didn't have the money to move in. He told me he would take my situation to the church's board of directors to see if they could help.

Before I left for work the next morning, Dr. Coleman called me back. "Well, the board reached a decision. The church will loan you $300 and give you $300."

"Thank you!" I hung up the phone and cried tears of joy.

A day later, I picked up the check and took it to the manager of the apartment. I signed the lease and arranged a move-in date. I hummed, sang, and smiled my way through the next two days. On the third day, I was at work when the manager of the apartment called.

"Yes, is everything okay?"

"Well yes and no. Something just popped up. It seems that you owe back rent on a previous apartment. You've got to take care of that bill before we can let you rent this one."

"How much do I owe and who do I owe it to?"

"It says here that you owe $800." She told me whom to contact.

The negative thoughts came back: *See, I told you that you weren't getting no apartment. You'll never get ahead. You don't have enough faith and God ain't heard a word you said.*

I ran out of the office, down the hall, and into the bathroom. I checked to make sure that I was alone and then locked myself in one of the stalls and cried out to God, "Help me, please. I can't go to the church for help—again. Where am I going to get $800? You know I've burned all my bridges. This is all too hard for me, God. Just too hard. I feel so weak." I blew my nose, dabbed cold water on my face, and went back to the office.

On my break, I called the real estate agent I owed. I practically told the man my whole story and then said, "Can we work something out?"

There was silence. Then: "Well, since you are calling us, and not many people with a debt this old even bother to call with a desire to pay, let me talk with my manager and see what he authorizes me to do in your case. Hold on."

I prayed fervently for those next seemingly endless minutes. Then—

"Hello, miss?"

"Yes, I'm still here."

"My manager said that if you send us a check for $300, we would consider your debt paid in full."

"Thank you! God bless you." I wrote down the information. As I hung up, the thought hit me: *Where am I going to get $300 more from?*

This time, I called *700 Club*'s Operation Blessing. I had seen on television how they blessed folks with things that they needed, so I figured maybe they'd bless me. When a lady answered the telephone, I told her my dilemma and asked if they would be willing to help. The woman on the telephone told me that they would check out my story and call me back.

Twenty minutes later she called back, "We checked out your story and I'm pleased to tell you that a check for $300, made out to the company you owe, is in the mail."

Glory! My moving day got closer with every prayer I prayed.

A few days later the manager of the apartment I wanted to rent called. "We got a fax from your old landlord informing us that you paid your debt to them."

"Great! When do I move into my new apartment?"

"Well, the owner of the property said that she would feel better if you had a co-signer."

"A co-signer?"

"Yes. Perhaps you could ask your parents or a friend."

She didn't have a clue that getting somebody to co-sign anything for me was impossible. "Okay, I'll call you back."

This had to be that one last straw that people talked about that broke the camel's back! God would truly understand if I gave up now. I sat down on the floor, put my face in my hands, and sobbed like a milk-less baby. But I prayed anyway. "God, I'm tired, but still I turn to you. You've got to do it for me. I got nobody else to turn to."

The very next day, I got another phone call at work. It was the senior pastor, Dr. Coleman. "You know, I was thinking that you might need a co-signer."

I opened my mouth but nothing came out.

He continued. "I just wanted you to know that if you do need it, the church is willing to co-sign the lease so that you can get into an apartment."

I told him that I did need a co-signer. He also suggested that since I worked so far outside the city, he and a board member would go to the management office, sign the lease, and pick up the keys for me. "You can stop by the church this evening after you get off work to pick up the keys."

At about 8:00 on a frigid February evening, I stepped off the bus and walked past the liquor store—past the doctor's office—made a joyful right turn—and sashayed up the concrete walkway to my new apartment building. With the turn of my new key in the new lock of my new apartment door, I entered my Promised Land—Apartment Number 1—and into a new personal and intimate relationship with God. I sat down on "my" beautiful carpet-less floor and wept like a middle-aged previously childless mother with a newborn.

Oh, how hard it is sometimes to press our way. The way gets dark sometimes. We wonder if God really hears our prayers. And if He does, why does it take Him so long? We want things to come to us easier. We don't want to press our way. Our strength may wane, our hope may fade, our faith may waver; but press on we must! Pray and step, step and pray. Prayer by prayer, and step by step, we start to realize that God does hear our prayers and He does answer right on time—in His perfect timing.

In the midst of the process, we find that we can persevere—that we can endure—and that God will give us exactly what we need at the exact moment that we need it. Theory becomes fact as we practice the spiritual principle of faith in our daily living situations. We learn to walk out our faith—to live by faith and not by sight. Then, we pass that message of encouragement on to the next person God puts on our path who needs to learn how to press their way. Thus, our lives start to align themselves with the pure purposes of God.

Dear Heavenly Father: Thank you for loving us all the same. What you do for one you will do for another. We are reminded, today, that You are the same yesterday, today, and forever. You hear our cries. You shut up the lies of the enemy long enough for us to hear Your sweet Voice in your words, "I am with you always. . . . When you call upon me, I will hear you and I will answer you because I love you and you are precious to me." Amen. So be it!

"Fear not, for I am with you;
Do not be dismayed, for I am your God.
I will strengthen you,
Yes, I will help you,
I will uphold you with My righteous right hand."

Isaiah 41:10 (New King James Version)

With a
Child's Heart

"Mommy what is this?"

"Let's open it up and see, baby?"

My eight-year-old son, Michael, was spending the weekend with me. I had been in recovery from drug addiction for nearly five months and born again a little over a year. Everything was new to me, especially being a mother. From the age of two, his paternal grandmother and father had raised my son. I had moved into his grandmother's with him and then moved out without him. I was still feeling pretty bad about that. So here we were, my son and I getting to know each other. He was so cute. Now, I know all mothers say that about their children. But really, he was cute!

It was Saturday morning and we were both still in our pajamas. I was in the kitchen about to start breakfast when he brought a maroon plastic pouch in to me.

"Unzip it, sweetie."

"Ooh-wee, Mommy, look," he said with such wonder as he saw the pouchful of crayons, markers, pencils, and pens. "You got some paper?"

"Let's see." I went into the bedroom and found a 9 × 12 piece of white cardboard. I handed it to him.

"I'm going to make something real pretty for you, Momma."

"Okay, baby, you do that. I'm going to fix us some breakfast."

"What you gonna make?"

"I'm making us some pancakes. But I'm not making ordinary pancakes, I'm making Mommy's famous, melt-in-your-mouth pancakes from scratch."

The radiant smile on his face almost made me weep. "Yay! Pancakes!"

It seemed the boy could do anything and I thought it was all so precious. When I looked at him sometimes, I thought of all that I had missed by not having him with me and yet I also thought about just how much he was spared from by not having lived with me. Addiction is ugly.

He turned and went to the table in the makeshift dining room in my tiny one-bedroom apartment. "I'm going to draw while you cook, okay?

"Okay." I went into the kitchen. I could hear the radio in the background and I sang along with my oldies but goodies. I knew all the words to every song. My mind flashed back to when I was a young girl. I could almost hear my mother hollering up from the bottom of the stairs in the house where I grew up, "Girl, turn that music down. If you knew your books like you know those songs, you'd really be all right." I kept right on singing in front of the bedroom dresser mirror to my audience of one. Singing one soulful tune after another into the hairbrush that I held in my hand pretending that it was a microphone. The smell of the sausage frying brought my mind back to the present moment.

I mixed the pancake batter to the rhythms and thanked God for giving me another chance at being a mother. I wondered, *Did my son understand why I left him with his grand-*

mother? Would he ever forgive me for not being there for him like other children's mothers were? Whenever we had a quiet moment I would try to explain it to him. "You know your mommy was sick then, baby; but I'm better now. It's going to be different now." But I could never really explain it. I didn't quite understand myself how I could have let the lifestyle get control of me like it did.

My son would look at me like he didn't care about anything I tried to find the words to say. He was just glad to have his mommy back in his life. His soft looks of love would melt my heart. I always looked forward to our weekends together. As I flipped pancakes and listened to the sausage sizzle in the pan I was lost in my thoughts. It all smelled so much like a real home. I wondered *Could I possibly provide a good home for him one day?*

My thoughts were interrupted by that sweet little voice again. Michael stood in the doorway of the kitchen. "Mommy, how do you spell penetrate?"

I couldn't have heard him right. "How do you spell what, Michael?"

"Penetrate. How do you spell penetrate, Mommy?"

Yes, I did hear him right. "And why do you want me to spell that particular word, honey?"

"I'm doing something; but I got to know that first."

"Okay." I thought, *Now don't panic, Stanice. But he's only eight years old. What is my eight-year-old boy doing that he needs to know how to spell penetrate.* Now because I was closer to the streets, with only a few months off drugs, than heaven, being born again for a short time, my mind went straight to—what my parents used to call—the gutter. I mean, when I hear the word "penetrate," I only had one frame of reference. *So what was my boy penetrating in that living room.*

"Mommy! So. How?" Michael brought me back to the moment.

"Well, son, let me see what you're doing. Maybe I can help you."

"No, Mommy, I can't let you see yet. It's a surprise!"

I took a few steps toward the doorway where he stood just to try to stretch my neck and peek into the living room. Michael, who stood to about my waist, pushed me just enough to let me know that I wasn't going into the living room without going through him. *Lord, help me, how do I handle this situation?*

We tugged a bit. I thought that maybe I could turn it into a tickle game. But he wasn't having it. The boy was determined not to let me see whatever was in that living room.

Finally, I surrendered. "Okay, Michael."

He readied his pencil and little scrap of paper. I talked slowly so he could write it down. "Penetrate is spelled p-e-n-e-t-r-a-t-e."

The happy camper held his little scrap of paper with his newly spelled word and ran back into the living room. Here was my chance—

"Now don't come in, Mommy! No peeking." Busted, I reeled my neck in and went back to my pancakes.

After a few minutes, I noticed it was mighty quiet in the living room. "Are you all right, Michael?"

"Yeah, I'm okay. Don't come in yet."

I finished cooking and put the food on the plates and was about to pour the milk.

"Mommy!"

I turned around and there was Michael in the doorway again.

"Look, Mommy. I made this for you."

He proudly held out his freshly created sign. Sandwiched between two large red and blue hearts were the words: Mom and Son—Nothing can penetrate our love.

Tears trailing down my face, I gently pulled him to me. I just hugged and rocked him in my arms. "Michael, this is the most beautiful work of art I have ever seen. Thank you, baby, so much. I love you so."

"I know, Mommy. I love you too."

Never in a thousand thoughts did I think that the incredible relationship that my son and I share would be possible. I believe that the weekend this story took place, was the beginning of our relationship's healing process. Through years of keeping my word, no matter what, showing up when I said I would, listening to him, becoming vulnerable with him, and sharing similar experiences allowed us to grow as a mother-son team, in spite of the fact that he continued to live with his father and paternal grandparents. It has not been without its blunders, heartaches, and tears, as you will come to see in other stories that I will share with you, but all in all, God has worked everything for our good. I just kept praying and kept trying. As Michael would not give up on me, I refused to give up on us.

I found in my faith-walk journey that many of us have done things in our past that we are not proud of, are embarrassed about, or even feel a residue of shame when we think about the selfishness and self-centeredness of some of the bad choices we made. However, some of us have also experienced the unconditional love of a child, whether our own or someone else's, and as a result of looking into these forgiving faces our cooled hearts are warmed and we get a glimpse of God's unconditional love and forgiveness.

Now, the hardest part for me has been to be as easy on myself as my child and God have been on me. All of us make mistakes; it's a part of life. But we get up and move on to the next thing carrying the lesson with us in hopes of making the next decision wiser than the one before it. All of us fall down sometimes, but we need to get back up, not beat ourselves up over it. We need to be gentler with ourselves, as well as with others. "Be easy on the people," a friend once told me. Why are we so hard on others? Perhaps because we are so hard on ourselves.

By praying and believing that if we have a child's heart and faith, a change will come—eventually it will. Perhaps even sooner than you think.

Dear Heavenly Father: Thank you for the unconditional love of a child. Thank you that they look past our flaws and see beneath the surface to our hearts—just like you. Love covers a multitude of sins. We get a glimpse of your face in their eyes and it frees our minds to believe that anything is possible. We are your children and what a wonderful Heavenly Father we have in You. There is peace and joy in Your presence. Today, we come to you as children, to thank you, because nothing can penetrate our Love. Amen. So be it!

In that hour, Jesus rejoiced in the Spirit and said,
"I thank You,
Father, Lord of heaven and earth,
That You have hidden these things from the wise and prudent
And revealed them to babes.
Even so, Father, for so it seemed good in Your sight."

LUKE 10:21 (New King James Version)

Precious
Moments

"Mommy! Grandma wants to know what time you gonna pick me up."

"Tell her about 6:30."

"Wait a minute. Grandma! My mommy say she coming at 6:30. Okay, I'm back."

"We're going to have a great time, Michael. Plus your mommy gonna sing real good for you, okay?"

"Okay, Mommy."

"I love you. See you later."

"I love you too."

I was getting used to being with my son again, even though it was mostly on the weekends. Still less than one year off drugs and in his life on a regular basis, I didn't have the mommy thing down pat. My hope was that it would get better. In the meantime, I called him when I said I would call and went by to see him when I said I would. He was learning that Mommy's word was good. It never had been before. Many a day, my son waited for me to come and I did not show up. I had missed the measles and mumps; but now God was giving me another chance and I was grateful.

That night we were going to a talent show together. I would be like all the other mothers that had their children with them. I wanted them to see my little boy and know that I was a mom too.

I had practiced for this talent show for weeks. A woman named Barbara Noonan, who had a thick New York accent, was directing the show. She said I had talent, although I did not think so, and that with hard work I could be one of the stars of the show. I said, "Sure, you're right." But I didn't believe her. Still, I showed up for every rehearsal. Although I had sung at a friend's funeral, I felt more comfortable singing in the seclusion of a shower. Give me a bar of soap, some running water, and the perfect acoustics of a closed bathroom—and Diana Ross look out! But Barbara believed I could sing in the talent show in front of all those people, so I believed in her belief and said that I would try.

During the earlier rehearsals, with my head down watching every step, I'd meandered onto the stage with microphone in hand and faced the back wall rather than the audience of ten to fifteen people. The song I attempted to sing was "Ooo Baby Baby" which was written and recorded by William "Smokey" Robinson. I knew all the lyrics and by the sixth rehearsal got pretty bold and even a bit animated while I sang; but I still faced the back wall. The people at rehearsals prodded and begged, "Stanice, turn around. You can do it. Come on, turn girl, turn!" In my heart, I really wanted to face the audience, but in my mind I was having a conversation with myself: *Now, you know you can't really sing They like you, that is why they are being so supportive. If you turn around, you'll know by looking at their faces that they really want you to sit down and shut up.*

Then one day at rehearsal it happened! I made a half turn toward the audience but now I was facing the stage door. A woman's voice echoed through the near empty theater: "I don't believe this woman. No, she didn't just turn to face the other wall. So what's this? You know every crack and crevice on the back wall and now you're going to study the stage door."

Barbara came to my rescue: "Leave her alone. In her own time, she'll turn around. She keeps coming back to rehearsals doesn't she? She knows that eventually she will do this."

Barbara had a point there. I did keep coming back. Maybe I would turn and face the audience sooner than I imagined.

Finally, about one week before the night of the talent show, as I sang, without missing a beat, I slowly turned around and faced the audience.

My friends in the audience cheered and clapped. "It's a miracle! Thank you, God!" Actually, I felt the same way—this had to be a miracle.

Then Barbara seized the opportunity. She demanded that I sing with feeling and move around the stage as I sang. She called out to the guy that I dated at the time, "Marty come on down." He practically ran down the aisle like he had been chosen to tell the millions of TV viewers at home what price was right.

"Sing to Marty, Stanice. There's your man standing right there. He's longing to know just what's on your mind. Tell him. Convince him just how much you love him. Tell him how you feel. Forget us. There's no one here but you and your man. Sing your heart out to Marty."

That almost worked. Maybe if I loved Marty, I could have been there and done that. But . . .

Somewhere around 4:30 on the day of the show, as I ate dinner, I thought about picking up Michael. It was hard for me to accept all he had been through because of my lifestyle and that he didn't live with me even though I was clean and sober.

As these thoughts overwhelmed me, I picked at my dinner and tears began to fall into my food. I hated when our time was over and I'd have to take him back. It seemed that we said goodbye too much. Mommies and sons shouldn't have to say goodbye every Sunday or at the end of a weekday visit. They were all "visits." It was hard learning to live with the consequences of my actions. My mind understood that—but my heart ached at such an unnatural situation.

I scraped my food into the trash can and decided to get dressed instead of moping. I put on a borrowed black off-the-shoulder evening dress, black feather boa, and black patent leather pumps. As I stood in the mirror and applied my makeup, I promised God and myself that, for my little boy, I would sing like a star. *"Tonight, my son is going to be proud of his mommy!"* I blotted my lipstick and as in the movie *All That Jazz*, I looked in the mirror and said, "Show time!" (I have always been a bit dramatic.) I smiled as I thought of my mentor, Dorine, who would laugh and say, "Stanice, don't go Hollywood on the people."

Since I didn't have a car yet, my son and I went to the talent show in a taxi. He never minded whether it was on the bus or in a cab; it was clear to me that he was just glad to have his mommy back. That was a gift of God, as far as I was concerned. The way he looked at me just lit up my life and made everything easier to bear, including the burdens I put on myself. To Michael, I was special. I'd see those graciously gentle eyes and know that saying yes to a life of faith in God, through Jesus Christ, and having my son were the two best decisions I ever made!

When we got to the auditorium where the talent show was to be held, I proudly introduced my son to everybody. However, I thought he would be more outgoing than he was, but he clung to me, almost hiding behind me. As I held him close, I realized just how little I knew about my boy and I thought, *How would I pry loose the secrets that the lost years held? What were his favorite colors? What did he absolutely love the most to eat? What frightened him? What brought him joy? But my son will be waiting for me; I'll think about all this tomorrow.*

I found seats up front and, when it was time for me to go on, I kissed him and went backstage.

Barbara, the director, said, "Stanice, you can do this. You're going to be just fine. I believe in you. Now, go sing your heart out."

There was no sense in me telling her that my mouth seemed too dry to sing, the butterflies were waging a battle of the wings in my stomach, and that I felt like I needed to go to the bathroom again. She would just tell me that it was all in my mind. Maybe she would be right that it was all in my mind; but what I tasted and felt was fear with a capital F.

As I stood behind the curtain I wondered, *If I back out of the show they'll understand. They can't make me sing.* But then I peeped through the opening in the curtain and saw my son. I knew I had to go through with it. *"God, help me. Take away the fear and stop the trembling. I want you and Michael to be proud of me."*

The MC finished his jokes and then announced, "Is everybody having a good time?"

It sounded like a chorus of thousands of people shouting, "Yes! Woop! Woop!"

My heart jumped a beat. I wrung my hands repeatedly, not knowing what else to do with them.

And then that dreaded moment of moments. The MC's voice reverberated throughout the auditorium. "And now we really have a treat for you. Just back from her European tour—straight from the airport to grace our meager stage—put your hands together and let's give her a warm, wonderful welcome . . ."

With me standing middle stage, the curtain slowly opened.

"Here she is, ladies and gentlemen. Our very own Stanice."

As I looked out over the audience, my whole body seemed to go numb. *My God. Look at all these people. There must be over three hundred here tonight.* It was standing room only. They clapped. Men and women shouted, "That's my girl." "All right now!" "Go for it, girl!"

I thought, *Right, wait until you hear me sing, you'll regret that you came.* And then it was like an angel tapped me on the shoulder and reminded me to focus on my son. Once I saw him standing smiling and clapping, I knew I could do anything. I felt like I could fly if I really wanted to!

In the next moment, music filled the air—melodious chords of keyboards, the lilting strums of guitars, the slow beat of the drums, and the soft sweeping of the snare. The perfectly timed rhythms seemed to slip through a shutter to my soul. As the stage crew lowered the lights in the auditorium, the audience seemed to hide away. As they raised the gold and red sultry lights on me, I seemed to board the music in the air. I opened my mouth and the sounds signaled that I was about to take flight. My contralto voice widened and swallowed the song whole as I sang. I hit the low mellow notes and rolled them on up like never before. *"Ooo-Ooo-Ooo baby baby. Ooo-Ooo-Ooo baby baby."*

All my thoughts came in notes, rhythms, and a longing in my heart to sing to the man I always looked for but never seemed to find—until that night. By that time I started moving all across that stage, pleading Smokey's heartfelt lyrics. I kept singing and motioning to the crowd, bringing them deeper and deeper into the song with me.

The audience went wild. Shouting. Screaming. I sang that song! I flipped and flung that black boa. My shoulder played peek-a-boo with the black evening dress. I perspired from the heat of the lights. But none of that mattered. I was gone—in flight. I ad-libbed for five minutes after all the verses were all sung out. Some say I even got down on my knees. And they may be right; I don't remember. It was my world and everybody was welcome to it! With that last *"Oooooooooooooo,"* I started low-range and ended up amid the stars.

I breathed and was jolted out of my trance by the sound of thunderous applause. I felt like I was born for that moment! The lights in the auditorium came on. Everyone stood up. Some people jumped up and down and some waved their arms, whooping and hollering. I looked at my son as he clapped and jumped around excitedly. Although I couldn't hear him above the crowd, I saw his lips making the words, "Mommy, Mommy."

During the last curtain call, I raised my head to the sky, opened up my arms and looked toward heaven with the applause as a perfectly laid-down soundtrack. I said, "You heard me, God, you really heard me!"

Many of us have something that we've always wanted to do or be but were afraid to try. There came this time in my life where other people believed that I could and it was infectious. There are people in our lives that encourage us to the point that we start to believe, "Yeah, maybe I can do this thing." For me, that simple little talent show was the beginning of my stepping out of my comfort zone and doing something I always wanted to do—sing for somebody other than myself in a shower stall.

We all have to decide to take that first step. No matter how tiny that step may seem to us, it's a step in the right direction toward the plans that God has for our lives. Once we are willing, and it is our actions that show our willingness, we will find that we do not have to take the steps alone. My experiences have proven to me that God is a God of everyday step taking. As I trusted, God showed up at every turn—through the director, through my son, through the friends that encouraged me. At the moment that we call out for help—we must believe in our hearts that help is on the way. Watch how God works. Help can come from where we least expect.

Dear Heavenly Father: Thank you for the precious moments of grace when we feel Your presence so strongly. The moments when we know beyond a shadow of a doubt that you hear us, know us, and love us. Thank you for the tender moments with our loved ones and friends who spur us on. It is awesome how you surround us with people who believe in us even when we don't believe in ourselves. We see Your love in their eyes. We feel Your touch when they wrap their arms around us, hold us as we cry, and tell us, "It's gonna be all right." They help us come to believe in the realness of you and in the nearness of you. These precious people, no matter how few, help us to feel our worth in You. They remind us that we were not born by mistake but that we are part of Your master plan. Each of us has something to give to the world that no one else can give in quite the same way that You enable us to give. You just planned it that way and we are grateful. What mercy and love you shower down on us! Amen. So be it!

Brethren, I do not count myself to have apprehended:
But one thing I do,
Forgetting those things which are behind
And reaching forward to those things which are ahead,
I press toward the goal for the prize
Of the upward call of God in Christ Jesus.
Therefore let us, as many as are mature, have this mind;
And if anything you think otherwise,
God will reveal even this to you.

PHILIPPIANS 3:13–15 (New King James Version)

Carrie's Comforter

I climbed the steep stairs up to the semidetached brick home that I had climbed so often when I was a kid. I always loved to come here. Unlike my parents' house, love lived in this home. This was the first day that I had been there in about five years. Once I had crossed that thin line between recreational drug use to addiction, family and friends were replaced with "half-on-a-package partners" and "cohorts."

I knocked on the wooden door. The wind was whipping my legs. I should have worn a long coat. I knocked again. I heard a woman's voice. "Wait a minute. I'm coming." The voice grew louder. "Who is it?"

"Carrie, it's me. Stanice."

Through the windowpane located high up on the door, I saw those hazel brown eyes that belonged to my godmother, Carrie, peering out at me.

I heard that laugh of hers that always sounded like some-one was tickling her. "My Lord! Neicy is that you?"

"Yes, it's Neicy." That's what my family calls me. It always sounded so babyish to me but today it sounded like a wake-up call reminding me that I was still part of a family.

She unlatched the three locks on the main door, then flipped the lock up on the storm door and let me in.

"Hi, Carrie."

"Well, baby, look at you. Don't you look good." She hugged me tight.

It was like she hugged the guilt I felt for not being a better goddaughter right out of me because I just started crying. "Carrie, I missed you. I'm so sorry I haven't been here for you."

"Baby, it's all right. You're here now. That's all that matters."

I attempted to explain but she stopped me.

"Hush, now, sweetie. I'm not mad. I was worried about you but I heard you doing good now."

"Yes, I've been clean for over a year now. I don't drink or use drugs."

"Well, baby, I'm certainly glad to hear that. Now, are you hungry? I fixed a nice dinner today and there's a lot left over."

"Okay."

I sat down at the dining room table and ate while she sat across from me and watched me eat. I'd catch her smiling each time I looked up. We talked and she caught me up on who in the family was doing what.

"You know I've been here by myself since my Sam died. I tried having a boarder one time; but it didn't work out. I like my privacy and I guess I'm just set in my ways."

Carrie and her husband, Sam, who was actually my cousin, never had kids. They treated me like I was their daughter. I had never experienced a couple that seemed so in love with each other as Carrie and Sam. They were like peanut butter and jelly, cornbread and fish. I could not fathom one without the other. I knew there had to be a tremendous gap left in Carrie's life without Sam. "It's strange not having Sam here. I miss him."

90

"Yeah." She changed the subject. People said she wouldn't talk about Sam. I guess we all have our way of not dealing with what aches us the most. Nobody knew that better than I.

That day was the beginning of a new relationship between goddaughter and godmother. I knew that I owed her amends for not being there to help her through her difficult times, so from that point on, I'd stop by, do her shopping, clean up her house, whatever she needed done. She had arthritis in her hands and legs, so I would rub them. I felt I had to make up for lost time.

Of course, she would try to give me money, and sometimes I would really be pressed, but my spirit just would not let me take it.

One day I was upstairs cleaning the bathtub and she hollered up the stairs, "Now, Neicy, you got to let me give you some money for cleaning the bathroom."

I hollered back, "No, Carrie. If I let you give me money, that would be my reward on earth and God won't reward me in Heaven."

"Say what?"

"I can't explain better than that, Carrie. That's just where I am right now. We read that chapter the other day in Bible study."

"Well, bless your heart," she said.

On my next visit, I was sitting in the living room on the cream-colored sofa that looked as good as the day Carrie and Sam bought it in the 1960s. I'm sure that was due to the plastic slipcovers that were starting to stick to my arms and legs. Carrie sat in the dining room with her chair turned with the back against the wall. We were talking like we usually did but this time there was no laughing. And I thought I was being funny. I liked to make her laugh. But this day, I could tell she wasn't really present in the moment with me. She was deep in thought about something. Every now and then she would lean her head back against the patterned wallpaper and just stare off into empty space.

"Carrie, is anything wrong?"

"No, baby. I'm okay."

"No, you're not, Carrie. Something is wrong. Do you hurt somewhere?"

"I don't want to bother you."

"Bother me, please. Talk to me."

I got up and took the few steps into the dining room. I saw that her eyes were watery. I got down on my knees in front of her and took her hands in mine.

"You are not okay. Tell me what I can do to help you."

She leaned forward in the chair. "Neicy, I miss Sam. I miss my handsome Sam."

Her hazel eyes seemed to stare through my eyes and into my soul for a solution to her inconsolable pain. I searched my mind for the words but there were none. I could not relate to a loss as great as hers. I just held her hands as she rocked and cried. I laid my cheek on her hands. I wished I could draw the pain out of her heart into mine, if but for a few minutes. I wanted to take her burden, give her some relief of what must have been years of suffering without her Sam. Yet I was powerless to help this precious woman who had loved me all of my life, so I just rocked and cried with her.

Suddenly, she broke the silence with a riveting question. "Neicy, when I die will I see my Sam?"

"Carrie, I—"

"Neicy, I'm afraid to die because I'm afraid that I still won't see Sam. Will I see my Sam? I've wanted to ask someone that question since the day he died almost five years ago."

Her question was bigger than I was. I was a baby in the

things of faith. *"Father God, I don't know what to say—what to do—help me."*

I grabbed a napkin off the table and dabbed the tears falling from her eyes—then mine. "Carrie, I don't know much. But I do know that God loves you so much that He will give you the desires of your heart. Right now, in Heaven, God weeps with you. He knows that the greatest desire in your heart is to see your Sam."

"Really?"

"Yes, really." At that moment, the thought just came into my mind: *Go to the car and get your Bible.* "Carrie, I'll be right back. I'm just going to the car to get something that I think God wants me to get for you."

"What?"

It didn't matter whether or not she understood what I was saying. I wasn't even sure that I had understood correctly myself but, nevertheless, I went to the car and came back up the steps with my Bible.

"Carrie, I believe that God wants me to show you something I read not long ago in my Bible. Maybe it will answer your question." I went to the index and found the page where First Corinthians started. It helped that my Bible had chapter headings, and over the 15th chapter the heading read, "The Resurrection Body." I started at the 35th verse and read word for word, as it was written, and let her look on with me.

By the time I got to Verse 51, I noticed that her mouth was agape with awe of what she was hearing. Her body was more relaxed; her sobs had become a gentle weeping, like she expected what came next. With my next breath, I read on:

"Listen, I tell you a mystery: We will not all sleep, but we will all be changed—in a flash, in the twinkling of an eye, at the last

*trumpet. For the trumpet will sound, the dead will be raised imper-
ishable, and we will be changed. For the perishable must clothe itself
with the imperishable, and the mortal with immortality.*"

I looked deep into her hazel eyes and saw hope where
only minutes before there was despair.

"Keep going. Don't stop."

I passed the Bible to her. "Why don't you read from here?"

She wiped her nose, "Get me my reading glasses off the
buffet over there."

I did and then sat at her feet as she continued the reading:

*"When the perishable has been clothed with the imperishable, and
the mortal with immortality, then the saying that is written will come
true: 'Death has been swallowed up in victory.'*

"Neicy, I've been to a lot of churches and I've never seen
this! Never heard this!"

"It gets even better, Carrie, read on."

"Where, O death, is your victory? Where, O death, is your sting?"

"My God!" Carrie shouted out as she looked up toward
Heaven, raising both hands. "Thank you! I never knew. All
these years I never knew." Like a child on Christmas morning, my seventy-year-old godmother hugged the Bible to her
chest and smiled at me as tears ran down her unblemished
cheeks.

A few minutes later God gave me the blessed opportunity
to pray with my godmother as she began her new journey of
faith and personal relationship with God.

We shared lots of wonderful and happy times after that
day. Where before she would never even leave the house,
she looked forward to me coming to pick her up.

That Christmas, she met me at the door in a jazzy red suit.
She was beautiful and her hazel eyes sparkled with new life.
My mom was cooking Christmas dinner and Carrie was my
date. We had a wonderful time laughing, singing, and just

talking about whatever and nothing. We were together again, and that was all I cared about.

A few months later, I got a call from my mom. "Neicy, Carrie died last night."

It felt like someone hit me in the chest with a sledgehammer. I gasped for breath. "Oh no, Momma."

My mother gave me the details and after I hung up, I fell across the bed and cried. While I settled in to cry all night, another option came to my mind. I got up off the bed, went to the bookcase, and got my Bible. I read out loud the 15th chapter of First Corinthians and recalled the day when the Lord gave Carrie and me a glimpse of Heaven.

I imagined Carrie and Sam walking hand in hand together down a shimmering street of gold. I smiled and whispered into the air, "Carrie? I told you God would let you see your handsome Sam."

When we experience an ache in our hearts left by a loved one who dies, it seems like the pain will never end. It can feel like the void left by that person will never be filled. We go over in our minds the last time we saw them, what they said, and what life was like with them. It tears our hearts apart to feel what life is like without them. We want to change the unchangeable, take the moment of their last breath on earth back so that they will be with us again, and never have them leave us again. Reality hurts so much sometimes and even though we realize that what we want to be true is not true, we want it nonetheless.

It is during these comfortless times that we can seek a comfort far beyond what any person has the power to give— God's comfort. He promises us that "Blessed are those that mourn, for they shall be comforted." The eyes of faith call for us to look beyond what we can see, touch, or even feel. The eyes of faith stretch to look to the invisible God who promises never to leave us nor forsake us. With the eyes of faith, we come to believe that what He promises, He will deliver. In that knowledge, we are comforted and, because of that comfort, we will, in time, comfort others with the same heartache.

Dear Heavenly Father: Thank you for the people you have placed in our lives who have loved us all our lives and the ones that have only just begun to love us. Give us the capacity to love as we have been loved—to love others as you have loved us—so compassionately and unconditionally. Thank you for Your Word that is alive and does not come back void but does exactly what you sent it to do. We praise you for the way the Holy Spirit prompts us to share our faith with others. Without you there would be no gift of faith to share. You are our HOPE. Amen. So be it!

"I will not leave you comfortless:
I will come to you."

JOHN 14:18 (New International Version)

Steal Away

Tat-tat-tat-POW. Gunshots, but no one in my dream got shot. I heard the loud and angry barking of dogs. Louder. This dream seemed so real although there were no visuals. Only the barking of what must have been a pack of dogs . . . growing louder. Louder. Angrier. I sat up in my bed covered only with the darkness of night. The barking was coming from outside my window. Muffled sounds of men. "Look over there," one voice said, drowning out the other voices with its urgency. Through my curtains, the white beams of flashlights crisscrossed like the spotlights at Grauman's Chinese Theatre on Academy Award night.

What was happening? I slowly made my way to the window, tiptoeing like I was the one who shouldn't be there. The barking grew louder, joined now by the steady whirling of a police department helicopter hovering overhead. A few feet from the window and POP, POP, POP, POP, in rapid succession. I fell to the floor, grabbed the cordless phone off the glass-topped nightstand, and crawled to the bathroom, the safest place in my apartment. Why? No windows! I knew the drill all too well. This was just another night in a neighborhood under siege by the dope boys. This was nightlife on Kennedy Street, Washington, D.C., USA.

Once in the bathroom, I shut the door, recited the 23rd Psalm, and really emphasized the part, "Yea, though I walk through the valley of the shadow of death, I will fear no evil for thou art with me." I learned that Psalm and how to pray right there in that windowless bathroom on Kennedy Street.

To this day, the bathroom is my prayer closet. Usually after about an hour, it would be safe to come out. By this time it would be like 4:00 A.M., and then I had to try to get back to sleep because I had to go to work later that morning. Tired and weary, I had no choice but to lean on the Lord to get through the day. This went on for most of the eight years that I lived there.

I used to wonder sometimes and actually ask Him, "God, make a way for me to get off this street," but the only reply I would get as evidenced by my paycheck was, "No, not yet." And even though most of the time I was alone in that apartment, I learned that I was never alone. God comforted and protected me, and chased away all my fears. I learned what it meant to have God as my refuge. Being under God's protective wing was no longer a far-fetched theory, but a daily fact of life for me.

In the middle of those years somewhere, I remember volunteering to present a workshop on the effects of drug addiction at a community center in a housing project. It was in a neighborhood that I did not want to go to. My neighborhood was like Opie's Mayberry compared to this one, which was "Gunfight at the O.K. Corral" territory.

As I turned into the debris-and-glass-strewn parking lot, children ran between the abandoned cars seemingly unaware that this was not a traditional playground. I was met by a middle-aged woman who shook my hand and then led me to the center, which turned out to be an apartment on the first floor of the building. I felt out of place and it appeared that they may have thought I was out of place, too. As I looked around at everyone in jeans and T-shirts, I realized that maybe I should have worn something other than my mint green silk pantsuit.

Toward the middle of my presentation, the discussion deviated from my outline and we ended up discussing how to cope with living in a neighborhood under siege. I took a deep breath and realized that I was right where I was supposed to be. I could relate to everything they said and I had some experience, hope, and strength to share with them *but only because of* the grace of God, who works all things together for the good of those who love Him. Yes, all things . . . including providing a shelter for me on Kennedy Street, Washington, D.C., USA.

We don't have a clue most of the time what God is showing us or why things happen as they do. All we can do is learn to trust that it's enough that He knows and in God's time we will see just how he has worked everything—the good and the bad—together for our personal and collective good. I guess that's why it's called having faith. We can't see it, touch it, taste it, or even understand how it works. Faith just is! And with faith all things are possible, including peace in the midst of the storm, courage instead of fear, hope for the future, and the ability to live in the fullness of joy in the present—regardless of what may be crashing all around us. With the eyes of faith, we see that in spite of what we may not be able to see in the natural realm, in the spiritual realm—all is well with our souls.

Dear Heavenly Father: Thank you for providing us with safety under the shelter of Your protective wing. You know all things. You see all things. We have such limited vision and all that we can do well, sometimes with a few reminders, is to fix our eyes on You. We don't know whys, whens, or even hows of life, but we are learning that you know all things. Help us focus on the fact that we are your children, Heavenly Father, and as your children, we could not have a more loving and powerful Father than You. It is Your perfect love that casts out every fear, stamps out every anxiety, quiets every question. We are in awe of Your Greatness and astounded by Your tender loving care of us, the sheep of Your pasture. Amen. So be it!

"For My thoughts are not your thoughts,
Nor are your ways My ways," says the Lord.
"For as the heavens are higher than the earth,
So are My ways higher than your ways,
And My thoughts than your thoughts."

Isaiah 55:8–9 (New King James Version)

Walk by Faith

"Girl, you got off drugs and lost your mind. You mean to tell me that you're going to Los Angeles, California, with only $40 and a round-trip plane ticket? You're crazy."

Elated about being in recovery and on a new faith-journey, I felt like I could walk on water. So Los Angeles on $40 made a lot of sense to me. Plus, someone gave me round-trip plane tickets so that I could go to the twelve-step program international convention. What other signs did I need to know that I was to go to L.A.? God cracked a door and I felt it my duty to push it wide open.

"Momma, I'm going to be all right. God will take care of me."

My mother shook her head and said, "Yeah, right."

In preparation for the trip, I called the convention committee, explained my limited financial situation, and asked for an indigent registration packet. The woman on the phone said, "No problem." She took my information and told me to pick up my free packet at the registration table when I arrived.

Now, I must confess my faith wavered. My mother's words echoed in my mind. So I called my dad and asked him to help me out with a little money.

He said, "You're crazy! You're going where and with what? I've got a bill from the IRS on the dresser now. And your momma is taking all my money. We've been divorced all these years, and I'm still paying that woman alimony. That woman . . ."

As I listened to him vent his problems and resentments, I wondered why I ever called him because the results were always the same. I felt worse after talking to him—if you could call it that. There was nothing two-way about our conversations. I cut him off with my usual, "Okay, Daddy. I'm sorry I bothered you."

Then I called my mother back. I didn't understand why I always offered myself up to my parents as a living sacrifice for their unresolved pain.

"You know I had to go to court again about my money. He's late again! I know that your father gets a hefty retirement check but I still can't get my money. I was married to that man for twenty-six years. Twenty-six years, Stanice. He doesn't realize that he got off easy. That man—"

"Momma! Can you help me, please?"

"Ask your daddy. He's got plenty of money."

"I already asked him. He said he didn't have any money."

"That don't make no sense, you can't get nothing from that man. He owes you!"

"Momma!"

She took a deep breath. "Well, I don't have it to spare. You know all I have to depend on is my job and myself. What's gonna happen to me when I get old? I sure can't depend on you or your brother. Did you know your cousin Mark bought his mother a microwave last Christmas?"

"Momma, come on now. I haven't asked you for anything in years. Why won't you help me?"

Then I crossed the line of no return. I continued, "Why is it that you always help Stan Jr. but not me? He asks you for money all the time and you give it to him. All he does is mess it up. Here it is I'm trying to do something positive with my life now and you always say no." I waited for the wrath of Ginny to fall.

"Well, you're a woman now and standing on your own two feet. But your brother needs me."

"Have you ever wondered why that is? Have you dared to consider that by enabling the thirty-year-old boy all his life you may be the main reason he won't cross the threshold to manhood?" I thought but I dared not say it out loud.

"Okay. Whatever. I'll see you when I get back from California."

The following Friday, I drove to Washington Dulles Airport and parked my car in the long-term lot and boarded the plane. I made a mental note to save some money to pay for the parking upon my return.

The flight attendant welcomed me with a toothpaste-commercial smile. I excused my way to the window seat. I felt alone in my struggle to remain drug-free. I also thought that maybe my parents were right about my being crazy. I buckled my seat belt, looked out the window, and silently prayed, *"God, please stretch this little bit of money I got and provide a place for me to stay while I am in L.A. I'm depending on you to show me that you can and will meet my every need. My own parents think I'm crazy to do this but I truly believe that you will make a way for me. One more thing, God, please carry this airplane under your protective Wing. You know I love to fly but I love safe touchdowns even more."*

Once we landed at L.A. Airport, I went to the baggage area. I dreaded carrying my suitcase because it was packed with more stuff than two people could wear in a month of weekends. While I waited, I searched through my purse and I could not find the flyer with the location of the convention. It seemed that I had packed everything but the flyer.

I heaved my overworked garment bag onto my shoulder and headed for the bus stop in front of the terminal.

I went up the steps of one of the many buses that was parked at the curb. "Excuse me sir, have you been taking a lot of people that hug each other a lot to a particular hotel today?"

"It's funny that you should ask that. Yes, we all have. You're right too," he laughed. "They do a lot of hugging. This one guy even said, 'You look like you need a hug.' Of course I backed up. I don't play that. But yeah, they're all over at the Anaheim Convention Center."

"Well, sir, that's where I want to go," I said as I clumsily boarded the bus, dragging my luggage up the steps and down the aisle behind me.

The driver looked at his watch and shouted back into the almost empty bus, "I'll be leaving in about ten minutes."

As we got close to the Convention Center, I saw hundreds of people hugging each other and talking in groups. This was the annual international convention, so there were people of every color, nationality and persuasion. There were punk rockers, Western, Afrocentric, rich, famous, and poor folks like me. As I stepped off the bus, I heard snatches of conversations in English, Spanish, Italian, French, Southern drawls, New York accents, and languages that I was not familiar with. We may have been different in a lot of ways but we all shared the common bond of learning how not to use drugs one day at a time. The thought of that energized me and assured me that I was not alone!

As I followed the signs to the registration area, I didn't see anyone that I knew. I felt the strain of major jet lag and my shoulder throbbed from the weight of the bag. All I wanted to do was lay my body down to rest. This walking on water was hard work.

My feet felt like pins and needles were being thrust through them as I limped my way to the registration desk.

"My name is Stanice, and I called last week and was told that an indigent registration package would be waiting here for me."

The young white woman with spiked stark black hair flipped through boxes of manila registration envelopes. "I'm sorry but I don't see your name on any of these packets."

"That can't be right. I called and the woman on the telephone assured me that there would be no problems. That a package would be waiting for me to pick up."

"Let me ask you this," she continued. "How long have you been clean and in the program?"

"Two and a half years," I said quite proudly.

"Well, that's where the problem is. Maybe she didn't know, but indigent packages are only for newcomers—people with no more than six months clean."

"But you don't understand. I called and came here all the way from Washington, D.C. There must be—"

My words gave way to the overwhelming desire to walk away—defeated. But where would I go? I realized it was time to take another leap of faith. I reluctantly reached into my purse for a $20 bill and handed it to her.

"Just give me a basic registration, please."

As she went for one of the thinner envelopes, I knew that basic meant no tickets for the banquet, spiritual breakfasts, dances, or talent shows.

At that moment, I heard my name called out. "Stanice! Is that you?"

"Yes! Yes!" I turned around to see the one person in the sea of people that knew me.

To my surprise, it was Barbara, the woman who had given me the airplane tickets.

We hugged and jumped around holding each other and laughing like teenagers.

"I can't believe I found you in this crowd, Stanice. Here!" She handed me a manila envelope. "I took care of your registration, I couldn't get you a full package but at least it's $20 you don't have to spend."

"Oh, Barbara, this is awesome. Thank you so much. Which reminds me . . ."

I quickly turned back around to the counter and looked at the woman who was about to hand me the envelope.

"I won't be needing that packet now. It's already been taken care of. May I have my $20 back, please?"

I turned back around. Barbara was gone. As I scanned the room, she seemed to have been swallowed up by the crowd.

Bewildered and a bit irate, I mumbled, *"Now what, God? You know I don't have a place to stay."*

My head throbbed from lack of sleep and my stomach gurgled in impatience for its next meal. I felt alone in a sea of people. My strength gone, I wanted to drop to the floor, stretch out, and just cry out, *"God, please show me where I can lie down for the night."*

I'd been to other conventions and remembered that people without rooms were always welcome to sleep in the hospitality suites. I considered them roomless shelters and roomless I was.

With renewed hope, I walked a few more steps and stopped a couple of women. "Excuse me. Do either of you know where the hospitality rooms are?"

When the two of them looked at each other, it was apparent that neither of them knew. They shrugged their shoulders and said in unison, "No."

I walked on toward the entrance and dragged my luggage along by the strap. *"I can't take another step."* Tears welled up in my eyes. *"Oh, God, I can't go on."* The room appeared to whirl around me. I heard a crescendo of voices and saw one

big blur of faces that seemed to melt into one another like a kaleidoscope. I held my registration envelope tightly in one hand and whispered, *"But, God, you promised!"* But had He really promised? Or had it been my own wishful thinking? I recalled my mother's and father's voices saying, "Girl, it's official now. You are crazy!"

In the next moment, I felt a tap on my shoulder. With tears streaming from my eyes, I turned around. Thank God! A familiar face! It was Clifton Neal, a guy from back home.

"You okay?"

I grabbed the man around his neck and hugged him tight. "No, I'm not okay." And then the floodgate of emotions burst open. "I'm three thousand miles from home! I don't have anywhere to stay and very little money. I'm tired, hungry, my feet hurt, and my head feels like it is about to explode. To top it off, I feel stupid for coming here like this. I just can't go on, Clifton." I took a deep breath, sighed, put my head on his shoulder, and sobbed like a baby.

He patted my back, as if to burp me. "It's going to be all right. Now stop crying. You gonna make me cry and you know my image can't handle that."

I looked at him and smiled.

He grabbed the strap of my luggage. "Come on. You can stay in my hotel suite. There's plenty of room. It's not far from here. I can sleep on the couch."

"Are you sure?"

"Yeah, I'm sure." He tugged at the luggage. "My God, what-all you got in here? It wasn't safe enough to leave the kitchen sink at home?"

He always made me laugh.

Clifton shouldered my luggage and carried it the four long blocks to the hotel. As we walked I thought, *Here was the guy that people, including myself, laughed at back home because he talked funny and had different views. Every time he shared his*

story, he made mention of some woman with her wig turned around backward that he was in love with. Yet God chose this man that I ridiculed to help me. Boy, you never know where your help is going to come from.

I felt ashamed. "Cliff, I haven't been nice to you in the past and yet you're doing this for me. I've laughed at—"

"You ain't telling me anything that I don't already know. I know what people say behind my back and to my face sometimes; but it don't matter. I know how folks can be. Hurt people hurt people. I just do what I got to do to stay clean one day at a time and don't worry about what other folks say. For most of my life, I worried about what people thought about me. I'm free of that now."

He saw my tears, which must have been glistening under the streetlights. He stopped, set the luggage down on the sidewalk, and hugged me. "You're gonna be all right. You're learning and the bottom line is you ain't using drugs no more. So it's okay. Everything is okay."

Clifton was a perfect gentleman that night. The next morning he gave me a key to the room. "My room is your room so come and go as you please. Checkout time is 11:00 A.M. Sunday."

"Thank you so much. I don't think I could have gotten through the night without your help."

"No problem. Do you need anything?"

"No. I'm fine." I didn't tell him that my return flight wasn't until Monday afternoon.

As I walked back toward the convention center, a steel gray late-model car pulled up to the curb beside me.

More familiar faces from home peeped up at me.

"Hey, girl. We didn't know you were coming."

"I didn't either until the last minute. A friend gave me round-trip tickets."

"Great. You want to go to breakfast with us?"

"Well, it depends. Where are you going?"

"Don't worry about it. Breakfast is on me," the woman in the front passenger seat told me. "We're celebrating. I got a promotion last week. Come on and get in."

After breakfast they dropped me off at the convention center. As I walked into the lobby, I saw Tina, another woman from Washington. We hugged and talked a few minutes. Then she said, "Stanice, you got a ticket for tonight's banquet?"

"No."

"Well do me a favor and take this one because I'm going to a restaurant. I'd hate to see the ticket wasted."

I wondered, *Do they know my situation? Was a message posted on a board somewhere that read "The fool arrived in L.A. last night with only $40, so look out for her"?* I realized my fertile imagination was in overdrive and headed in the wrong direction. So to get centered, I sat in on a few workshops.

As the day went on it became more and more evident that God had landed in L.A. long before I did and had set everything in motion to reward my faith.

By day's end, without my asking, people gave me tickets for admission to the talent and comedy shows, dances, and Sunday breakfast. In addition, friends invited me to stay in their room in their luxurious hotel on Saturday night. So when I returned to Clifton Neal's room to retrieve my luggage, I left him a thank-you note and a ticket to the comedy show.

On Sunday morning, the convention concluded with the spiritual breakfast. After the speaker, most people prepared to leave, including my friends whose room I shared the night before. Only a few people had Monday flights out and I was one of them. I hugged my friends, said goodbye, and dragged my luggage toward the hospitality room. I figured I could hang out there until the convention committee put me out or God revealed my next blessing.

Then I heard a man's voice. "Can I help you with your luggage?"

"Well . . ."

"Where's your car so I can load it for you?"

"Well, I . . ."

"Did you call a cab to take you to the airport or something? Where are you going?"

"I'm not sure; I haven't been told that yet."

By the look on his face, my last statement confirmed it for him: I was not wrapped too tight. I felt it was time to confess.

"You see, I do know where I'm going. Back to Washington, D.C. However, my flight doesn't leave until tomorrow and I don't know where I'm going to stay until then—at least not yet."

"Well you can have my room. I'm paid up until tomorrow."

"Yeah, right." I was quite apprehensive about this one. Sounded like a line to me.

"No really. I originally planned to check out tomorrow but my manager paged me and requires my presence on the job tonight. So I need to leave within the hour," as he looked at his silver Rolex.

"Really?"

He smiled, showing a gorgeous set of pearly whites. "Yes. Really!"

"But you could get a refund from the hotel."

"Yes, maybe so; but I don't think that this is a coincidence. I've been clean over ten years and I have seen God work in some pretty mysterious ways during that time."

"What's your name?"

"I'm Jonathan. And yours is?"

"Stanice."

"I'm pleased to meet you." We hugged as he sought help on the pronunciation of my name.

111

"Stan, like in Stanley. That's my dad's name. And just tack on 'niece.'"

"Oh! Stan—niece. Okay. Come on, it's the hotel right over there across the street."

As we made our way through the lobby, I still wasn't feeling too comfortable with this solution, but there was still time to bail out; however, people who knew him stopped us every few seconds, and that relieved my mind somewhat.

"Hey, Jonathan, see you at the next convention."

"Okay, Matt. It was awesome again this year wasn't it?"

The man agreed and they hugged. Two minutes later it was some women, then another man, then two men, all who knew Jonathan. He introduced me to most of them. I started to feel more comfortable. As we made our way across the street, I saw a few of my friends from home and made it a point to introduce them to Jonathan—just in case.

When we got to the hotel, he told the woman at the desk to look out for me because he was leaving and I would be staying in the room. We went upstairs. He finished packing his bags and made sure that I was settled in.

He gave me his room entry card and one of his business cards. He instructed me to call him collect when I got back home so he would know that I got there all right.

I got teary-eyed as I thanked him. "This is so incredibly special. What you're doing and all."

"Hey, it's okay. We got to look out for one another."

"How can I repay you? I'll send you some money when—"

He cut me off with a wave of his hand. "No. You just look out for someone else when you can that's all. Just pass it on. You're going to be all right. Put the extra lock on the door." With that Jonathan left the room.

I wept tears of joy as I looked around. It seemed each room God provided was plusher than the one before. I sat down on the California king-size bed and prayed. *"Thank you,*

Lord. You have been so good to me at every turn. I'm not crazy. You are to be trusted!" I opened up my purse and counted my money. After the bus ride and a few other little things, I still had $33 and some change.

My stomach must have heard me counting my money because it growled a reminder that it had been too long since breakfast. I walked over to the mahogany writing table, picked up the hotel menu, and stretched my body out on the royal blue chaise lounge that overlooked the pool. As I looked at the prices on the menu, one thing became very clear to me—I would not be eating at this hotel.

"What now, Lord?"

I walked through the hotel lobby and out into the warm night air in search of a fast food restaurant. I bought a small hamburger and fries. I thanked God for it and savored every bite like it was filet mignon broiled medium-well and a baked potato stuffed with sour cream and chives.

The next morning as checkout time approached, I showered and packed my luggage with the few things that I had taken out. I took the elevator down to the lobby and went to turn in the key and ask for the shuttle to the airport.

"I'm sorry, miss, but the shuttle just left a few minutes ago. Did you call last night to schedule special transportation?"

"No, I didn't know that I needed to."

"Well yes, otherwise the shuttle leaves every hour on the half hour. So the next one will be leaving in about fifty minutes."

She must have seen the disappointment on my face because she said, "Well let me see what I can do."

She went into the back office. After a few minutes, she came out with a man who was taking off his brass lapel pin that identified him as a hotel employee. He came around to my side of the counter. He introduced himself and explained that he had just finished his shift and could drop me off at the airport, since he passed it on his way home.

I accepted. He heaved my bag to his shoulder. "So, judging by your luggage you've been in L.A. for about a couple of weeks huh?"

"No, not quite."

I waited at the front door while he went to get his car. He drove up in a white midsize convertible with the top down. As the hot Santa Ana wind whipped through my hair, I noticed people looking at us as we drove down the freeway. Even in L.A., a black and white couple was a novelty.

The more we talked the conversation became easier and more revealing.

"So are you married?" I asked.

"My wife and I are about to be divorced."

"Oh, I'm sorry to hear that."

"Yeah, me too. I love her but it just hasn't worked out. I really hurt her and she hasn't been able to forgive me."

I listened as he talked. Soon our conversation turned to God. He talked about how empty his life was and no matter what he did nothing was filling it up. He confessed that he thought marriage would do the trick but it didn't.

"Yeah, I know. I've been there. I had a hole like that in my life at one time too. Then, I found out that God loved me and wanted to fill that void. Or maybe it was the other way around—God found me."

All too soon, it seemed that he pulled up in front of the airport at the curbside check-in. He reached into the glove compartment and hit the trunk release button.

"Thank you so much for the ride. I really enjoyed talking with you. I'm going to pray for you and your wife. God can turn the whole situation around, if you ask Him. He's always waiting to hear from us, you know."

As he grabbed my bag out of the trunk, he turned to me. "What time did you say your flight was?"

I looked at my watch. "I've got well over an hour before flight time."

He smiled. "Have you eaten yet?"

"No."

"Well, how about I park the car and we go into the terminal and I buy us some lunch?"

"Okay. Are you sure?"

"Yes. I'd like that."

I ordered a Philly-style steak and cheese smothered with grilled onions and green peppers, potato salad, and a large soda. He ordered the vegetarian's delight, whatever that was. Although it didn't look appetizing, it was quite colorful. We laughed and talked like we were old friends.

After lunch, he walked over to the arrival/departure monitors and checked on the status of my flight. Over the loudspeaker, the perfectly modulated baritone voice announced that my flight was now boarding. My new friend and I exchanged addresses and telephone numbers in case he was ever in D.C. or I in L.A. again. We hugged.

"It was so good to meet and talk with you. Thanks for everything."

He smiled. "The pleasure was all mine. You really helped me a lot."

As I walked toward the boarding ramp, I stopped, turned, and called out to my new friend, "I guess God planned it this way. That we should meet and help each other. God works in mysterious ways, you know."

He smiled and nodded in agreement.

Once inside the airplane, the tall flight attendant with perfectly straight teeth welcomed me aboard. I excused my way to my window seat, buckled up, stared out of the window and prayed. *"God, thank you for taking such good care of me while I was in L.A. You met my every need. Bless those people that you used to help me. Help my new friend and his wife fall in love with each other all over again. Heal their marriage and make it brand-new. I know you can do it. Now, please make these skies as friendly as the airline claims they are and get me home safe—"*

My prayer was interrupted by a woman's perfectly pitched voice over the plane's loudspeaker.

"It seems that we have overbooked this flight. For those who volunteer to get off this plane, we will provide you with passage on the next flight and a round-trip ticket good for anywhere United flies within the continental United States."

It sounded like a great deal to me. I silently weighed the variables. No one was waiting for me at my destination airport. I drove myself to the airport and parked in the long-term lot. The scale tipped in my favor and I popped straight up out of my seat like a bagel in a wide-slotted toaster.

"Excuse me, miss. I'm up and headed straight for the door. Consider my seat available."

"Great! Thank you so much. If you go to the ticket counter, they will give you the voucher for your free round-trip flight and set you up for the next flight out."

I briskly walked to the ticket counter. The next flight was in forty-five minutes. I felt a sudden surge of faith that moved me to search for an airport gift shop. I bought three souvenirs—a magnet for my mom's refrigerator, a bookmark for my dad, and a felt pennant for my son's bedroom wall. I thought this was a good time for me to start a tradition for my son: a collection of pennants from wherever his mother traveled. The souvenirs were tokens of my new faith in God's ability to provide. In my heart, I knew that this trip symbolized a new beginning for me of walking by faith and not by sight. It was no longer a theory that sounded good; it was the key to my living a fuller life.

With the departure gate in sight, I saw people in line and boarding. I ran to the counter. A bit short-winded, I announced, "I'm one of the people who gave up their seats on the last flight. Do I get on this flight?"

"Yes, you can board now."

More straight teeth greeted me and this time their owner escorted me to my seat, since it wasn't identified on the ticket. I followed her and almost bumped into her because she stopped before we made it through the curtain that separated first-class from coach.

"Here you are." She pointed to a window seat in first-class. "Can I take your bag and put it up for you?"

"Sure." *Had she made a mistake? First-class? Me?*

"Enjoy your flight," she said as she handed me slippers.

"Now, God, you really have outdone yourself," I thought. *"I have never flown first-class. Plus, free round-trip tickets for a flight anywhere in the continental U.S. good for a whole year."* As I contemplated the places I could travel to, the possibilities excited me.

The attendants treated me like a queen. They served me cordon bleu, roasted red potatoes, and steamed veggies on a china dinner plate. I told the attendant to put a hold on the peanuts. "Sorry, I couldn't possibly eat another thing. But thank you, though."

As I ate, I chatted with the older, impeccably dressed white man who sat beside me. By the blasé look on his face, perhaps he had grown stale from his many frequent flier miles in first-class seating; but with the wonder of a child on her first trip to Disneyland, I perked him right up. A half hour into the flight, we talked and laughed like we were old friends.

After the plane touched down and came to a stop, I said goodbye to my newest friend and thanked the flight attendant.

"You made me feel so comfortable. And by the way, you have an inspiring smile."

My luggage arrived at Dulles International before I did, and was waiting for me when I got to the baggage claim area.

I took the free shuttle to the long-term parking lot. On my way out, I paid for parking and still had a couple of dollars of my original $40 left.

As I drove, I tuned in a gospel station and sang along all the way. When I got home, the first call I made was to my son. Then I called my mother and father.

"Mom, I'm back. I'm exhausted and going straight to bed now but I'll come over to your house tomorrow and tell you all about my trip."

"What? You actually went?"

"Yes. And by the way, I brought you a little something back from California. I got to call Dad now to let him know that I'm back and brought him something too. I love you. Good night." I hung up the receiver.

Sitting on the side of my bed, I took a few minutes to visualize my mother sitting on her sofa with her mouth wide open in awe of what she just heard and my father in front of his TV shaking his head and saying, "That girl is something else."

As a postscript to this story, as if this wasn't enough for you or me, I got a letter postmarked Los Angeles, California, about three months after my trip. I carefully opened the envelope, and inside was a letter that read, "Stanice, I have great news! About a month after I drove you to the airport and we had lunch, I found God or, rather like you said, maybe He found me. God brought my wife back to me and we are not getting a divorce. She forgave me and we are more in love than before. It's true! God does work in mysterious ways, His wonders to perform! Thank you for sharing your experiences with me. May He always bless you. Sincerely . . ."

Tears fell softly onto the letter and a prayer of thanksgiving tiptoed out of my heart and went up to God.

If we had a dollar and donut for every time that we doubted our decisions, we would all be rich and fat. For a minute, it looks like everything is going to work out and then POOF— in an instant, the hope flickers and fades. During these lapses of faith, we can either give up or hold on and press our way.

Even though it may seem easier to just give up, there is something inside us that kicks in and makes us hope for the best anyway. We hope against all hope. Maybe that something *is* faith kicking into another gear. It is this wait-and-wonder time that we have to pray our way through. "God help us make it through this." After all, the only one who knows the outcome or who can change the outcome is God; so we might as well go to the source.

When we seek God's will for our lives and look to His Power to supply just what we need at the moment that we need it, we learn that with Him being our Helper all things are possible. Yes, doubt enters sometimes; however, we can only doubt what we believe to be true.

Some of us constantly pray, "God I need more faith. Please give me more faith." Perhaps we have all the faith that we are going to get and it is just a matter of exercising the faith that we have so that it can strengthen to the point where it will see us through anything and everything. Perhaps faith is like a muscle that atrophies if not exercised; but with a steady regimen of push-ups and pull-ups, curls and crunches, it becomes firm, strong, and fit enough to get us through the present and press us on toward the future.

Slowly, we learn to trust God as we step out on faith and do that next step that we know to do. God will always meet us right there in the middle of the step. Perhaps it is the stepping out in faith that takes us to a new level of faith—out of words and into action.

While it is true that "without faith it is impossible to please God," we can also look at that truth as "with faith, however small, it is impossible not to please God." We never know how we will be blessed, where, or who God will use to bless us. That's why it's a good thing to treat every person as we want to be treated.

Dear Heavenly Father: Thank you for going both with us and before us. Thank you that there is no place that we can possibly go to where you are not there too. Thank you for the gift of friendship and the people that you place in our lives that walk out your love and care for us. So today, we confess our doubts, for only in confessing where we really are can You move us forward to where we really need to be. Although we don't know what's around the bend, we know who is the maker of bends and everything else we can see and don't see. Your love and care for us is truly amazing. As we learn to walk by faith and not by sight, thank you that you allow us to take toddler steps toward you until we get our bearings and learn to walk, run, and soar with wings like eagles. Continue to teach us your ways all the days of our lives. Take us further still in You until we discover like Abraham discovered that you are indeed Jehovah-Jireh, God our provider. Amen. So be it!

But without faith it is impossible to please Him,
For he who comes to God must believe that He is,
And that He is a rewarder of those who diligently seek Him.

HEBREWS 11:6 (New King James Version)

Light in the Dark

On Friday September 6, 1996, at 3:00 A.M., I got a wake-up call that I will never forget! The ferocious winds accompanying Hurricane Fran sledgehammered my sweet dream. I awoke to a world void of light and no silvery moon. I was in the basement of a wood-framed house surrounded and held captive by flag-pole-tall bending and breaking pine trees—disoriented, scared, and alone. It was like living inside the color black.

Fear choked me as I crawled through the house in what I hoped was the direction of the bathroom. Death knocked at the windows and doors begging for entry. But I wasn't answering. I bumped into every wall, felt each sharp corner of furniture, and shouted in an attempt to drown death's call. "Yea, though I walk through the valley of the shadow of death, I will fear no evil; for You are with me; Your rod and Your staff, they comfort me" (Psalm 23:4, New King James Version). I shouted the same verses repeatedly with *ouch's* mixed in like choruses. I knew that if I could get to the bathroom, which was in the center of the house, I would be safe.

As I crawled and listened to the hurricane that raged all around me, I realized that it could very well be my last night on earth. I felt the coolness of the ceramic tile under my hands and knees as I made it to the safety of the windowless bathroom. I felt the toilet seat, propped myself up, and grabbed the Bible and mini-battery-powered clip-on book light out of my magazine rack. I turned to Psalm 119 and read, "Your Word is a lamp to my feet and a light to my path."

In the background, I heard the crackling and thump of snapping trees. Thunderously loud wind, crashing glass, and tree branches slashed all around the wood-frame house. Through my tears, I recited out loud, "Your Word is a lamp to my feet and a light to my path. Your Word is a lamp to my feet and a light to my path."

Yet, still—I thought of death.

I wanted one more chance to tell my mother, father, and especially my son, Michael, "I love you." No excuses. No long talks. I wanted them to know that I genuinely loved them—since forever—and until forever is no more. And then something happened.

Peace washed over me like the warm waters of a baptismal pool. It was like God wrapped His loving arms around me like a loving father comforts his child awakened by a nightmare. The wind seemed muffled. Time stopped. Whether I lived or died did not seem to matter. An incomparable light flooded my spirit. The tiny book light shone like a beacon illuminating the vast night sky that surrounds it, beckoning the troubled ships to shore.

I whispered a prayer, "Even if I die, I know that you are with me. If I live, you are still with me. Whether I live or die—all is well with my soul and for that truth I am grateful." I stretched out on the bathroom floor and fell asleep.

A loud tapping sound woke me. I opened my eyes to the light of dawn filtering through the slit at the bottom of the bathroom door.

A muffled voice called out, "Are you okay in there?"

I got up off the floor, walked to the living room window, and shouted, "Yeah, I'm all right."

I had all intentions of saying more; but as my eyes focused it looked like a war scene from a Vietnam documentary. Yards strewn with felled trees reminded me of a childhood game of pickup sticks. Debris was everywhere. The roof of the house across the street was missing. Telephone poles leaned on tall pine trees like dominoes waiting to fall. A huge tree trunk lay where it crashed—inches from my porch.

With tears in my eyes, and praise on my lips, I walked to the phone, picked up the receiver, and to my surprise I heard a dial tone. I quickly dialed my son's number.

The voice on the other end—"Hello."

"Hello! Hello! Michael, I love you so much!"

In the darkest hours of our lives, we can hold on to God's words and know that weeping may endure for a night; but joy comes in the morning. Whatever we go through, we are not alone. God sees! God knows! And perhaps above all—God's love dispels all darkness. If we focus on the love of God and not on the circumstances that may surround us, we can make it through to the light on the other side of the mere thought of God.

Dear Heavenly Father: Thank you for never leaving or forsaking us. It is so very good to know that you have stationed guardian angels all around us like a protective hedge and remind us that you are here with us even now. We are so very grateful that You hear our cries and You can even taste the saltiness of our tears, as we cry out to the only help we know—You. We need you to light our path so we might not stumble and grope around lost in the dark. Hold us near—be the light that chases away the darkness from our lives. Amen. So be it!

Your word is a lamp to my feet
And a light to my path.

PSALM 119:105 (New King James Version)

*

TRUSTING IN GOD'S PERFECT PLAN

*

God Sees Way
Down the Road

It all started with my writing a thank-you letter to the CBN *700 Club* in Virginia Beach. I reported how my life had radically changed after watching a dramatization of an ex-addict's life on one of their telecasts. I wrote that I had prayed like he did and asked God to come into my life and live His life through me. I excitedly wrote that I had not used drugs in over sixteen months and that my life was getting better by the day. I also thanked them for paying an old bill, which cleared the way for me to move into my new apartment, as well as referring me to people who gave me furniture for my apartment and clothes to look for a better job—which I got!

As I walked to the mailbox on the corner, I had thoughts of thanksgiving to God for using a television program to reach me with the hope and promise that could be found if I surrendered my life—botches and all—to Him. I had erroneously thought that I had to clean myself up first and then go to God, which is why I probably never sought Him. I never could clean myself up no matter how hard I tried.

I felt glad that God had quickened my heart and mind to write the letter. I walked back to my apartment and went on with the next thing to do in my new faith-walk. I did not give the letter another thought.

Two weeks later, Linda Volcano, a producer from *The 700 Club*, called.

"We received your letter. I'm calling to find out if are willing to share your story with our viewers."

"For real?"

"Yes, I want to come to Washington with a film crew and shoot a video dramatization of your story. Like the one that you saw that made a difference in your life. We are giving you the opportunity to share with people how it was for you and how a personal relationship with God has changed your life."

"My, my!"

"So, will you? Can we set a date to come up and do this?"

"Yes! Sure! I'd love that!"

We discussed the details. After I hung up the telephone, I immediately picked it up again and dialed my mentor, Dorine.

"Dorine, you won't believe this! *The 700 Club* called me! They want to film a dramatization of my life story."

"Well, all right now! I believe it, baby 'cause you never know what God is gonna do or has in store for us. That's wonderful!"

"But . . . but I'm scared, Dorine. I don't know if I want everyone to know what my life has been like. Plus, they said I have to reenact the drug usage scenes. With syringe and all! But she did say that the syringe would not have a needle and that they will use oregano for the marijuana scene. And headache powder or something instead of heroin."

"So! There you go. It looks like everything's already been taken care of."

"Yeah, but I will remember. I'll be rolling a pretend joint and have a syringe in my hand. Suppose it will make me want to use drugs again?"

"Then you just go to a twelve-step meeting, let the group know, and it will pass just like it has. Where is your faith,

Stanice? God is not going to give you such a marvelous opportunity to tell people about what He has done in your life and not take care of you. It's time to put your talk into action. You say you trust Him, right?"

"Yeah!"

"Then, trust Him! You have been prepared for such a time as this. You never know who will see this video and who it will help. That show is seen all across the world. Just help somebody like somebody helped you!"

"Okay, Doe. Thanks. I love you so much."

"I love you, too, baby. It's gonna be all right!"

Several weeks later, Linda and the *700 Club* film crew arrived. I had asked my son's grandmother to get him out of school early, as there was to be a scene with him and me together in my new faith-walk.

Anyway, the taping went well. The fear left me, as I stayed focused on how God had set this all up way back down the road. I felt like I was reliving it; but the hope I had in the now far outweighed the despair that I had felt in the then. It was like I was asking God to spare me and help me all over again. As I prayed like I had done that day well over a year before, it was like I was praying it for the first time. I forgot all about the cameras surrounding me. It felt like I was relaxing in a semiprivate hot tub filled with the bubbly, steamy waters of peace and pure love.

Somehow, I knew too that this was only the beginning of God's perfect plan for my life.

Several months later, the show aired on New Year's Day. It was part of a telethon called *New Beginnings*. Joy-tears streamed down my cheeks and a multitude of "thank-yous" sprang from my lips as I watched my story on my new nineteen-inch color television in the solitude of my apartment. I couldn't help but think about the goodness, grace, and mercy of such a loving God who saved a wretch like me.

A few weeks following the broadcast, I got another call from *The 700 Club*. They had such a resounding response from people who saw my story and made the decision to surrender their broken lives to God that they wanted me to come to Virginia Beach to do a live interview. So I did that.

In addition to the video and interview, *The 700 Club* included my story in a booklet called *Changed Lives*, and formatted the video into several different languages so it could be viewed in other nations.

In the meantime, I was still so overwhelmed with gratitude that I felt God was leading me to write another letter and mail it in care of *The 700 Club*. However, this letter was to Buddy Baird, the guy whose story I had seen that changed my life.

About two months later, I got another phone call from *The 700 Club*. They wanted me to come back on the show for another live interview. This time I would get a chance to meet Buddy, as we would be interviewed on the show—together!

While all this was going on, God was still working His wonders behind the scenes. Two years after the first airing of my story, I got a call from my ex-husband, Clem, whom I had not seen in over twelve years. I didn't even know where he was, if he was alive, and if he was alive I had always wanted the opportunity to ask him to forgive me for the part I played in the breakup of our marriage. And now here he was on the other end of my telephone line.

"Stacey?"

"Yes." Immediately, I knew his baritone voice.

"This is Clem, your ex-husband."

"My God, I know! How did you find me? How did you know where I was?"

"My wife and I were looking at *The 700 Club* over a year ago and I saw you. I said, 'Honey, that's Stacey! My ex-wife!'"

I seized the opportunity. "Oh, Clem, can you ever forgive me for all the hurt I caused you and your family?"

"Stacey, I forgave you a long time ago. I knew you were in trouble even then, but I had no idea it would get so bad for you. I prayed for you, though. Even though I never knew where you were, I always prayed for you because I knew that God knew. And when I saw you on *The 700 Club*, I knew that God had answered my prayers."

"Clem," I managed to get out of my throat that was choked with tears.

"It's all right. You just keep doing what you're doing. Somehow, I always knew that you would be all right."

"Thank you, Clem."

"Take care, Stacey."

"You too."

"Goodbye."

"Goodbye, Clem."

Our vision is so limited. Have you ever left the house a little later than you should have in order to get to an appointment on time? Your anxiety level rises as you check your watch and the traffic slows to a crawl. Then ahead there are the flashing lights of emergency vehicles. A terrible accident comes into view. Suppose you had left on time or a few minutes earlier than you did? Could it have been you being cut out of the mangled car?

Or perhaps you had your mind set on staying at home; but instead you reluctantly consented to go somewhere just to appease that loved one. But by night's end you were really glad that you went. There was something that happened that you would have missed out on if you had stayed at home.

Or perhaps you've taken a job you really didn't want but later you met someone or came across an opportunity that might not have presented itself had you not been on that job.

Or perhaps, like Clem, you are praying for someone and as the years slip by your prayers seem futile. Clem had no way of knowing where I was physically or spiritually but God knew exactly where I was and what I needed.

Yes, God sees way down the road. He has a plan that encompasses far more than we could ever think or imagine. Plans for the good of not just our individual selves—the me generation that we are—but for all. He loves each one of us like we were the only one He has to love—if we only have faith!

Dear Heavenly Father: Help us to trust You in our everyday living situations. Direct our paths and order our steps toward the plan that you have for our lives. We are grateful for how you provide everything that we need and so many of our wants. We don't know what our future or even the next minute may hold for us; but we are learning that You hold it all. Because You go before us, after us, alongside of us, we have nothing to fear. Strengthen us, encourage us, and give us the hope that we need to move forever forward with our lives. So often, we ask you to do things for us. Well, today, we humbly ask . . . what can we do for you that will encourage someone else's faith-walk?

> Many, O Lord my God, are Your wonderful works
> Which You have done;
> And Your thoughts toward us
> Cannot be recounted to You in order;
> If I would declare and speak of them,
> They are more than can be numbered.

PSALM 40:5 (New King James Version)

His Eye Is
on the Sparrow

I was living in North Carolina when Tom Fuller came into my life with the grace of a flat rock skimming across the surface of a still lake. I can still feel the ripples of our times together circling out from those touch points.

"Hey there, Stanice," Tom said in his Southern drawl. "I been watching you for a while and I like the way you handle yourself. I've heard you speak a few times and I really got a lot out of what you shared."

"Thank you. Your name is Tom, right?" He stood six feet nine inches tall, 250-plus pounds, and had the prettiest mop of silver hair.

He nodded and smiled. "Well, well, you finally got my name right! I think you've called me every name in the phone book." With his fingers, he brushed back the wisps of hair that fell across his face. "I was wondering . . . I've heard you say you ride horses."

"Yeah. I sure do. But what were you wondering, Tom?"

"Well, there's a rodeo at the State Fairgrounds in Raleigh. I've always wanted to go to a rodeo. So, I was wondering, would like to go with me tomorrow evening?"

"I've watched them on cable TV; but I've never been to one. Yeah, I'd love to go."

The next evening, filled with the excitement of going to my first rodeo, I dressed up in my finest western wear. White shirt with metal tabs and tassels, pointed-toe cowboy boots—everything but a cowgirl hat.

Tom was prompt and drove us to Raleigh. He pulled the car into the State Fairgrounds' sprawling parking lot filled with pickup trucks and SUVs. I noticed something else—I seemed to be the only African-American within sight. My date, Tom, was a white man born and raised in North Carolina. I felt a bit uncomfortable—we were way below the Mason-Dixon line. I was about to discover if I'd returned to the Old or New South.

Most of the men, women, and children carried mini Confederate flags. Tom and I walked toward the arena surrounded by Confederate flags on T-shirts and tags, jaws bulging with tobacco, and smiles stained brown from snuff. I lost my footing on the gravel but Tom caught me by the arm and kept me from falling. "Are you okay?"

"No, I'm a bit paranoid right about now, Tom."

"You're gonna be okay. I got your back." He took my hand in his as we walked toward the box office. As I waited off to the side for him, fear gripped me. Men, women, and children stared at me with looks that I interpreted as, "What are YOU doing here at OUR rodeo?"

My mind flashed back to the prior week's newscast. *"We have tragic news to report this evening. While walking down a street, a black couple was fatally shot. It is believed to have been a hate crime. More on that story tonight at 11:00."*

As we entered the arena, the smell of animal dung wafted heavily in the air. Vendors hawked their wares—everything from horse bridles to cotton candy.

"Stanice, come here," Tom called out. "These are some nice cowboy hats."

We tried on hats, modeling them for each other, joked, and laughed.

"Which one do you like, Stanice?"

"I really like this green one. It's an Australian Outback style, I believe." I put on the felt wide-brimmed hat and adjusted the tan braided stampede string under my chin. "Yee-haw!"

"You look real good in it, sweetie. It's yours," he said as he paid the man. "No need for a bag," he instructed the vendor. "Looks like she'll be wearing it tonight."

We walked to our center box seats. The lights dimmed. The sound system squelched and came alive. "Good evening. Welcome to the best rodeo this side of the Mason-Dixie line. And now, Billy Bob will lead us in the cowboy's prayer."

Well that's nice, I thought. *A prayer. Maybe I am in the right place, after all.* I bowed my head and closed my eyes. I couldn't quite make out what Billy Bob and the crowd were saying, so I prayed my own prayer.

The crowd said, "Amen."

Then, out from the stall, came a galloping horse complete with a rhinestone cowboy in the saddle and a huge Confederate flag strapped across his chest. The crowd cheered and the music blared. *"I wish I was in the land of cotton, old times there are not forgotten, look away, look away, look away, Dixie land."* If I had not been there, I would not have believed it. After prayer came "Dixie."

After a few verses and choruses, the galloping horse stopped for a few minutes in front of each section of the grandstand. As he stopped, he turned his horse toward the section, and the people stood up, cheered, and loudly sang along.

I nudged Tom. "You know I'm not getting up when the cowboy comes over here, right?"

"Yes, I know."

This whistling, shouting, and singing went on for a few sections, then the cowboy stopped the horse in front of the stand next to ours. People stood, cheered, and waved their mini Confederate flags. The cowboy yanked the bridle, turned the horse, and slowly rode and stopped in front of our section.

I didn't move. Tom didn't move. I heard no cheers from the people in our section. No one stood up in the rows in front of us. I looked at the people in the rows to our left—then our right—then I slowly turned my head and looked at the rows directly behind us. Not one person in our section stood up—not one person made a sound.

In fact, I noticed that the cheers of the other sections grew weaker. All eyes were on our section. As I looked around each white face made eye contact with me. The children followed their parents' lead. I witnessed the dazzling light of compassion and respect in their eyes.

With a slight smile, I nodded, *"Thank you."* I looked straight into the cowboy's eyes. He reared his horse up on its hind legs—tipped his hat and rode on to the next section.

The next section whooped, hollered, cheered, and waved their little flags. Tom looked at me, smiled, and took my hand. I breathed a sigh of relief and rested my head on his shoulder.

After our first date to a rodeo, Tom asked me out again and I said yes. However, at the last minute, I made up a lame excuse and called off the date. After all, he is white, I am Black, and we were in the South. Old or New South, I didn't know which, and I was too afraid to find out. I didn't like the way people stared at us and whispered to each other whenever we were together—black and white. I imagined the conversations went something like this: "Honey, look at the nigger with that white man. How dare they flaunt such an atrocity!" and "Look at sistah girl with that white man. What a waste!" and "Remind me, Henry Joe, to bring this couple up at the Klan meeting tonight. Something has got to be done before this disease spreads and other nigrah girls think they can get away with dating white men." I imagined breaking news interrupting regular TV programming: "Black woman from up north found hanged in Durham, North Carolina. More on News 5 at 11:00."

I really liked Tom and he was my friend. I knew I owed him an explanation of why I canceled our date on such short notice but couldn't see how that would be possible. I had never confronted such issues nor did I want to. I just wanted the feelings of fear and confusion to go away. It was a long sleepless night in Durham.

The next morning, I telephoned Omie Brown, a child-hood friend. I told her about Tom and confessed my fear.

Omie listened and then said, "Stanice, from what you told me, this guy has character. Let me tell you something. You know I have owned and bred horses for a long time. I have been to many a horse event and let me tell you I have seen black men with white women; but I have never, in all these years, seen a white man bring a black woman to any one of these events. What it tells me is that Tom Fuller is a man of character. Plus, God's Word says that 'God has not given you a spirit of fear but a spirit of power and of love and a sound mind.'" She took a breath and continued. "And another thing, you don't know why God put Tom in your life. You're thinking one thing and it might be something entirely different. But if you don't see this man again you will never know God's perfect intentions."

The following Monday, I called Tom and asked to take him out for coffee. We met at a fast food restaurant. I confessed to him that I had lied and that it was fear that kept me from honoring our date. I told him my fears stemmed from the possibility of being a multiracial couple in the South. As I sat at the table across from this gentle giant, I could feel my fears, like legions of vampires, dying in the light of exposure.

I reached for his hand. "I'm sorry. That wasn't fair to you . . . The way I handled the situation. I should have at least talked to you about my thoughts and feelings."

We made a date to go to the museum in Raleigh the following week. The wall was broken—I let Tom in.

As we sat talking between sips of coffee, I realized I wanted to know more about Tom and I wanted him to know more about me.

He shared his thoughts and aspirations with me, and then he asked, "What are some of your hopes and dreams?"

I hesitated, looked down at the table, and from way down deep in my soul, I looked at him and said, "I want to be a published author. Actually I wrote a manuscript before I left Washington and came here to live. Even had a publisher. But I turned them down."

"You what?"

"I turned them down. Honestly, I was afraid I couldn't handle the rewrites they wanted me to do. I know so little about the craft of writing."

"Stanice, after you become an established author with many books to your credit, you may decide to exercise the option of turning down a publisher; but not your first book. I repeat—*not* your first book."

"Well, Tom, what's done is done."

"Let me share something with you: It's always easier to get another book published once you are published. So you need that first book."

"How do you know?"

"I just know."

"Well, maybe it's too late for that book, but I still want to be a great writer one day. I've just got so much to learn and I don't exactly know where to start."

"No, it's never too late. And, well . . . I can help you get started."

"Help me? What do you mean? How?"

"I'm a writer. A poet, mostly; but I've written screenplays, and I was a professor at a couple of universities."

"Say what? You're lying? Really?"

"'Tis a fact, my friend. If you're really serious about learning, I'll teach you what I know about writing."

I felt the tears welling up and my throat constricting. "You would do that for me?"

"Yes. I have a feeling that you have it in you to become a great writer. With a lot of hard work, of course. When would you like to start?"

I reached into my purse, pulled out a pen, and spread a clean napkin on the table. "How about right now? Now is always a good time."

For the next two years, I was a writer apprentice to Tom. We'd meet once a week at a Denny's. He gave me one-on-one lectures on the craft of writing. After a while the waitress knew our schedule.

"Hey there! How you two doing tonight?"

We'd all chat as we followed her to our usual secluded corner of the restaurant. She'd always spread out our essentials on the table, smile at us, and ask, "Your usual coffee with whipped cream on the side?"

God works in mystifying ways. God used Tom to ignite my smoldering dream and, just as I asked, He made it plain enough for a fool like me to understand.

Many of us desperately want to be filled with the capacity to dream but life's hard places have taken the air out of our sails. Many of us have dreams but fear and procrastination prevent us from taking that first step toward the realization of the dream. Many of us have a dream but get bogged down with the everyday stuff of life and lie down on the side of the road and forget why we are on the road in the first place.

But this day, let us listen to the small, still voice of God as He speaks through the people, places, and circumstances that He sets in place and motion to help us get to where He has already prepared a place for us to be—living our dreams.

We must listen for God's encouragement and provision within the opportunities that come, the doors that open, and the doors that shut. It's as if God says to us, "Here, my child, walk this way. I know you don't understand it now, my chosen one, but I had to shut that door, so that I could lead you to this one. Come. This is the better door and I already opened it long before you got here. Everything's been prepared. I love you. Don't be afraid. Walk on through. I'm here with you and I'm already there with you."

Dear Heavenly Father: We thank you for the marvelous plans that you have for each and every one of our lives. Remind us that as long as there is breath there is hope and that our hope is in You. For those of us with vision for our lives, make it progressively clear. For those of us that lack vision, infuse us with your individual, tailor-made dreams. Give us the power, wisdom, and resources needed to carry our dreams through to fruition. And, above all, help us to never forget from whence comes our help. We thank you now for what you have done, are doing, and are about to do. Amen. So be it!

This is the confidence we have in Him,
That if we ask anything according to His will,
He hears us,
And if we know that He hears us,
Whatever we ask,
We know that we have the petitions that we have asked of
Him.

1 JOHN 5:14–15 (New King James Version)

God Alone
Knows the Plan

I moved back to Washington after living in North Carolina for what seemed the two longest years of my life. Now I was jobless.

"But I don't want a temp job," I told my lifelong friend Omie over the telephone. "I want a permanent job."

"That's what you want, Stanice. But what does God want?"

"Look, Omie, I need a full-time permanent job with benefits and that's what I'm looking for."

"How do you know that God won't bless you as a temp?"

I hung up the telephone disappointed that yet another friend didn't understand my needs. She had a permanent job and so did the two other friends that suggested earlier in the week that I sign up with a temp agency.

In the stillness of that night, I rolled from one side of the bed to the other unable to sleep. Three people had made the same suggestion. Perhaps they were right. Maybe God was speaking to me through my friends. I was reminded of a bit of wisdom a dear friend once shared with me: "If one person tells you it's a horse, maybe it is a horse, but if three people tell you it's a horse—saddle up!"

The next morning I called a temp agency and scheduled an interview. Two days later I had my first assignment as an executive secretary at *USA Today*'s *Baseball Weekly*. I replaced the temp they had, who had been selected for jury duty. In other words, I was the temp's temp.

On the third day of the assignment, the executive editor, Lee Ivory, came over to my desk and said, "Stanice, you're doing such a great job, we'd rather not have the other temp come back. Would you consider being the temp until my assistant comes back from maternity leave?"

"Yes, I can do that."

When I told the temp agency that I was staying, they locked me into the $10 per hour and refused to raise it to $13 per hour as previously promised. Since I had already given my word that I would stay on at *USA Today*, I stayed and worked that job like I was a full-time permanent employee. No excessive lunch breaks, long personal calls, or unnecessary days off. I was there and I worked to the glory of God for three months.

On the last day of the assignment, they announced that a birthday party for the executive editor was about to start in the conference room. I went in, looked around at a room full of smiling people that I had come to know. It was standing room only.

"SURPRISE," we shouted in unison. The executive editor took center stage. With a wide grin he said, "The party is for you, Stanice! It's our way of saying goodbye and to show our appreciation for a job well done."

A party for the temp's temp? I opened my mouth but no words came out. I was overwhelmed with joy and wonder that translated to a steady stream of tears. I put my hands over my face in an attempt to push back the tears but it didn't work. I cried and struggled for the words to say, if there were any.

As I enjoyed the party, I knew that they didn't know the story behind the story. I had informed the agency that I had applied for permanent jobs at *USA Today*. I understood the game. If I'm not a temp, then the agency can't make any money off me. This reality explained my next assignment. The agency had called the morning of the party and instructed me to report to Greater SE Community Hospital, which was at least twelve miles from *USA Today*.

The next day, I went to my new assignment. Three days later, the woman that I was working for came to me and said, "Had I not just hired someone for this position, I would hire you. You're really good."

I thought, *"Now what's up with your timing, God?"* But later that same day, I received a telephone call from *USA Today* asking me to interview for not one job but two.

One week later, on May 4, 1997, I was working as a *USA Today* full-time permanent employee with benefits. There I was—a writer with a dream of being a published author—amongst writers and editors in a creative environment.

By July 1998, writing diligently before and after work—with the strength and resources that only God could have provided, I had finished a manuscript and book proposal. Tom Fuller, my writing coach, and Tamara Holmes, an assistant editor at USAToday.com, in their spare time, graciously edited my work. I submitted the proposal and sample chapters to two publishers. Within a few days, Learning Publications, Inc., asked me to send the complete manuscript. A week later, they offered me a contract to publish. I accepted.

Meanwhile, God also blessed me to excel on the job. In December 1998, I was promoted to editorial assistant of USAToday.com.

With dream still in tow, on April 30, 1999, I became a published author with the release of my first book, *12-Step Programs: A Resource Guide for Helping Professionals*.

On my job during the day, I developed editorial, technical, and marketing skills especially as they relate to the Internet.

At night and sometimes way into the early morning hours, I wrote stories from my life's experiences and distributed them daily on the Internet. I also used the knowledge gained at USAToday.com to build myself a website, *www.stanice.com*, to distribute and market my first book, as well as my stories.

In 1999, it became clear, with prodding from my son and friends, that the life stories that I wrote and e-mailed were the beginnings of my next book. Before the year's end, God provided an agent and a contract to write what is now my second book, *I Say A Prayer for Me.*

On Friday, August, 17th 2001, I worked my last day for USAToday.com. Blessed going in and blessed going out. A season ends; a season begins. Yes, God truly blessed this temp's temp immeasurably more than I could have asked, thought, or imagined.

Have we put God in a box? Do we think He couldn't possibly bless us while we are doing something we don't really want to do? It's said that losers do what they want to do, but winners do what they have to do. Do we have horses that we need to saddle up so we can ride off into the perfect will of God for our lives?

Dear Heavenly Father: We thank you for using the people that you placed in our lives to give us guidance. Sometimes we are so busy looking for signs that we miss the wonders that you are so ready to perform—if we surrender. Help us to hear you in the small, still whisper and not have to wait for you to shout in the thunder. Help us to let go of our own agendas and yield ourselves to yours. Amen. So be it!

Now to Him who is able to do exceedingly
Abundantly above all that we ask or think,
According to the power that works in us,
To Him be glory in the church by Christ Jesus
To all generations, forever and ever. Amen.

Ephesians 3:20–21 (New King James Version)

Our Steps
Are Ordered

There is one thing I've learned—I may think that I'm going to a place for one thing and then God shows up and gives me much more than I could have asked, thought, or imagined. In New York City, not too long ago, this truth came alive for me.

It was a Monday morning. I took the shuttle flight to La Guardia Airport from D.C. for a speaking engagement. As I walked down the ramp and into the terminal, I scanned the crowd for my friend Stephanie Cruz.

"Stanice, over here!" There she was, a tall, pretty, willowy black woman with signature freckles.

I made my way through the maze of people. "Hey, girl." We hugged.

"It's so good to see you. You look fabulous!"

"Thanks, Stephanie. So do you."

"I'm illegally parked right out front so we better hurry before my car gets towed."

I soaked up all the sights as we drove through the streets of Harlem. It felt good to be in New York City. I had looked forward to this little trip for a while.

When we got to Stephanie's apartment building, a uniformed doorman greeted us. I had no idea that apartments in Harlem had doormen. Once inside, we talked about what was going on in each other's lives and shared our hopes.

"Tonight, after you speak, there is a woman that I want you to meet. Her name is Kimm McNeil. Kimm and her sister, Roxanne McNeil Johnson, promote a lot of events and they are always on some radio or TV show. I told her all about you and your book."

"Oh, yeah?"

"Uh-hum. You'll like Kimm. Maybe tonight you two can talk and she can give you some ideas about getting publicity for your book."

"Ah, Stephanie, thanks."

"Hey, sure. We got to look out for each other."

Later that evening, we went to the church where I was to speak. Stephanie introduced me to a lot of people. Others just came up and introduced themselves and everyone gave me a hug. I felt so welcome—so in-the-right-place-at-the-right-time. The place was filling up with people of various ages and races. By the time the program started, the huge room was packed. There were a few other speakers, each dynamic; each gave an inspiring message of hope. When it was my turn, I walked to the platform with a short prayer in my heart, *"Father God, you know what we need. I don't. So, I'm going to open my mouth and I need you to fill it up."* As always— He did.

After the program, on the sidewalk in front of the church, groups of people talked and laughed.

"Stanice, come here. Let me introduce you to Kimm." Stephanie brought me over to a lovely black woman.

"Kimm, this is Stanice."

"Hello, Kimm."

Immediately, with one dazzling smile, she put me at ease. "Hi, Stanice! Stephanie told me so much about you."

We talked and, at the right moment, I pulled a signed copy of my book, *12-Step Programs: A Resource Guide for Helping Professionals*, out of my purse and gave it to her. We continued to talk and she told me about a book entitled *The Personal Touch*.

"Stanice, it's a wonderful book that will inspire you and inform you about the publicity game. It's by a woman named Terrie Williams. She's an African-American sister who started her own public relations agency."

"Wow, that's all right!"

"Yeah. As a matter of fact her first clients were Eddie Murphy and Miles Davis and she's been pulling in all the big names ever since. The sister is awesome!"

In the meantime, Stephanie was rounding up those of us who were going to dinner. She had made a reservation at the Shark Bar, a famous upscale African-American–owned restaurant on the Upper West Side. We got into our cars. Stephanie and I rode together.

We found a parking space close to the restaurant and as I got out Stephanie told me, "Bring a copy of your book and a few of those cards with the photo of you on them promoting your book. Stanice, you never know who you might meet."

I followed her instructions and said, "Sure, you're right. Thanks for looking out for me, Stephanie. I'm so new at this."

We crossed the street and met the group in front of the unassuming restaurant. A line of us, men and women, followed Stephanie into the foyer and waited there while she went over and talked with the smiling hostess. After a few minutes, Stephanie walked over to us and started counting heads. "Well, the good news is they have the reservation; however, they can't seat us until all thirteen of us are here and there are three still missing."

None of us, including Stephanie, understood the rationale behind that move. But we were a pretty accepting bunch that night after all that good stuff we had heard at the anniversary celebration and it was a nice warm night, so we filed back outside and waited. We laughed and talked about how wonderful the anniversary had turned out. "Here they come," someone said. "That's them pulling into the parking space across the street." We all got excited at the thought that we were finally about to eat. It was close to 9:30.

All thirteen of us filed into the restaurant. This time we were in there long enough to experience the decor and ambience of the place. As the hostess led us through the restaurant, I noticed what appeared to be parchment walls that showcased an impressive collection of black and white photographs. The hostess smiled graciously and seated us in a private dining room. Stephanie had made sure that I sat next to Kimm. We each ordered. While we waited for the food, we zoomed in on the hot sweet potato muffins.

We were having a great time getting to know each other. We were about five minutes into our dinner when a woman came into our dining room and headed straight for Kimm.

"Hello." Kimm got up and the two of them talked quietly.

Stan, one of the guys at our table, spoke to the visitor too.

I smiled at the woman and went back to eating my food. As I was bringing a forkful of collard greens to my mouth, I felt a tap on my shoulder and Kimm's voice. "Terrie, you won't believe this but not a half hour ago I was telling Stanice here," as she nudged me to get up, "about you."

It still didn't hit me. For a moment, by the looks on their faces, everyone knew something that I just didn't get. Maybe it was late and I hadn't finished sending nourishment to my brain.

"Stanice, this is Terrie Williams, the woman I was telling you about earlier."

It was all happening so fast. "Hello, Ms. Williams." I

smiled and gave her a firm handshake. "I don't believe this. This is great!"

"Hello."

I was speechless.

Kimm took over. "Terrie, Stanice just had her first book published . . ." And she went on from there. I just stood there.

Terrie smiled, probably sensing my numbness, and asked, "What's the title of your book, Stanice?"

"*12-Step Programs: A Resource Guide for Helping Professionals.*" Then I leaned down and got one of the flyers off the floor beside my chair and handed it to Terrie.

"I'll check it out."

"Thanks. It was a pleasure meeting you." I sat back down.

Kimm and Terrie continued talking a little while longer. Then Terrie said goodbye to everyone and walked out.

Kimm looked perplexed. "Stanice, why didn't you say more?"

"I didn't want to impose. I figure she might be as hungry as I was and would want to get to her meal." I started in on my dinner again.

A thought hit me: "*Why didn't you give her a copy of the book? Like duh, Stanice. Hello?*"

I turned to Kimm. "I should have given Terrie my book, huh?"

"Yeah! I figured you didn't give her a book because you didn't have any with you. I would have given her the one you gave me but you signed it and wrote my name in it."

"I've got a copy under the table."

"You're kidding."

"No! Do you think it's too late for me to give it to her? Did I miss the window of opportunity here?"

"Stanice, get up and take it to her now! She's in here somewhere. Find her!"

I hesitated but everyone around the table urged me on. "You can do it," came from one end. "Go for it, girl!" came from the other end.

I got the copy from under the table, stood up, and declared to my tablemates, "I can do this!" What they didn't hear was the quick prayer I mumbled as I walked to the doorway of our private dining area: *"Lord, you know exactly where she is, find her for me, please."*

I turned the corner into the dimly lit main dining room to begin my search. "Oops! Excuse me." I bumped into somebody—I couldn't quite see who.

"No, excuse me." The woman's voice sounded familiar.

"Oh my goodness, Terrie!"

"Stanice?"

"Yes! I was just coming to find you. I wanted to give you a copy of my book. I'm so new at all of this. I didn't know what to do."

"And I was just coming back to get you!"

"Really?"

"Yes." She held out my card. "This looks great!"

"Thank you, that means a lot coming from you." I handed her my book.

She leafed through it. "This is wonderful! You've got to tell me more."

She led me over to an empty table and we sat down. "I want to know how you came to write this book. Tell me something about you and your background."

We talked for about ten or fifteen minutes. I gave her my work and home numbers. "How long will you be here in New York?"

"Well, my plan was to go back tomorrow morning in time for work, but I'm sure I can work something out, if you think I should stay around tomorrow."

"I've got to think about all this. How to approach it. But I promise you, I will call."

"Thanks so much for taking the time to talk with me."

"It was my pleasure. Your book will help a lot of people."

As I walked back toward the dining room, I heard someone call my name. It was Terrie. "I promise to call you."

"Okay."

I wanted to shout right there in the middle of the restaurant, "Thank you, Jesus!" But I controlled the urge and shouted on the inside instead. I believed I could fly back to our dining room.

When I walked into the room, everybody's mouth was agape.

"Girl, we can't believe it! You were with Terrie all this time?"

I told them everything. We were all in awe at the mighty power of God to order our steps and bring together His plan, which is *always* more than we can ask, think, or imagine.

A few days after I got back home, Terrie Williams kept her promise—she called.

Think back to instances in your experience where you have been in the right place at the right time. Some of us chalk these up as simple coincidences, but are they? Or is God ordering our steps?

When we yield ourselves along with our plans, hopes, dreams, and desires to God, He will order our steps. We can hold on to God's promise that if we delight ourselves in Him, He will give us the desires of our hearts.

Dear Heavenly Father: We too are in awe of You. We thank you for all you have done, are doing, and are about to do. We love the creative ways that you provide for us, lead and guide us. Thank you for keeping your promises. Thank you for taking the time to create wonderfully individual plans for each of our lives—plans for prosperity and not disaster, plans to give a future and a hope. Amen! So be it!

Trust in the Lord with all your heart,
And lean not on your own understanding;
In all your ways acknowledge Him,
And He shall direct your paths.

Proverbs 3:5–6 (New King James Version)

What You Give to God
Is Never Lost

Something incredible happened Friday evening, November 5, 1999. Something so incredible that the evening is etched in my mind forever. I met God at the Lost-and-Found counter.

I was at work and it was getting close to quitting time— 6:30 P.M. I pretty much resigned myself to staying late, as had become my norm. However, by 6:45 a pressing desire to leave flooded over me. I can't explain it but I knew not only that I needed to go, but also I knew that it was not for home that I was bound.

What seemed to just drop into my mind like a fisherman's net was that I needed to go to McKenna House to a twelve-step group meeting that had been my regular group for years when I first stopped using drugs. I was so compelled to go that I immediately stopped what I was doing, turned off my computer, grabbed my briefcase, and walked briskly to my car in the underground garage. I felt like I was on the brink of something wonderful happening.

As I drove to the meeting in my brand-new turn-of-the-century Tampa blue pearl Mitsubishi Gallant, I pondered just how far God had brought me.

I recalled the tiny efficiency apartment where I had lived more like an animal than a human being. I remembered the endless nights and excruciatingly painful days when I couldn't break free from the death grip that addiction had on me. I thought of the lonely and empty years trapped in the vicious cycle of living to use and using to live. I recalled the degrading and unbearable nights filled with the smells of cheap cologne and the whiskey breath of faceless men. I remembered my reflection in the mirror, an aging black woman with self-inflicted needle puncture wounds trailing my neck, arms, hands, legs, and feet like the black stitches that held Frankenstein together.

I recalled looking out at the sweaty and huffing marathon runners pacing themselves up the hill right outside my window and feeling like an inmate on death row looking out the bars of my self-constructed prison. I retasted the fear in a cotton-dry mouth that I learned to live with every day of my existence. I was afraid that I wasn't blessed enough to die, but instead I was cursed to "misery-away" somewhere in a glass-strewn alley under a flickering street lamp surrounded by rats and stray dogs. I remembered the look on my son's face as he sat on his grandmother's porch waiting for his mother to show up, wanting to believe that I would, but fearing, as usual, I wouldn't get there before his bedtime, if I got there at all.

I wept as I contemplated the infinite magnitude of God's love and mercy that He showed to me as He reached down from His Heavenly Home, gently scooped me up in the palm of His mighty hand, and lifted me out of the dismally dank and dark pit that was my life. I immersed myself in the thirst-quenching thoughts of God's daily sweet kisses that sear this brand-new life in me. As I drove from one stop light to the next, one right turn to the other, on every stretch of the road from my office to McKenna House there was a knowing inside me that I was now bathed in sunshine, oiled down in love, and dried in the cool breezes of hope and a fruitful future.

As I approached my destination, I wondered with the innocence of a child on Christmas morning, *What is waiting for me at McKenna House? Why this overwhelming expectancy?*

Of course, I tried to figure it out. Anything else would not be true to my character. *I will at least get to see the old friends that got clean with me.* The "old-timers," they call us now, as we referred to those who came before us who paved the way in learning how to live life without drugs. Oh, what a long way God has brought so many of us. Whether others realize who or what brought them through is not my business. I know that I know God brought me through. Man could not do for me what God could only do—save a wretch like me. *What is waiting for me at McKenna House?*

As I pulled into a parking space, I thought of the neighborhood: This was where I took my bus ride to the addiction treatment center; across the street was the apartment building where John Smith locked me in the tiny, windowless bathroom in an attempt to keep me from using drugs; where we both discovered on that stifling hot, near unbreathable August day, there ain't no mountain high enough and no pit deep enough to keep a full-blown junkie from getting high. Eventually, it was where my mattress and black-and-white television set with the coat hanger antenna had been tossed onto the sidewalk because I failed to pay the rent. It was also where Jesus Christ had a predestined appointment to free me from the heavy chains of addiction that clanged around my neck and clamped down my life.

As I skipped up the steps to McKenna House, I wiped away the joy-tears and rejoiced in the discovery that I was walking in the gift-journey to recovery.

Once inside, I received the hugs and smiles of my friends who had journeys of their own that God allowed them to

I Say a Prayer for Me

share with me and the friends that I hadn't met yet who were just starting out. A prayer in my heart went up that their roads to recovery would be as rich and fulfilling as mine has been thus far.

After the meeting, Melvin came over, hugged me, and said, "I'm so glad you're here. Remember that poetry I told you about? Well, it's in my truck. Wait right here and I'll go get it." He turned and walked briskly out the door.

I stood frozen in my tracks. I wondered, *The poetry? Could it be? I had forgotten what he had said over a year ago. Was it really my poetry?*

According to Melvin, in the late 1970s, while at a university in Washington, D.C., he found a yellow binder in one of the study rooms. Upon opening it, he found that it was full of poems typewritten by Stanice Anderson. He read some of them, decided that he liked them, and took the binder home.

Eventually we met; however, I was introduced to him as Stacey, my nickname. When our paths crossed again in the mid-1980s, I had returned to my birth name, Stanice, but I still had my first ex-husband's last name. In addition, he had long since forgotten about the yellow binder.

Then, in 1998, as Melvin moved into a new house, he came across the yellow binder. As he revisited the poetry, he recalled that I had shared in one of my talks my lifelong passion for writing. In that moment, he realized that I had to be Stanice Anderson, the author of the poetry he had found twenty years ago. The next time he saw me, he told me the story about the yellow binder and promised to put it in his truck so that he could give it to me.

One year later—God got both of us in position to bless and be blessed—and this was the night! I waited for him outside on the front steps of the meeting place. My pulse raced and my head felt light as I watched Melvin briskly dodging traffic as he made his way across the street. When he reached the steps, he smiled and handed me an envelope that seemed to shimmer under the bright street lamps and car headlights.

I pulled out a stack of paper with a yellow cover and back page bound by black plastic spine. Memories flooded my mind all at once like a dam bursting. As I held the manuscript in my hand, I remembered punching the holes and binding them. I opened it and saw my words stamped in black on the page by the metal keys of a typewriter. The names of the poems: "Discovery: Phase One," "Nalunga," "Gone," "A Fading Memory," "The Asphalt Jungle," "Man's Elegy," "In the Beginning," "Reflection of a Fool." Tears welled in my eyes. I had not seen my words or felt my rhythms in over twenty years.

I recalled details, like the clothes I wore when I wrote "Reminiscence"; what I felt when I penned the words to "The Song My Heart Sings"; how raw my heart was when I poured out my poem "Remembering" to my son's father.

Inside the yellow binder was also an indexed section that contained lyrics to songs. I had long forgotten that I wrote lyrics, that there had been a time when music played itself in my heart constantly. All the poems and lyrics had dates no later than 1976, the year my son was born.

I turned and hugged Melvin. "Thank you so much. Never in my wildest dreams would I have thought I would ever see these poems again. God used you to give them back to me . . . or maybe they were never really lost."

As we talked and marveled at how all this had been orchestrated, I realized that nothing in God's keeping is ever lost! When He knew that I was ready, He brought my poems back to me.

Our faith falters sometimes and we think that all is lost, whether it be a situation, a thing we cherished, or a person;

but You, Father God, have *the last say* in everything. You know the desires of our hearts even before we realize that a desire even exists and You delight in granting those desires.

We sometimes get impatient and say *"Hurry up,"* or *"When, my sweet Lord, when?"* Or we get depressed and feel the weight of dreams deferred. Or we resign ourselves to believing that it's too late and that the desires of our heart will never be realities. It seems like when we get to any of those points, God sends somebody, some music, a painting, a gorgeous sunny day, a smile—He can use anything and any-one—to remind us not to give up five minutes before the miracle happens, because with God all things are possible and His timing is perfect! He's never a minute too late or a second too soon.

Dear Heavenly Father: How magnificent and unchanging is your love and care for us. We are like lost poems sometimes ourselves but whatever it takes—the whole universe and a heavenly host of angels are at your command—You use Your resources to find us and bring us back in fellowship with You. We thank you for rekindling our lost dreams, birthing new dreams, and repairing shattered hopes. We are grateful for how you guide us to the right place, at the right time, and for Your right purposes. We are learning more every day that what we yield to You is never lost! Amen. So be it!

But, beloved, do not forget this one thing,
That with the Lord one day is as a thousand years,
And a thousand years as a day.
The Lord is not slack concerning His promise,
But is longsuffering toward us,
Not willing that any should perish
But that all should come to repentance.

2 PETER 3:8–9 (New King James Version)

※

COMPASSION

※

One Day at a Time—Forever

I refused to wear black. Instead I wore a pale pink and white Angora sweater with a winter-white wool skirt. I sang that glorious morning like I had never sung before. "One day at a time, Sweet Jesus, that's all I'm asking of you, Lord. For my sake help me to take one day at a time."

"Amen!" the congregation said in unison. I walked past the choir, down the carpeted steps, and stopped briefly at the shiny white coffin where the shell of Mary Jane lay. I carried with me the essence of the woman Mary Jane safely in my heart. As I took my seat on the pew, I knew that Mary Jane was in Heaven smiling at me. "You were right, Mary Jane."

Months prior to this, Mary Jane picked me up to take me to a support group meeting as she had often done. "Hi there, Pretty-Girl-That-Can-Sing."

"Why do you always call me that? You never call me by my name."

"Baby, to me that is your name." She smiled, shifted gears, and pulled off into the traffic.

I really liked this woman. I had been clean and sober for less than a year, compared to her twenty-plus years. Mary Jane was a petite fifty-something and had a face like a black angel. She was funny, spry, drove a jazzy mauve car, and had her own home, which she often shared with women early in recovery until they could get on their feet. She sort of cackled when she laughed, and left people mesmerized as she told dramatic stories about her life. We'd listen and learn. It was rumored that she had cancer, but she never talked about it, so I never brought it up.

"So, are you enjoying your new life in recovery?"

"Yeah. It gets hard sometimes; but overall, I'm enjoying not using drugs one day at a time."

"It wasn't easy for me either in the beginning and some-times not even now; but it does get better. You just hold on to the fact that it does get better because *you* get better." She took one hand off the steering wheel and patted the back of my hand. "You're gonna be all right."

The next time I saw Mary Jane she was a lot thinner. "Hello. It's so good to see you." We hugged. "I've asked Dorine, how is the Pretty-Girl-That-Can-Sing?"

"How you been doing, Mary Jane?"

"Oh, I'm going to be all right. My spirit is up, it's a lovely day, so therefore all is well."

We sat down and talked mostly about me. She wanted to know what had gone on in my life since she had last seen me.

After that, I would see her from time to time and she'd be sporting a totally coordinated outfit. That woman could dress! She had style and always kept herself in a brand-new pair of shoes. I think she bought shoes like I bought books—totally to the extreme. But she was walking a bit slower and I noticed grimaces of pain on her face, but from somewhere deep down inside she would continue to pull out smiles for everybody.

Then I heard she had moved out of her house into the house of a friend, who was also a nurse, because she was mostly bedridden and couldn't climb stairs. I went to visit. Her friend answered the door. "It's Stanice," her friend shouted.

"No, you mean it's the Pretty-Girl-That-Can-Sing," a voice shouted back.

"That Mary Jane is a trip, ain't she?"

"Yeah. You gotta love her."

The woman led me to the dining room, now converted to a bedroom to accommodate Mary Jane. Medicine bottles lined the buffet and a portable toilet with handrails sat in a corner of the large room. Mary Jane lay there in the bed smiling radiantly at me. She had this uncanny way of making people feel special and loved. After spending time with her, you felt like you could do anything you set your mind to. It was a rare gift God had given this little woman.

"I brought you some of my famous, homemade, anointed, chocolate chip walnut cookies. I gotta fatten you up, woman."

"Well bless your heart."

"I put in plenty of sugar, and loads of butter. And I prayed for you all over that cookie dough."

"You're something else! They smell wonderful. I guess I'll have to change your name to the Pretty-Girl-That-Can-Sing-and-Bake."

"Oh, Mary Jane." We laughed. From that time on, I baked cookies for her.

A few weeks later Dorine called me. "Mary Jane called. She wants us to come over to see her tonight."

"Okay, I'll be ready by the time you get here."

While Dorine drove, I cut the silence. "Dorine, she's getting better. I know she is."

"I don't think so. I take her to chemo every week. She seems to be getting weaker to me and she told me that the cancer has spread. She's in pain most of the time but she tries not to let on. That's just the way she is."

I looked out the car window and silently prayed for Mary Jane's healing.

Her friend opened the door. "She's having a rough night tonight but she insists on seeing you, so go on in." As we walked toward the dining room, we heard the sound of footsteps ascending the stairs.

"Dorine."

"Yes."

She strained for those words and dug deep for the smile. "And where's the Pretty-Girl-That-Can-Sing?"

"I'm right here, Mary Jane."

Dorine dragged a chair beside the bed and sat holding Mary Jane's hand.

"I'm dying you know."

I felt the uncontrollable urge to stop her next thoughts. "No! Don't say that, Mary Jane, because I asked God to heal you."

"And He will, baby."

"Then why are you saying—"

"Just listen. I asked both of you to come here because there are some things I want you to do for me."

"Anything," Dorine said. "We love you."

"Yes, I love you, Mary Jane."

"You first, Dorine. I want you to handle the funeral." She handed Dorine a sheet of notebook paper. "Everything you'll need to know is on this piece of paper." She pointed to a beautiful light-colored suit that hung in the doorway. "That's what I want you to have them dress me up in."

This is all too hard for me, I thought, and contemplated how to make my break for the door.

"Stanice. Stanice!" Dorine's gruff voice forced my mind back from planning my escape.

Dorine nudged me closer to the bed. Mary Jane reached for my hand. Sitting on the side of her bed, I allowed a silent prayer to escape instead, *"God, please give me strength."*

"I'm gonna need you to sing," Mary Jane commanded.

"You mean right now?"

"No, at my funeral. I want you to sing 'One Day at a Time.' I love that song!"

"But I don't even know the words to the song."

"You can learn them."

I turned away because I couldn't hold back the tears another moment. She gently pulled my chin around and looked deep into my tearing eyes and said, "Please sing that song for me. Sing it so I can hear it up in Glory."

"Mary Jane, I can't do that."

"You can and you will because I believe in you, my Pretty-Girl-That-Can-Sing. Now let's pray."

Mary Jane wanted to sit up so we helped her. We held hands, bowed our heads, and I waited for one of the great women of God to pray. Silence. I peeped at them. They were both looking at me.

Dorine was the first to break the silence. "Stanice, you pray."

I had never led a prayer with other people present before. Mary Jane and Dorine both took my hands in theirs, bowed their heads. I bowed my head. Silence. I peeped and each of them was looking at me.

"Well . . ." they said in unison.

"What? Pray out loud?"

"Yes! Stanice," Dorine offered as she smiled and shook her head.

"God help me." At that moment, it was like the butterflies in my stomach all took flight at the same time and came out of my mouth as words. I really prayed that day. I mean, I just told God all about it! It was like an out-of-body experience. I heard my voice, but I couldn't believe that it was me praying. "Amen! Hallelujah!"

We all breathed a sigh and looked at each other with tears streaming down our faces and collecting under our chins. Mary Jane pulled me to her shoulder. "If you can pray like that, you can sing my song."

The next day I bought the sheet music but I still didn't want to learn the song. In my mind as long as I didn't learn the song, Mary Jane couldn't possibly die.

For the next month, we visited Mary Jane in the hospital. She writhed in pain and the sparkle in her eyes was fading. Her world was filled with monitors, pills, and nurses that intruded with behind-the-curtain medications.

Then, late one night, I was home on my knees at the side of my bed. "God please. I'm scared. I'm selfish. You know that I am. I don't want Mary Jane to leave me. Who will make me feel I can do the impossible? Who will make me feel special? I need her in my life. It's just not fair. You put her in my life, please don't take her away." I had no words left to express how I felt. I cried, moaned, and rocked.

In the next moment, an unexplainable calmness came over me. A peace covered me like a warmed sheet on a doctor's cold examination table. Deep within my thoughts came such an unselfish thought that I knew that it was not mine. It had to be a thought from the very mind of God: *"Let her go. Let me heal her in my way and in my time."*

I responded to the gift-thoughts with a prayer. "Lord, I thank you for Mary Jane. I know that you will heal her, whether you decide to heal her and leave her here on earth or heal her and take her to heaven. Your will be done."

I got up off my knees and went straight for the telephone and dialed the number for the hospital. "Hello, is this the nurses' station?"

"Yes."

"I know it's late but I'm calling to check on Mary Jane. Is she resting well tonight?"

"Who is this?" I told the nurse who I was. She remembered me from my visits, and the nurses on that wing of the hospital knew Mary Jane.

"I'm sorry to have to tell you this but Mary Jane died peacefully in her sleep about five minutes ago. One of the other nurses is calling Miss Dorine now."

"Thank you for being so kind to my friend Mary Jane." I hung up the phone.

I sat down on the side of the bed and through my veil of tears I noticed the sheet music on my night table. I reached for it and allowed my love for Mary Jane to etch the song in my memory and heart. "One day at a time Sweet Jesus, that's all I'm asking of you, Lord for my sake help me to take one day at a time."

All of us yearn to be loved and accepted for who we are right where we are. Hopefully, we all will at some time or another have people with hearts like Mary Jane in our own lives. People that believe in us even when we haven't grown enough to believe in ourselves. People that make us feel special and worthy. I believe that those of us that have experienced the grace of God through the voice and actions of another will be given opportunities to do and be the same for someone else.

It's said that to whom much is given, much is expected. Someone, somewhere needs our love and kindness today. May we be unselfish enough to give the love, kindness, and support that has been so freely given to us. May we live our lives as nobly, courageously, purposeful, and compassionate as the Mary Janes of this world.

Dear Heavenly Father: Thank you for the people that you place in our lives for whatever reasons and during whatever seasons. May we embrace the lessons that you want to teach us as we allow You to touch us through them. We say, "Yes to Your will, Lord, and yes to Your way." Teach us to loosen our grip on the temporal and to cling to the eternal—You and Your will for our lives. Thank you that when our time on this earth is over that it will mark, for us, a brand-new beginning. Amen. So be it!

When the perishable has been clothed with the imperishable, and the mortal with immortality, then the saying that is written will come true: "Death has been swallowed up in victory." Where, O death, is your victory? Where, O death, is your sting?

1 CORINTHIANS 15:54–55 (New International Version)

Bittersweet Surrender

There is at least one in every workplace—that one difficult person who seems to just rub you the wrong way.

Not long ago, I worked as an office manager for a small
African-American–owned business. As far as I was concerned,
I was in charge. Nothing happened in that office without
my knowing about it. I did payroll, employee orientation,
accounts payable and receivable, ordered supplies, quelled
employee disputes, and worked as much overtime as I
wanted. Then one fateful Friday it happened.

The owner of the business, a tall, willowy, dark-complex-
ioned man, came over to me and announced, "Stanice, I've
got a new business partner."

"Oh, yeah?"

"Yes. My mother."

I thought, *Now, isn't that precious. His mother, a silent business
partner.* So I said, "That's really nice."

He continued, "She'll be working here in the office as vice
president of administration."

"Really?"

"Yep. She starts on Monday."

"And what Monday would that be?"

"This coming Monday. I want you to train her. I want her to learn everything that you do, including the financial software system."

"Sure. No problem."

"Now, Stanice, you'll still be the office manager; but it may mean your role will change a little bit. But with all that you have to do around here, I'm sure you'll welcome the help."

My whole body went numb and my thoughts took flight. *His mother? Vice president of administration? Doesn't he get it? I don't need any help and I definitely don't need change. I'm fine. This office is "my show," and I'm not keen to share the spotlight.*

I left work that Friday evening for what ended up being the shortest weekend of my work career. I seemed like I blinked and it was Monday morning.

I drove to work and parked my car in front of the building. I noticed a van in the parking lot that I had never seen before. It had to be his mother's. I sat there in my car, turned off the radio, and prayed to God for the strength to get through the day. When I got out of the car I was fully convinced that all was well with my soul.

I walked into the office. "Good morning," I greeted one of the guys that worked for the company.

"Hey, how you doing, Stanice?"

"I'm blessed!" I smiled and kept walking.

A tall, willowy, brown-skinned, middle-aged woman stood in the doorway of my boss's office. It had to be his mother. He looked like she spit him out. She introduced herself.

The first couple of days we butted heads like two rabid rams. It was a small office, and every step that I took—there she was. I had my way of running the office and she had her own ideas of how the office should be run.

She was constantly over my shoulder saying, "Why are you doing that?" and "I wouldn't do it that way if I were you." Then there was the "I take care of that now."

She wouldn't even let me make a simple bank deposit anymore. I felt like she thought I was going to steal something from her son. *Didn't she know my history? Didn't she know I'd been there almost two years and there had never been a dime unaccounted for?*

My overtime all but stopped. My patience with her went from tissue-paper-thin to nonexistent. My answers got short and curt.

One day as I sat at my desk preparing an invoice, she came and stood over me and said, "Stanice do you have a problem with me?"

I looked up at her; but before I could answer—

She hovered over me, raised her voice, and moved her long slender neck from side to side. Bending over me with her index finger about two inches from my face she hurled out, "You are an employee of this company. My son and I own this company and we sign your check. You don't seem to understand that you don't run nothing!"

At the very least, I wanted to jump up out of my chair and dislocate the index finger she pointed in my face. Everything inside of me wanted to say, *"I'm out of here! Take this job and stick it where—"* But I sat there and silently sent up a rescue-me-from-myself prayer. *"Lord, please help me stay in this chair and keep my mouth shut."*

From my chair, I looked up at her and said, "You know what? You are absolutely right. I don't run anything here. I am an employee of this company and I'm grateful that I still have a job. I have not handled this whole situation well at all and I'm sorry. You tell me how you would like to see things done." I couldn't believe I had said that.

She lowered her hand, her voice, and parked her neck in neutral. She told me how she expected things to be run and, to the best of my ability, I did just that—but nothing more. With each day that passed, my dislike for my boss's mother evolved into borderline hatred.

Each day, it got harder to conceal my true feelings. Hatred consumed me from the inside out. It was contrary to all I professed to believe. I felt like I was perpetrating a fraud—and in my heart I was. Unable to stand it any longer, I took my feelings to God. Even though I knew that He knew, I confessed all that I was feeling and asked Him to forgive me and to take away the awful feelings.

As I was down on my knees, it seemed like the Lord shone a flashlight into the recesses of my heart. I did not like what I saw. It was not my boss's mother that was the problem—it was me and the condition of my heart. It is always easier to put the blame somewhere else—but to look at my role in whatever the situation—that's a whole 'nother thing.

I had to search within myself and identify what was really going on that made the ground fertile enough for the seeds of hate to take root. I admitted to God and myself that I was jealous, envious, stubborn, and unwilling to submit to her authority. I was also angry with God and myself that I was not further down the road in my life and career than I thought I should have been. I was insecure and felt threatened by my new boss. So, I asked God to forgive me. Just like His Word says, He forgave me on the spot because when I'm faithful to confess falling short of what He would have me do, then He is faithful to forgive me and wash me clean of the thing that I am confessing. However, there was still something that I needed to do to work out my own salvation.

What permeated my mind next was the story in the Bible where Jesus washes the feet of his disciples. I reached for my Bible on my nightstand and turned to the index to find out exactly where the story was. I asked God, *"Why has this story come to my mind?"*

I found the story in the 13th chapter of John. I started reading at Verse 1 and read to Verse 8:

It was just before the Passover Feast. Jesus knew that the time had come for him to leave this world and go to the Father. Having loved his own who were in the world, he now showed them the full extent of his love. . . . Jesus knew that the Father had put all things under his power, and that he had come from God and was returning to God; so he got up from the meal, took off his outer clothing, and wrapped a towel around his waist.

After that, he poured water into a basin and began to wash his disciples' feet, drying them with the towel that was wrapped around him.

He came to Simon Peter, who said to him, "Lord, are you going to wash my feet?"

Jesus replied, "You do not realize now what I am doing, but later you will understand."

"No," said Peter, "you shall never wash my feet."

Jesus answered, "Unless I wash you, you have no part with me."

I imagined Jesus going around the table to each one of the disciples and washing their feet—including the feet of Judas Iscariot, who Jesus knew was born to betray Him. I read on—starting at John 13, Verse 12 through Verse 17:

When he had finished washing their feet, he put on his clothes and returned to his place. "Do you understand what I have done for you?" he asked them. "You call me 'Teacher' and 'Lord,' and rightly so, for that is what I am. Now that I, your Lord and Teacher, have washed your feet, you also should wash one another's feet. I have set you an example that you should do as I have done for you.

"I tell you the truth, no servant is greater than his master, nor is a messenger greater than the one who sent him.

"Now that you know these things, you will be blessed if you do them."

I closed the book. I knew, in my heart, that I needed to apply the principle of the story to my particular situation if I was to get the full benefit of the reading. So reluctantly I tried to visualize washing the new vice president's feet. The thought of lifting her long dark brown feet in and out of a bucket of water was beyond my scope of possibilities.

I confessed to God, *"I'm just not there yet."*

All that night I couldn't get the image of me washing that woman's feet out of my head. I felt like I wrestled with an angel. Back and forth we went.

"Stanice, you must."

And me saying, *"Oh, no, not that. Anything but that."*

I tried to barter with the angel because I could visualize buying the woman lunch or giving her a compliment—but washing her feet? That was asking too much.

The next day at work I still had the images of the story in my mind. I even found myself glancing down at her feet. I shuddered.

Later that day, I discussed my dilemma with my friends over lunch. Of course, they thought I had lost my mind to even be considering such an exercise. It became apparent that this was between God and me.

Every night that week, I reread that story. At first I focused on the promise of Verse 17, *"Now that you know these things, you will be blessed if you do them."* I wanted that blessing part. But I knew that to get the blessing I had to embrace and put into action all the principles that the example set, including: love, humility, mercy, and submission. The promise was conditional, it meant: *"if you do them, you will be blessed."* The blessing was the fruit of the labor.

In the presence of the Lord, that very night, as I lay in my bed between healing and sleep, I visualized myself washing her feet. *"Yes, Lord, I see now. Thank you for teaching me YOUR WAYS."*

When I went to work, it was like I was seeing and hearing her for the first time. I heard her anxieties. I listened for her softness and her love—both were present. I saw the actions of a woman who was as out of her element with me as I was with her. I saw a mother who loved her son so much that she had given up her good government job to come and help him in his time of need. I saw a woman who sought to protect her son like a lioness protects her cub. *Would I not do as much for my own son?*

From that point on we got along. A few months later on Christmas Eve she handed me an envelope that contained a beautiful card with a handwritten note: *"Thank you for all you have done for the business and for training me. You went out of your way to help me and I'm grateful."* Also inside the card was a $50 bill. I hugged her and felt genuine love for her. I realized, at that moment, that God had changed my heart.

Yes, there is at least one in every workplace—that one difficult person who always seems to rub us the wrong way. We just need to follow Jesus' example to make sure that we are not that one.

Borrowing from the twelve-step recovery programs, there are four steps that come to mind that can be used as tools to help us have a better and more effective relationship with God, other people, and ourselves. Step 4: *"We made a fearless and moral inventory of ourselves.*" Step 5: "*We admitted to ourselves and another human being the exact nature of our wrongs.*" Step 10: "*We continued to take a personal inventory and when we were wrong promptly admitted it.*" And Step 11: "*We sought through prayer and meditation to improve our conscious contact with God as we understand Him, praying only for the knowledge of His will for us and the power to carry it out.*"

If we are not right with God and ourselves, it's impossible to have healthy relationships with other people.

Dear Heavenly Father: Thank you for speaking into our hearts your Word of Truth, even though that Word cuts like a two-edged sword sometimes. We thank you that you love us enough to tell us the truth. We are learning that it is for our eternal good. Thank you for your patience and your mercy. You teach us by example the way we should go. Your sheep know Your voice even though sometimes it takes us a while to trust it and trust You. Amen. So be it!

Remind the people to be subject to rulers and authorities,
To be obedient, to be ready to do whatever is good,
To slander no one, to be peaceable and considerate,
And to show true humility toward all men.
At one time we too were foolish, disobedient, deceived
And enslaved by all kinds of passions and pleasures.
We lived in malice and envy, being hated and hating
one another.
But when the kindness and love of God our Savior appeared,
He saved us,
Not because of righteous things we had done,
But because of his mercy.

Titus 3:1–5 (New International Version)

If It's Broke,
God Can Fix It

"Momma, what did you do today?" I've found that our visits together are longer if I stay in the waters of shallow conversation.

"Not much. So, what kind of book is this that you're writing?" my mother interjected.

I really didn't want to go there with her. "They're just stories, Momma."

"Stories? What kind of stories?"

"Life stories. I write about my experiences." I dared not say any more.

She shifted herself forward onto the end of the sofa, craned her neck, looked into my eyes as if to peep beneath my surface.

She took a deep breath. "Well, I'm telling you now! If you write anything about me and brutality, I'm suing you!"

Still in a relaxed position on the love seat across from her and with a slight smile, I said, "You know what, Momma? I don't doubt that one bit."

I turned the conversation back to safer waters. "So, Momma, when did you move that étagère? I like it there."

For the rest of our visit, the conversation never returned to my writing. We both found safety in not discussing my stories further.

As I drove home, I realized that we had both come a long way compared to where we were—at least we could stay in a room together for longer than five minutes. I also realized that her statement to me was spawned by fear.

I understand, now, that people do strange things when motivated by fear. Fear of the present—the future and growing old—or of being alone. Although some people would never admit to being afraid, it's evident in their actions, words, and, especially, in their eyes. It's like when my mom and I are talking sometimes and I look into her eyes—they are vacant. The essence of the woman is not there.

However, I know she loves me. It's just hard for her to show and receive love. I'm learning that it is better to understand rather than be understood. But it's hard sometimes to love people right where they are—just as God loves us— right where we are.

There was something else that I distilled from my mother's statement. She admitted there was some brutality going on. This was the second time that she admitted that something was not right in the way I was raised.

Months prior to this visit, I dove headfirst into treacherous icy waters by confronting her over the telephone.

"Momma, why did you beat me and treat me like you did?"

"That was thirty years ago. You're damned near fifty. Get over it! That's the way Grandma raised me. I got over it! I raised you just like she raised me. Look, you abandoned your son and he still loves you. Get over it!"

The conversation deteriorated from there and I hung up without saying goodbye. My whole body seemed to be novocaine-numb for a few minutes, and then I cried like a two-year-old.

God always knows what I need when I need it because, within minutes, I heard my twenty-three-year-old son's key in the door turning the lock. I ran to him and cried on his shoulder. I told him as best I could what had just happened and how I felt. It was strange, but I also felt relief because the brutality was finally out in the open. Secrets die in the light of exposure.

The fits of rage that my mother displayed were not something that I had imagined or remembered wrongly. For many years, I thought that had I been a better child or a wiser adult then I would not have brought forth the "wrath of Ginny." Or if I treaded lightly in conversations or told her enough times that I loved her, then it would have been received and I would not have been physically or verbally battered.

I thought back to a conversation I had with my father when I was in my thirties. I wanted to make amends to him for all the harm I caused him and my family. Basically, I ended up apologizing for being born.

He looked at me in what was one of our few tender moments and said, "Stanice, it's not all your fault. You grew up in a very dysfunctional home."

My ears had to be lying. Could this be my perfect father, the head of my perfect family, confessing the true state of my past home life? I was relieved and angry. Why hadn't someone told me before now that the way I was raised was not normal? All those years I believed that I was the only thing wrong with the family.

In that moment, I understood what a friend told me once. "What you may or may not do to a person can be the catalyst that brings out the rage that is already in their hearts."

I don't know everything that went into the mix of my mother's life; but somewhere along the line, she was hurt so badly it left a gaping wound that festered and oozed onto her family, as we were the closest to her. It was nothing personal, hurt people—hurt people. Misery does love company.

I am not a victim because when I look back over my life, I see that because life got tougher for me my faith got stronger. It's partly because my mother and father raised me like they did that I am who I am. I'm a survivor, fighter, and overcomer!

In addition, I appreciate the wonderful relationship I have with my son. Not having a good relationship with my mom taught me that I have to work at my desire for a good relationship. That it is a two-way street where we both have to want it so bad that we're willing to communicate, be flexible, listen, share who we are, where we are, where we hope to go, and sacrifice. It means listening more than we talk. It means sharing our fears, inadequacies, joys, blunders, and victories. It means becoming vulnerable.

A few weeks later, I was still a bit disturbed by the exchange with my mother that day about my stories, so I talked with my childhood friend Omie.

"Stanice, you've got to write a story about you and your mother. You are not the only one who struggles with a relationship with their mother. God will use your story to free someone else up to love their mother regardless of what has happened in the past or what is going on now."

"But, Omie, I don't want to hurt her and I definitely don't want her to sue me! You know Ginny."

"Look, Stanice, you are accountable to God. You must obey Him! The devil doesn't want you to see the love that is there between your mother and you. He wants you to remember only the pain; but there is something warm and wonderful that happened between you and your mother. You've got to search your heart and memory to find those things. Then you will get your breakthrough."

"Okay, Omie. You're right. Because more than anything, I

would love to have a close and loving relationship with my mother."

Omie reassured me that with God all things are possible, as she shared with me a story of another friend who now has a great relationship with her mother.

After I hung up, I prayed and asked God to do for my mom and me what it seemed we could not do for ourselves—come together in love and unity. *"I'm willing, God, to search for the good and let go of the bad."*

A few weeks after I asked God to show me the good days with my mother, I was driving down a road in Durham, North Carolina, and memories flashed through my mind like the 8mm movies that my father used to make of us. With my eyes on the road, I reached over to the passenger side, fumbled in my purse, pulled out my trusty micro–tape recorder, and spoke the thoughts in my mind. As I spoke, the projector in my mind started to roll scenes from days long gone.

I saw my mother and me, no more than ten years old, in Atlantic City on the Scrambler amusement ride—me on the outside squeezing my mother into the corner as the ride gyrated and whirled around on its metal tentacles. I heard our laughter stroking the late evening ocean breezes like Van Gogh stroking the colors off the palette and onto the freshly prepared canvas. I loved being with my mother. There was never a dull moment with her.

And then it happened! In my mind, I saw it again. My mother's wig flew off her head and disappeared into the crowd. The ride was minutes from over and I could see the childish embarrassment all over my face, and the man who stood at the gray metal gate surrounding the ride smiling and waving the wig in one hand.

He yelled as we whizzed by him. "Miss! I caught it!"

My mom and I looked at each other tenderly and then burst out laughing. We laughed so hard that we almost peed our shorts. I recalled that she always took the time to take my brother and me on vacation, even when my father was too busy with his work.

Fast-forward and I was about eleven years old, and my mom and I were on the train, headed for yet another few summer weeks down to where she grew up in Broadway, North Carolina. She had prepared her usual shoebox of fried chicken, hard-boiled eggs, and other goodies to eat on the train, as we "Negros" were not yet allowed in the dining car. I felt her warm breast as I slumped up against her to take a nap as the train clattered its way south. I always felt safe with my mother.

Fast-forward and I was thirteen and she was teaching me to sew.

"Stanice, you cut along this line. Now, you try it." My mother knew how to do so many things well and was always willing to teach me.

Fast-forward. We were in the neighborhood drugstore, after church, sipping on a fountain cherry Coke and ordering double-dip scoops of black walnut ice cream.

A man noticed her striking beauty as he passed by. "So how are you sisters today?"

"That's not my sister! She's my mother!" I staked claim, as I was always proud to do, because she was so beautiful and youthful. We chatted like sisters and loved like mother and daughter.

Rewind. Starting at about eight years old. I saw my mother sitting at our mahogany piano, tickling the black and white keys with her long caramel-colored fingers, tapping her feet on the pedals in 4-4 time, and singing out in a raspy soprano voice, "Lord, I searched and I searched. Lord, I cried and I cried. I searched and I searched until I found the Lord. My soul . . . just couldn't be contented. My soul . . . just couldn't be contented. My soul . . . just couldn't be contented. Until I found the Lord."

While she sang, my brother and I ran around the coffee table listening for the music to abruptly stop so that we could claim the side-arm chair. I loved musical chairs! My mother used her gifts to give us joy.

She ministered to my spirit with every song that she played and sang. It seemed that each song pulled up and parked in my heart. My mother planted the seeds of the need for God in my life a long time ago.

Fast-forward, and I was an adult. In my mind, I heard my voice on the telephone that day.

"Momma! Please come over here. I've got to talk with you right away."

"What is it, baby?"

"I'll tell you when you get here."

Within half an hour she knocked on my apartment door. I opened the door and saw a face of compassion and love for her daughter who evidently needed her.

Crying, I went into my mother's arms. "Momma, I'm pregnant!"

For some folk, this would be a jump-for-joy day; but my situation had extenuating circumstances. My husband, Clem, had left me about eight months prior after only three months of being married to me. I was in a relationship with another man, Michael Tucker, whom I loved and I believed loved me. And this was whose baby I carried.

"I thought I was just getting fat; but I'm three months pregnant!"

"What do you want to do?"

"I want to have this baby."

She hugged me tightly. "So, I'm going to be a grandmother. That's all right with me, baby. I love you. Everything's going to be okay!"

"I love you too, Momma."

Months later, when my new son, Michael Tucker, Jr., and I

needed a place to stay my mother and father took us in. Because of her compassion and generosity, my son and I had a fruitful and merry Christmas. I still have photographs.

Fast-forward. Each illness or operation that I've had, my mother was there. Whenever she was called, she came right away.

How it must have hurt her that day, when police called to report that her daughter had overdosed on heroin. To see her baby girl, laying in the ICU wired with fluid lines, monitors, and breathing with the aid of a respirator because of a collapsed lung, must have been hard. I recall coming in and out of consciousness and looking up into her swollen, tearful eyes. I recall her holding my hand and stroking my hair. She kept watch over me, and how she must have prayed. God answered my mother's prayers and brought me back from the precipice of death—three times.

Another time I went into surgery for a biopsy of my breast. My son along with my mother followed the gurney, holding my hands, reassuring me that I was going to be all right.

"God is gonna fix it for you, Stanice."

"We have to take her into the OR now," the doctor told her—again.

Reluctantly, she let go of my hand.

It was like the floodgates of Heaven had drenched my mind in sweet memories of my mother. It was getting harder to concentrate on my driving.

Someone behind me beeped their horn and ushered me back to the present moment. The light had changed and it was time to move. I wiped the tears away with one hand while holding the steering wheel with the other. Overwhelmed with gratitude, I pulled into a shopping center parking lot, away from the rest of the cars, turned off the engine, and wept. *God, I thank you for answering my prayer."*

I realized in that moment that love does cover a multitude

of sins and that light and dark cannot coexist. *"Help me stay focused on the pure and lovely thoughts, as I see that within them lies the light that chases away the dark."* It's not the condition of my mother's heart that I am responsible for—but my own heart.

There in a Durham, North Carolina, shopping center parking lot, I made a conscious decision to let the hurt die and the love grow. The rest is in God's hands. Even though I was hundreds of miles away from home, I whispered into the warm Southern air, "God is going to fix it for us, Momma."

I still have hope for a better relationship with my mother; but I realize that we both have to want it and work for it. In the meantime, I visit, call, and pray for my mother and myself to be free of whatever chains us to past hurts.

May God help us to surrender our past hurts and lift the gaping emotional wounds up to Him to heal. He put us here on this earth to love each other and He will help us to do that. No, we didn't choose the families we were born into but we must trust God in all things and in all of our ways. Before we bog ourselves down with the unanswerable whys? of our lives, we need to remember God's promise: "And we know that all things work together for good to those who love God, to those who are called according to His purpose" (Romans 8:28) New King James Version.

It's so easy for us to remember the wrongs that people have done to us. It's even easier for us to forget the wrongs that we have done to others. However, it should be hard for us not to forget how God loves us so unconditionally. In spite of what we do—don't do—say—or leave unsaid, God loves us. He loves us so much, in fact, that if we offer our broken relationships up to Him, He will fix them—starting with the me that we see in the mirror.

Dear Heavenly Father: Remind us of Your love, especially when we don't get or give the love we feel we need within our families. Heal our hearts and mend our families. Help us to stay in touch with how you love us, so that our deepest desire will become to love others in the same way. Knowing that You love us, unconditionally, makes loving others so much easier. Thank you for the privilege of prayer and for the peace that emanates from a simple act of surrender. We are learning that we are welcomed—even encouraged—to bring anything and everything that concerns us to you in prayer. Amen. So be it!

**He heals the brokenhearted
And binds up their wounds.**

PSALMS 147:3 (New King James Version)

*

SURRENDER TO
GOD'S WILL

*

Make Your Bed Hard— You Gotta Lay in It

I had been back in my nine-year-old son's life and drug-free for all of six months the night of the talent show, and I found that it takes more than just the title of "Mother" to be a mother. I had much to learn, and that night the real lessons began.

After I gave what I thought to be a brilliant vocal performance of "Ooo Baby Baby," I descended into myself. I traded my responsibility to be a loving, considerate mother for the TV version of an insensitive and selfish pseudo-star. I am sure that God knew the moment that I walked out onto the stage that I was not ready for the spotlight; but I didn't have a clue. It felt like it was my night—singular.

Well, one song led to another. I was hot and I didn't want the night to end. I sang background for a group that performed after me. Then lead vocal with another, another solo, and then as I accepted the applause of the crowd, I looked over to the side of the stage, and there stood my nine-year-old son, Michael. It was 10:00 P.M. He motioned to me to come to him.

"Okay, baby," I said and shook my head in answer to him just in case he couldn't hear me over the applause.

When the stage curtain was drawn, I walked toward him. I thought, *What's wrong with him, he doesn't look like he's having a good time anymore.* "What's wrong, Michael?"

He rocked his small body as he whined, "Mommy, I want to go home."

"Okay, honey, but Mommy's got to sing one more song, okay?"

"No, Mommy, please take me home."

"Come on, baby, it will be over before you know it and then I'll take you home all right?"

"Okay," he said.

"Here, give Mommy a hug." I leaned down and he hugged me around my neck and walked back to his seat.

I don't even remember the name of the next song I sang— or the next—or the next.

I do remember that I heard whimpering off to the side of the stage: "Mommy, please."

"Okay, Michael, just one more song." The stage, music, and applause were like aphrodisiacs. They made me feel powerful like the drugs once made me feel—until they turned on me and showed me just how powerless I really was. Michael stood there looking at me and wiping tears from his eyes. I reassured him, "One more, Michael. That's all."

I wondered, *Why does what I'm telling my son sound so familiar? Where had I heard those words before? "Just one more." Had I traded one drug for another? No time to think of that now. I've got just one more song to sing.*

Michael stomped his foot and brought me back to his need. "Mommy, now! Mommy, I want to go home."

Poor baby, it was 11:00 at night. I could tell he was sleepy because his eyes become thin slits in his beautiful face when he's tired. *He looks so much like his daddy. His father's eyes reacted the same way whenever he was tired.*

"Mommy!"

Insistent little tyke. He probably got that from his dad too.

Suddenly, a grown-up voice invaded my mother-to-son talk as I had all but convinced him that the next song really would be THE LAST song.

"Stanice!"

I turned around. There was Barbara Noonan, the director of the talent show, with her cheeks puffed out and one hand on her hip. I thought, *What is her problem? How dare she use that tone of voice. Couldn't she see that I was having a private conversation with my son?*

"What, Barbara? May I help you?"

"Stanice, take that boy home! He's tired and he should be home and in his bed asleep this time of night."

"Barbara, please!"

I could smell the greasy potato chips that lingered on her breath as she stood almost nose-to-nose with me. As she reared her neck back, her freshly spiraled Jerri curls shook and shone under the bright corridor light. Like bullets, her words shot out of the barrel of her mouth: "Look, girl, you already sang your last song. Cut! That's a wrap! The show's over for you! Now, take that boy home."

"Barbara, listen! You—"

"No, Stanice, you gonna listen to what I have to say and I don't care how much you don't like it. You always talk about wanting to learn how to be a good mother. Well consider this your first lesson! Your child's needs MUST come before your own. Look at him. What are his needs at this moment?"

She was right. I didn't like her talking to me like that, especially in front of my son, but as I looked at his face pleading a trail of tears, the truth-tipped arrow of conviction pierced my heart and in that moment I realized that my actions were cruel. Tears welled up in my eyes.

I pulled Michael to me. "Okay, baby, Mommy hears you and we're going right now. I'm taking you home." I gently wiped his tears with my lips as I kissed his tears away. "Mommy's sorry. Go and get your coat. I'm taking you home."

I turned and hugged Barbara. And like a jaunting slap that brings a hysterical person back to reality, I wiped away my own tears and said, "Thanks. I needed that."

Barbara looked into my eyes. "You're gonna be all right, Stanice. You will learn."

I gathered up my things and my son and walked toward the door. As we made our way up the side aisle, people came up to me. One woman said, "Girl, you tore that song up! I didn't know—"

"Thanks, but not now. I've got to get my son home. It's late."

My son looked at me and wiped the remaining tears from his face. At that moment perhaps we both understood the unspoken. *Finally, Mommy's got it!*

Since it was so late, rather than trying to hail or call a cab, I asked a friend to take us to Michael's grandma's house—his home. The car ride was thunderously silent. My mixed emotions gathered in my body like storm clouds. I silently lashed myself with questions and admonitions. *How can you say you love that boy and yet treat him like that? See, you're not a good mother and you never will be. What's different? Maybe you don't use drugs anymore, but your life still stinks!* I had been wrong and I didn't know how I would ever make it right. I turned and looked in the back seat of the car. Michael was asleep. I leaned over the seat and gently positioned him so that he would be comfortable.

When we got to his grandmother's, the lights on the porch and the living room were on. How she must have worried. She opened the front door before we even hit the first step. I could tell she was mad by the way she cut her eyes at me— she had a right to be mad. Dazed and half asleep, Michael stumbled up the steps and fell into her extended and protective arms.

"Stacey!" With her Bermuda accent dragging out the "a." She still called me by my nickname. "What were you thinking? Having this child out this late! And you didn't even call! I didn't know what had happened."

"I'm so sorry," I meagerly offered.

"Yeah. Uh-huh. How many times have I heard that?"

Evidently, one too many times.

"Goodbye, Michael." I don't even think he heard me.

His grandmother sucked her teeth and closed the door.

As I walked back to the car, I prayed, "Lord, I took a beautiful night, unwrapped it, and then just threw it away."

When I got into the car, my friend said, "Are you all right?"

"No, I'm all wrong tonight. All wrong."

All the way home, down every street, in every house and store, on every person, and at every stoplight, all I could see was the tear-stained face of my son.

As I got out of the car, I believe my friend offered me some sugarcoated words of encouragement but I didn't take any of them. Bad mommies don't get dessert. "Good night. Thanks a lot," was all I said.

I looked toward my apartment building. No light on the porch for me. No one waited for me to come home. Still, as was my custom when I turned the key in the lock and opened the door I called out, "Honey, I'm home." I hoped that one day someone would be there to acknowledge that I was home—perhaps even my son. In the meantime, it was God and me; and even He had to be angry with me.

Later that night, I kneeled down at the side of my bed and sobbed into my orange bedspread. "Oh Lord, how can I be so old and so stupid? Help me please. I know so little and learning is so difficult and a slow process for me. I try to get it right and I mess up every time. I desperately want to be a good mother. Please teach me how because I have no earthly idea how this mother thing is supposed to go. Put into my heart a mother's love."

When I got up off my knees, there was a dark wet circle of tears. I thought about the many times I cried that same pattern into the bedspread during the six months since I had stopped using drugs. As I thought of how weak and vulnerable I felt most of the time, I realized that it had to be God that pulled me through many a night without using. As long as I didn't go back to my old ways of using to live and living to use there was hope. In spite of crying through so many nights, God always delivered fresh new mornings and a string of hope-filled one-more-days.

Is this what was meant by the grace of God? Is this unconditional love? The answer swirled around my thoughts like cotton-candy clouds on a clear spring day: "Yes, it's that and so much more." I smiled, as the truth broke loose inside me. I felt sure that God would not love me any less when I blew it than He does when I get it right.

In the next moment, I recalled something I must have heard someone say: *"God will always love you no matter what you do or don't do. Nothing can separate you from the love of God."* I wiped my tears and blew my nose, as it felt as if God wrapped His loving arms around me and emptied me of all my doubts. I felt like all was well with my soul.

As I got into bed, I reached over onto the nightstand to turn out the light and noticed the poster my son made for me a few months before. It read in big blue balloon letters: "Mom and Son. Nothing can penetrate our Love."

Nothing? I thought.

As my spirit absorbed the colored marker strokes of love on the poster, out of my heart leapt the unequivocal answer to my question: *Absolutely nothing.*

During the following months, I continued calling and visiting my son at his grandmother's. I believe that we both felt the damage of my actions, as there was not much said between us after the night of the talent show.

One day, as he rolled by me on his wobbly skateboard, I sheepishly asked, "Michael, how about you and I go to a picnic some of my friends are having—?"

Before I could get out when and where, he brought his skateboard to a halt and said, "No, Mommy."

I dared to ask and he dared to answer. This was the first time Michael said no to going somewhere with me and I was about to find out that it would not be the last no.

Over the next five or six months, whenever I asked him to go somewhere with me he gave me an emphatic "No." He offered no explanations, no questions, no "let's explore the possibilities." It felt like a "Just Say No" campaign. No! End of conversation—Period.

One day, feeling a bit stronger and bolder, I went a bit further and after his usual "No" I said, "Come on Michael, go with me. It will be all right. I'll ask your grandma, okay?"

"No, Mommy, I don't want to go."

"Why not?"

"Because."

"Because what?"

"Because—no!"

I'd like to think he was too kind to come right out and say, "because of that night at the talent show, Fool Mommy." I knew why; so I didn't press. Still, it hurt me each time he said no.

I started to understand that my blatant irresponsibility that night at the talent show pierced my son's heart, which, in turn, pierced my own. My heart and my son's were connected. When I hurt him, I hurt myself. When he hurts—I hurt. I alone was responsible for the tear in the relationship; and it was my responsibility to make amends. I made my own bed hard, now I had to lie in it—and it hurt!

Discouraged, it seemed like the bitter lesson would never end. I called my mentor and friend, Dorine Phelps, who had been a part of my life since I left the addiction treatment center. She understood my struggle to remain drug-free and build a relationship with my son. She always listened to me, answered my questions, and encouraged me.

"Dorine, will Michael ever forgive me and go somewhere with me again?"

"Stanice, that boy loves you! He forgave you a long time ago. Just give the boy time to heal. Both of you are learning each other. You just keep showing up, and in God's time— not your time—he will say yes. He has got to learn to trust you again."

"But it's so hard. And it hurts so much."

"It's okay, baby. Let it out. You gonna be all right. You just need to understand that it's not tell-and-show time any- more—it's SHOW-and-tell time! He's got to SEE your love in action. He's got to see that you are about him and not just yourself anymore. Just stop asking him to go places for a while. Don't press that boy, Stanice. Let God fix it!"

"Okay, Dorine. Thank you. I love you."

"I love you too, baby. Trust me when I tell you—it's gonna be all right by and by."

As I hung up the telephone, I looked toward heaven. "God, you really handpicked that woman into my life."

Well, I followed her advice. I'd go over to his grand- mother's house and we did things right there. It also gave me a chance to get to know his little cousins and friends that lived in the neighborhood. Before I knew it, I had lots of chil- dren in my life. I have always felt like a perpetual child; so I liked playing games like hopscotch, school, and red light with them. I also started sparking their imagination by inventing games like "Storyteller" where I'd start a story that I made up on the spot and each child's challenge was to finish the story. The most creatively told story won the applause, admiration, and affirmation of all who listened. I believe that was their favorite game, and it was definitely my favorite.

Every now and then, in the midst of these days together, I asked my son to go somewhere with me, but he still said no. It didn't hurt as much anymore because I enjoyed being with him and it didn't matter where we were.

On the eighth month after the talent show, I called Michael early one Saturday morning.

"Mike, would you like to go to a basketball Unity Day with me?"

"Yes, Mommy."

"That's all right, honey. Maybe the next time."

"No, Mommy, I said yes!"

"You said yes? Really?"

"Uh-huh."

"Oh Michael, that's wonderful. I promise to take you home when you want to go home, okay? You just say the word and we're out of there."

"Okay, Mommy."

"And how about this? Why don't you ask your cousin Kiesha to go with us? That way, you'll have someone your own age going along. How about that?"

"Okay. Yeah."

"You'd like that?"

"Yep! Oh man!"

"All right then. Put your grandma on the phone so I can make sure that it's okay with her."

He hollered out, "Grandma, my mommy wants to ask you something."

As I waited for his grandmother to come to the phone, I realized that I absolutely loved hearing my son call me

"Mommy," especially since I didn't hear it as often as some mothers do because he didn't live with me. My thoughts exposed my deepest desire: *Yet! He doesn't live with me YET.*

His grandmother came to the phone. Out of respect, I asked her permission to take Michael and Kiesha with me and gave her a reasonable time to expect us home. Wanting her to know that I had learned my lesson, I also told her that if at any point they wanted to leave before that time, I would honor their wishes. She was a bit reluctant, and I didn't blame her. I knew it was because she loved her grandson to whom she had been more of a mother than I had ever been.

On the day of the event, I took a taxi to his grandmother's house. As I watched the city sights from the back of the cab, from my heart flowed a silent prayer, *"Lord, please don't let me mess this up again. May I decrease and you increase in my life today."*

When the cab turned the corner and pulled up in front of the house, Michael and Kiesha waved from the porch and hurried down the steps to greet me. As my son wrapped his arms around me, I thought, *What a wonderful day this is!*

Since the community center was only a few blocks away, we walked, talking all the way. Once we got there, perhaps I was a bit too attentive at first. Every half hour or so I asked Michael and Kiesha, "Are you okay? Do you want to go home?"

"No," they answered each time as they ran, laughed, and played with their new friends in their own basketball game they had going on.

I watched from the bleachers and tears came to my eyes. *"Thank you, Lord, for giving me a mother's love that I can show my son. Lesson learned."*

A few hours later, I walked lightly on my aching feet to where they were playing tag, and said, "I'm tired. Can we go home now?"

Michael looked at Kiesha, then turned and looked at me. He smiled and nodded his head. "Okay, Mommy. We're ready."

Both of them took my hand in theirs and walked me toward the gym door. Mike yelled out to his new playmates as we passed by, "Hey y'all, we're going now, my mommy's tired."

Sometimes, we are so slow to learn the lessons that God would have us get into our spirits so that we can live more useful, fruitful, and abundant lives right here on earth. We tend to make the same mistakes over and over again, until we get tired of reaping the consequences. Like my grandmother used to warn me, "You make your bed hard, you gotta lay in it."

But with our eyes wide closed, we still insist on doing it our way. Then, after we make a mess of something and have to live with it, wrestle with it, cry, moan, and groan through it—just trying to get to the light that must be somewhere on the other side of it—hopefully, we eventually get to the point where we are sick and tired of being sick and tired. It is only then that some of us become open enough to confess to ourselves and God the possibility that "Maybe, I don't know as much as I think I know. So, I'd better try something different this time."

Yes, thank God for our hard beds. Sometimes they are necessary for our surrender to God's will instead of ours. In the meantime, God patiently waits for us to come to the end of our natural selves and call out for the supernatural help that is always just a prayer away.

Dear Heavenly Father: Though we admit that our lessons seem painful at the time that we are going through them, we take the time today to thank you for wrapping us and the lessons that we bear in Your love. We are learning that because you love us and know exactly what we will need for the road ahead that you correct and perfect us. We are coming to believe that your correction is not to punish us but to equip us for the plans that you have for our lives—plans for prosperity and not disaster—to give us a future and a hope! Thank you for the lessons that are blessings that will not only benefit us, but everyone and everything that we come in contact with. We are learning, ever so slowly, that it isn't just about us and that "we" is greater than "me." How wonderful that when You touch our lives, we are never the same again. Amen. So be it!

My brethren, count it all joy when you fall into various trials,
Knowing that the testing of your faith produces patience.
But let patience have its perfect work,
That you may be perfect and complete, lacking nothing.
If any of you lacks wisdom,
Let him ask of God,
Who gives to all liberally and without reproach,
And it will be given to him.
But let him ask in faith, with no doubting,
For he who doubts is like a wave of the sea,
Driven and tossed by the wind.

JAMES 1:2–6 (New King James Version)

*

LET GO
AND
LET GOD

*

Letting Go

Letting go is never easy—never.

Ever since I made a decision to turn my life and will over to God's care seventeen years ago, I have slowly let go of old perspectives, attitudes, and some of the people that populated my life.

Shortly after I had stopped using drugs, Pat, a woman who had been my get-high partner, somehow got my telephone number and called me. I knew that I couldn't stay drug-free if I continued to hang out with her.

"Stanice, meet me after work. You know I get paid today."

Hearing her voice coupled with "payday" brought back vivid images of hypodermic needles, and my body slumped with my head bobbing back and forth in a drug-induced stupor. My heart raced as I felt the twinges of agitation that always preceded the anticipation of the thrill of the chase to find the best heroin package on the street. *"God help me,"* my prayerful thought zoomed upward like lightning striking in reverse.

Immediately, my mind snapped back to my new drug-free reality. Determined to hold on to my new life free of the despair, degradation, and hopelessness that were a daily part of the addicted lifestyle, I focused on the grace and love of God, the hope I found, my son I had begun to build a relationship with, and my new friends who encouraged me and were willing to teach me how to be all that God had created me to be. I didn't hear much of what Pat said.

Feeling a jolt of heavenly strength, I said, "No, Pat. I don't use anymore and you don't have to use anymore either. God can change your life just like He changed mine, if you would only let Him. Why don't you meet me at a twelve-step meeting? Let me introduce you to some people God put in my life who help me not use drugs one day at a time. Just like we got high together? We can stay clean together."

"Okay, girl. What time and where?"

I gave Pat the time and address. That was over seventeen years ago. She has yet to meet me at a twelve-step meeting. A couple of times a year, she calls and I invite her to my clean-time anniversary celebration but she never comes. Pat's sister tells me that she does okay for a while and then goes back to the old lifestyle. I keep praying for her and my hope is that she will make it out of the bondage of addiction—alive.

Letting go is never easy—never.

I also had to learn to let go of old behaviors, especially since I had been such a promiscuous woman—it was a part of the lifestyle. I knew that I needed help to change, so I talked it over with my mentor, Dorine Phelps.

"How do I get through the lonely nights alone?"

She looked at me with the tender look of a wise mother. "Baby, you just have to pray, hold on, don't use drugs, and you will start to want something different for yourself."

A few months after trying out my mentor's suggestions, I walked to a party up the street from where I lived. A new friend was giving the party for her cousin, whom I did not know. I danced so much that I needed some fresh air to cool off, so I went out to the backyard. As I looked at the full harvest moon, I softly sang my favorite old song by Smokey Robinson and the Miracles, "Ooo Baby Baby." I was alone or so I thought.

During the second stanza, I heard singing coming from behind me—it was a man's voice.

I slowly turned around, without missing a beat in the song, and my eyes delighted in the most incredibly handsome, smooth-skinned Black man I had seen in a long, long time. The moonlight outlined his silhouette and seemed to make him shimmer. It was like a scene in a romantic comedy. It also reminded me of the commercial where the woman runs in slow motion through a large field of swaying wildflowers toward her man and then jumps into his opened strong arms.

We continued singing our duet, never missing a beat. We finished the song in perfect harmony. When he flashed that perfect smile, I felt like a teenager again.

He said, "We sounded real good together. What's your name?"

Melodiously I said, "Stanice."

"Stee-niece?" He fought for the right pronunciation.

I was used to people mispronouncing my name, so I offered the usual help. "No, Stan-niece. Stan like in Stanley. My dad's name is Stanley. My brother's name is Stanley and my mother's name is Stannette."

"For real?"

"No, I was just kidding about my mother. Her name is Ginny."

It broke the ice and we waded into a conversation.

"I've seen you before. You came to my cousin's celebration a few months ago. I asked her about you. I'd really like to get to know you better. And before you even ask, no I'm not dating anybody. Do you live around here?"

How presumptuous of him, I thought. But still I answered with a simple, "Yes."

"Do you live alone?"

"Yes."

"It's my birthday tonight and I would really like to spend it with you. Why don't we go to your apartment?"

"Is that what you usually do on your birthday, go home with a woman you just met?"

He backed up a few steps. "No. It's just you I'm feeling the need to be with. I don't know what it is but I'm just drawn to you."

"I'll tell you what it is. It's lust!" I said. At least it sounded like my voice. I couldn't believe I said that.

"No, you got me all wrong. Don't judge me by other men you may have met. But, hey, we can talk about that on the way to your apartment."

"No!" I said it so vehemently that I scared myself.

"Hey, Stan-niece, no problem." He twisted his words in like a knife. "It's your loss."

As he walked away, I wanted to shout out, *"Ask me again."* But I said nothing. He kept walking and didn't even bother to look back.

Stunned at the way I handled the situation, I stayed looking at the harvest moon and wondered why I felt like I had done something wrong and unnatural. After a few minutes, I went back into the party. I made my way through the crowd and upstairs toward the front door. As I put on my jacket, I wanted to find him and tell him that I had changed my mind but I didn't. Instead, I whispered, *"Lord, let him ask me just one more time, please."*

I walked slowly down the street toward my apartment, turned occasionally, and hoped to see him running to catch up with me before I made the right turn. It seemed colder going home than it did when I had walked up to the party.

The guy never called out and I never heard footsteps or a song from behind. I was alone—again.

Once I got home, I prepared for bed and prayed, *"God, please help me get through the night. I am so lonely."* I cried myself to sleep that night.

Letting go is never easy—never.

The next day I got dressed up in my finest royal blue suit and went to a banquet that I had looked forward to for weeks—alone. This was another exercise suggested by Dorine, about learning how to take myself out and not depend on a man to take me everywhere.

When I walked through the door of the banquet hall, I noticed at a table by the entrance the same incredibly handsome guy from the night before with his arm around a beautiful woman. She was staring up in his face beaming a smile and straightening his tie. He looked at me and lowered his head.

I held my head high and gracefully walked into the main room. Friends ran over to greet me with hugs. They suggested that I join them at their table. As I followed them, I whispered softly, *"Thank you, Lord, for last night 'cause I sure would have felt like a fool today."*

Letting go is never easy—never. But until we let go of the old, we cannot embrace the new.

My mentor once told me, "Girl, when God is ready to bless you—you gonna mess around and miss the blessing because you're all jammed with that." Whatever "that" is for us at any given time in our lives. She's right! Sometimes we hold on so tightly to the old, not realizing that, until we let it go, God can't move us to the next level of our faith-walk.

How can we press forever forward, when we insist on dragging into our present and future what I refer to as "blasts

from the past"? Whether these "blasts" are destructive behaviors, harmful relationships, or negative thought patterns,
we have to let them go. God stands ready to bless us. He
wants to do a new thing in our lives, if we are willing to let go
of the old.

How can we know what God's marvelous plan for our life
is, if we are busy trying to work out our own plans? Why not
surrender our plan to God by asking Him, "What is your plan
for my life that you predestined even before I was born?"
Trust God and let Him show you your uniqueness in Him.
There is something that only you were born to bring to the
world. Let go of your preconceived notions of what that may
be and allow God to bring to fruition His glorious plan for
your life that is far greater than anything that you could
think, ask, or imagine.

Fall back into the arms of God. Trust and don't be afraid.

Dear Heavenly Father: Thank you for giving us the strength and wisdom that we need to let go of the useless and harmful behaviors, people, and ideas. Letting go is not easy for us but with You we can do all things. Help us develop a closer walk with you. Talk us through the lonely nights and days. Remind us that we may be lonely but we need never be alone because You are forever with us. Amen. So be it!

Do not love the world or the things in the world.
If anyone loves the world, the love of the Father is not in him.
For all that is in the world—the lust of the flesh,
The lust of the eyes, and the pride of life—is not of the Father
but is of the world.
And the world is passing away, and the lust of it; but he who
does the will of God
Abides forever.

1 JOHN 2:15–17 (New King James Version)

Confession Is
Good for the Soul

Dear Daddy:

I do so enjoy your letters. I hope you don't mind but after the last family gathering I shared your letters with your grandson, Mike. It made his heart glad to know that you are proud of him. Lately, you have communicated your feelings in letters and verbally that I've always wanted and needed to hear from you. I guess it's natural and normal for a daughter to need validation from her father.

Even as I was growing up I'm sure you loved me though I don't recall you saying it. But if you did, maybe I was not open to receive the love. My life hurt so much of the time and I wanted to tell you—but I couldn't. I lived in the shadows somewhere between pain and shame. I could not break free no matter how hard I tried. I laughed and attempted to appear normal but the anger—the ache—the secret held me hostage.

Remember the first time I played hooky from school? I was fourteen years old and I just wanted to be like the other girls. I was tired of being different—of being a good little girl. It was too lonely. Well, something happened to me that spring day that forever changed my life. Childhood as I once knew it ended. I awoke a vibrant rose of youth that morning and by afternoon the petals were stolen and stomped on, leaving only the stem of prickly thorns lost somewhere between limbo and hell.

I went voluntarily on a dare with a girl that I thought was my friend to Northeast Washington. I had no idea that I was the virgin that was to be led to the rim of a volcano and sacrificed to appease the gods. We went to an apartment on Adams Street. There was one guy there who said some other girls were on their way. My friend said that she was going to the store and would be right back. I followed her to the door, but she wanted me to wait there so that I would be there when the other girls arrived.

I nervously sat on the couch as I noticed that the boy looked older than what she told me he was. He attempted conversation and then I heard sounds coming from the back of the apartment. Following the sound were voices—men's voices. Everything happened so fast. Down the short hallway came a man, then another man. That made three men and me. They seemed to have come out of the walls like roaches when you turn the lights on. I headed for the front door. I don't know who hit me first. Fists pounded into me, hands covered my mouth, and arms pulled my legs. They dragged me into the bedroom.

Then the air filled with cursing and shouted demands. "Shut up! I'll kill you if you scream."

I tried to fight but my legs and arms were pinned to the bed. "Please don't do this," I begged. "I'm only fourteen!"

"Didn't I tell you to shut up? Shut her up, man." Fists, then more fists pounded my face. I could feel my eyes swelling like dinner rolls on a hot day. Everything faded to black. Then, lights flickered like strobe lights and comets with endless tails. A combination of excruciating, pulsating hot pain and icy numbness surged through my body.

"Daddy! Daddy! Help me, Daddy!" I cried out to you; but you never heard me. You never came. No one came. No one helped me.

Drowning in a pool of shame, degradation, and pain, I wanted to die. I remember thinking, *How can I live with this? How will I explain to my parents or my husband one day that I'm not a virgin anymore? Everyone will know. God, why are you letting this happen to me?*

It felt like car doors slamming and smashing every part of my body at the same time. I hid myself as best I could under a fortress of thoughts, prayers, promises, wishes, and anything that would help me not be there in that awful and degrading place, with those horrible and brutal men. And then like I wished it—it was over. But it would never really be over.

The three men let me go; but I heard one of them tell my girlfriend, "Make her understand that if she tells—she dies!"

What no one could see was that something inside me had already died. My hope in a future and my desire to live through the present. My ability to love and be loved. My trust for anything that breathed—especially men and big girls that pretend to be friends. My belief in God who the preacher in the pulpit said had promised to never leave me nor forsake me. My belief that I was a worthwhile human being. All murdered and left inside me to rot. I was damaged goods; destined to be alone. Alone with the nightmare. Alone with the pain. Alone with the secret of what happened that spring. The stench began before I could get back home.

For years, I relived that rape almost every night in my dreams. As the nightmares haunted me, my pain turned to anger, which, in time, gave birth to rage. A red-hot rage directed toward men, who had the capacity to hurt me, women, who had the capacity to betray me, and myself, who had the capacity to let it all happen. I also felt rage toward God for allowing the rape to happen. I vowed never to be hurt again—never to trust again—and never to love God or human beings.

For a time, drugs and promiscuity seemed to help me forget. The succession of men and living life on the edge became my therapeutic answer to killing the secrets that would not die.

In addition, I soon found out that secrets grow in the dark. They fester like a cancer and eat away at the soul.

I chose men that would physically and verbally abuse me and were capable of doing the unspeakable. The dark men. I was raped again and sodomized at seventeen. Raped again at eighteen, and raped and beaten on several occasions by another man that I was in a relationship with for two years.

At thirty-four, hopelessly addicted to drugs and at what I thought had to be the end of my life, I was in my apartment. I had been in the bathroom shooting heroin in my veins for most of the weekend. Exhausted and sick of myself, I went to the refrigerator to get some Kool-Aid and as I passed by my thirteen-inch black and white TV set with the coat hanger antenna, there on the screen was a man talking about his drug addiction. He recalled the disgust he had for himself. He went on about the degradation, broken promises, and endless lies. But when I looked at his face and his demeanor it was evident he was no longer in a hopeless state of being.

Even on my black and white television set, he looked radiant, alive, and full of hope. So much so that it seemed I was seeing this man in living color. His tanned pinkish skin looked smooth and his brown eyes seemed so bright that they appeared to twinkle. I talked to the man on the television screen, *"What did you do? How did you get out of the despair so alive and free?"*

I forgot all about the Kool-Aid and sat down on my sheet-less mattress, which was on the multicolor-patched carpeted floor. I listened and was mesmerized by what I saw and heard. It was as if he heard my questions because his next words were, "I asked Jesus to come into my life. To forgive me for my sins, to live his life in me."

Desperate and already on the floor, I rolled over onto my knees and prayed the same prayer. It seemed as though a brilliant light flooded my apartment. It was as if the light was God stepping through my apartment door. Still on my knees, I told God all about my life— where it hurt—the bad things I had done and said— everything I could think of came pouring out of my mouth like someone had given me a shot of truth serum left over from the days of the Cold War.

I guess it was in my mind, but it seemed like I heard my name being called: *"Stanice."* It sounded like a choir of angels hummed my name to a celestial melody. I had long since given up my real name. Most people only knew me as Stacey. Thinking about my real name made me remember who I really was, where I came from, who my parents were. But it hurt too much to remember.

Maybe it was just in my mind and heart, but I recall having a conversation with God that night.

After I poured out my past, it was as if God said, *"I know, Stanice. I was with you. I've never left you. I love you. You have been mine from the beginning of time."*

Such a sweetness and weightlessness came over me. The fear, the self-loathing, the despair, and the hopelessness drained out of me. It was all replaced with a sense of peace, love, and forgiveness.

But you know me, Dad. I still fought the experience. I just couldn't believe that the God of the universe cared about me or had time for me. I felt that I had gone too far over the edge to be brought back. In my mind, I argued, *"But, God, you don't understand. I'm damaged goods,"* as I remembered the rape.

But every wall I threw up, God seemed to come through. *"I'll repair whatever is broken in your life—everything."*

No one can tell me that I did not have an experience with God that night. I recalled things that I had desperately tried to forget. The secrets seeped from my lips and died in God's light. I felt like I was being shown with every confession that I made that God had me in the palm of His hand from the beginning.

Dad, it had to be God because these thoughts I had were too insightful and pure for me to have on my own. I sensed Him saying, *"I knew you even before you were born. I knit you in your mother's womb. I made you Black. I set you in that family. I made you a girl and in the era, you were born. Nothing that has been has been by chance. While the boys of your era were being called to Vietnam, your girl-ness made you exempt. I did that.*

"And yes, I knew about the abortions. It was I who gave you the strength to get off that bed and call for help when that woman left you for dead. It was also I who did not allow those men who raped you to kill you. Yes, each time.

"It was I who brought you to consciousness in that infirmary at Fayetteville State when you OD'd off cough syrup. You did see a glimpse of heaven. It was not a dream. I allowed you to come back. When you OD'd off that heroin alone in your office on that Sunday, it was I who reminded the woman who found you that she needed her briefcase and sent her back to the office. You think she just happened by chance to come back and see your keys, know you were there, get the guards, and break through the door, and rescue you. No! It was not by chance. It was on purpose—my purpose.

"It was I, your God, who breathed life into your body in the ambulance the three times that you flat-lined. It was I who reinflated your lung after it collapsed. Once they got to the hospital, it was I that had your cousin Vicki on duty in the emergency room. She recognized you and called your mother."

The thoughts did not let up. *"Remember the time you felt your life leaving your body as John beat and choked you? It was I who stopped him before he killed you. And it was I who stopped you from going into that apartment even though you tried three times to put the key in the door. That spark you felt was my Spirit warning you of the danger waiting on the other side of the door. I alerted you to call the police and wait. When the police got there, do you remember they found him in the emptied apartment waiting for you to turn the key and come in? Again you were spared. I have never left you nor will I ever leave you.*

"And it was I that year that got you the temp assignment the day your buddy overdosed on heroin. You know that had you been with her you would have injected yourself first. She died but you lived.

"There have been many washed-out bridges on the roads you chose to take but I navigated you all around them. Some you know nothing about but know this, my child, I have a plan

for your life. While the evil one meant to harm you, I alone worked all things together for your good."

I found myself no longer wanting to fight. How could I fight such love, compassion, and grace? No one had ever showed me such a love as I felt in those moments. I felt like I had wrestled with an angel and lost. I surrendered and fell over limp on the sheet-less mattress, wept, and thanked God. It was that night that my new life with God was born.

Dad, I do want you to know that the rage is gone and I am no longer in bondage to my past. God healed the gaping emotional wounds left by the rape and enabled me to forgive the men who raped me. I understand now that it was not my fault and that rape is a violent crime perpetrated by people with a soul sickness. Therefore, I pray for these men, wherever they are, that they may know the love, forgiveness, and peace of God that found me.

I blamed you for so long for not getting me the help that I needed to get through the rape when it happened; but perhaps if I had told you and Mom exactly what happened you would have. Maybe the truth couldn't have been handled then. Maybe it was all too much for any parent to know. I understand now that maybe it would have hurt you to know that you were not able to protect your little girl. There is still so much I don't know. But one thing I do know is that I love you—always have and always will.

Dad, I guess you know now that I never mailed this letter to you. I was holding it until the right time; but you died before my right time came. I always wanted to tell you what happened; but I never got the courage until now—and it's too late. Now that you are with God, perhaps He told you for me. Or perhaps you are reading it over my shoulder as I type the words that I scribbled on a steno pad a long time ago. I don't know.

Until we meet again, let us both rest easy and leave the profundities of life to the Author and Finisher of Life—God.

Moving forever forward,
Stanice—proud to be your daughter and namesake.

If we do not expose our secrets to the light they will kill us slowly from the inside out. They are just too heavy for us to bear; but if we offer them up to God we will find the freedom that cannot be found in other things no matter how hard we seek. Sure, He knows them anyway, some of us say, but confession is good for the soul. It brings us out of the denial of what we've done or what's happened to us and allows us to move forever forward with our lives—in spite of—maybe even because of what has happened.

Otherwise, we are in bondage to our past and cannot move forward. True joy eludes us and love cannot seep through the tightly webbed fortress that the secrets spin around our hearts and minds.

There are other benefits of exposing the secrets. We find that we are not alone—that we are not the only one. We find others who have done the same things or had the same things happen to them and that they made it through. We start to believe that if they can overcome—surely, God being our helper—we can. If God forgives them—surely, we can be forgiven. If they can forgive the most hideous of crimes perpetrated on them—surely, God being our enabler, we can forgive. We discover that God's Love covers a multitude of sins and that darkness and light cannot coexist.

Perhaps God is urging you in your spirit to write someone a letter. Perhaps it's a letter to Him. Perhaps it's never to be mailed. Perhaps it is. That's between you and God. But write it like no one will ever see it. That way you won't worry about grammar but only what your heart has been yearning to express but knew of no safe way to do.

In my case, my letter wasn't meant to be mailed or it would have been; but I still believe that my dad read it. And my most fervent prayer is that God uses the letter to bless you, as it blessed me.

If there is no one that you want to write a letter to, know that God is always ready to hear from you. Write a letter to our Heavenly Father. Invite Him into your life, confess how you have fallen short of His perfect way, tell Him your secrets, share with Him your pain, hopes, dreams, desires. Cast onto the written page all your worries and anxieties. Ask Him to make clear to you the path that He has for you and His great love for you. Go on, tell God, *"That woman Stanice told me that you are real and care about me and every detail of my life. So, reveal yourself to me in a personal way. Show up for me like you show up for her."*

Write, pour out your heart, cry over your letter like I did. Then, if it makes you feel safer, burn it. Watch the smoke spiral up like incense toward the Throne of Heaven. Come away from the experience expecting and listening for God's response of unconditional, forgiving, and unchangeable love. Taste the glorious freedom of a personal and intimate relationship with God, the Maker of Heaven and Earth. And when the opportunity arises, and it will, share the letter exercise with someone else.

Dear Heavenly Father: Thank you for teaching us that our secrets die in the light of exposure and for setting us free from bondage to our past. We learn from our past and then move forward. We are grateful for the courage to speak and write the truth as we have come to know it so that you can make it perfect by adding Your unchanging Love. Grant us Godly wisdom that takes us to further heights in life and in You than we could have ever imagined. Amen. So be it!

Confess your trespasses to one another,
And pray for one another,
That you may be healed.
The effective, fervent prayer of a righteous man avails much.

JAMES 5:16 (New King James Version)

✻

FORGIVENESS

✻

Glimpse of an Angel

I drove a friend's brand-new white Supra through Rock Creek Park one warm and wet autumn day. The two-lane road was layered with orange and brown leaves. The earthy smell of dirt and fallen leaves hypnotized my nostrils. Someone whose head was barely visible over the headrest was driving a dingy white car in front of me.

Enough of this sightseeing, I need to get to work, I thought. I looked down briefly at the button on the console that the owner told me not to push while driving in the city. *After all,* I thought, *I am in the park surrounded by the city, not actually IN the city.*

No cars were coming in the passing lane. So determined to make my break past Mr. or Mrs. Need-a-Booster-Seat in front of me, I pushed the button, changed to first gear, and VAROOM! I jetted around the slow moving car. Then, I felt the control of the car being snatched from my grip like a driving instructor who'd had enough of his student driver for the day. The car had an agenda of its own and started spinning. Leaves were flying up all around me. I felt like Dorothy leaving Kansas in the cradle of the tornado. I wondered if I, like Dorothy, would wind up in an Oz I couldn't get out of.

Seconds felt like minutes, then time seemed to stop. The car kept spinning and swerving. Then it went off the road and up onto the glistening grass of the picnic area. BAM! One picnic table. BAM! A sapling snapped loose from its stringed confines. I fought to regain control but with each crunch, snap, skid, and turn I knew it was time to surrender whatever was next to God. There was this deathly silence and an equally deathly sight getting closer with every spin. "Jesus!" Rapidly coming to meet me must have been the biggest and widest tree trunk in the park. I closed my tear-filled eyes and waited to meet Jesus face-to-face. I saw chiseled on my headstone the words, "She died a fool."

Words filled my mind but there was no time for the words to travel out to my mouth: "God, forgive me." Suddenly, my neck snapped back against the headrest and the car abruptly stopped its death spin. I opened my eyes. I looked up and to the left. I was so close to that huge tree that I could see each layer and crevice of the wet, dark brown bark. I smelled the wet clumps of moss clinging to its side and counted the ants coming out of their hiding cracks. I felt on my tongue the grit of the shards of bark loosened from the tree. I tasted death and it made my heart pound on my chest for exit rights. Chill bumps covered my arms and I shivered and shook like on a cold December night.

I managed to steady my hands long enough to unbuckle my seat belt. I crawled over the console to the passenger side and slowly stepped out of the car. My legs felt like rubber bands and gave way. I fell onto the wet, cool bed of fallen autumn leaves. A bit dazed, I checked my body for damage. Not one scratch or droplet of blood! With my hand on the side of the car, I pulled myself up and surveyed the scene: a trail of broken picnic tables, saplings pulled up by the roots, small trees snapped like twigs, the deep brown earth furrowed with tire tracks and spirals. Just as I looked toward the road, the driver of the dingy white car pulled off.

I stood there with the morning mist dancing with the tears on my face. I turned around and looked back. The car had stopped no more than two inches from that mighty oak tree. I looked upward searching for the height of the towering oak and my head almost touched my back. I raised my outstretched hands to the sky and shouted, "Thank you, Lord."

In that moment, through the crooked leaf-starved branches, I saw a shimmer of light. The light surrounded what looked like the form and shape of a man. He sat there propped against a cluster of branches and looked straight at me. I squeezed my eyes shut and opened them again. The shimmer was gone. The man was gone.

For a few brief moments, I had glimpsed an angel.

Although I came out of the crash physically unscathed, what about the condition of my heart? There is the part of the iceberg that man cannot see but God can because He is the maker of the iceberg and the ocean floor it passes over.

I called Italy and told my friend Francesca, the owner of the car, "I had an accident and damaged your car pretty bad."

"Are you all right, Stanice?"

"Yes, not a scratch, but your car—"

She interrupted, "Don't worry about it. It's insured. We'll work it out when I get back." She gave me the insurance information.

I called the insurance company. "Yes, I have the policy up on the screen," the agent said. "There is a deductible of just $1,000."

"Excuse me. Did you say that there is a deductible of *just* $1,000?"

"Yes. The car is a part of a fleet on this business policy. Hello, are you there?"

I was there but my brain was busy calculating. Let's see, at eight or so dollars an hour *just* how many hours would I have to work to meet a $1,000 deductible even if I did not have rent, food, car note, or other living expenses to pay?

I got all the necessary information and hung up.

The next day I put the car in the shop. When Francesca came back to the States she got it out and stopped by to see me. "I understand that you can't pay the deductible in one lump sum."

We agreed upon an amount that I would pay every two weeks and I signed a promissory note. I made my payments the first month and then I started juggling monies, giving her partial payments and saying that I would catch up the next time. It went from there to no payments. Then I descended into not going to the places I knew she would be, and not returning her phone calls.

I justified it all and told myself, *"She's rich and doesn't need my money."* Yes, I could have been honest and done the right thing and paid her or at least renegotiated the payments into something I could afford, or even made the necessary sacrifices, like taking my lunch to work instead of buying it—but I didn't. Yes, I could have trusted God to provide all my needs—but I didn't. Ducking and dodging her seemed easier. And lying? It was just more convenient.

Or so it seemed until Christmas Day.

I made the same stop I made every year—Dorine's house. Dorine was my mentor and friend as well as Francesca's. When I pulled up to the house, whose white Supra was parked right in front? Yep, you guessed it. Francesca's!

I parked across the street from the house and sat in my car for at least fifteen minutes asking myself, *"Should I go in?"* and answering myself, *"No, fool, do not go in."* I turned the engine off. I started the engine. I turned the engine off—again. I started the engine—again. I did this until my brain pulsed in my head like one large gear running at top speed and then, SLAM! The gear locked and the conveyer belt of thoughts came to a screeching halt.

It was not until that moment of desperation and disgust with myself that I opted to pray. *"Lord, I know I've been running on my own will in this situation for months now. I've gone so deep you're gonna have to be the one to dig me out, please. You do for me what I can't seem to do for myself. Forgive me and show me what now."* The quiet of my soul finally at rest pervaded my car. I watched the laced snowflakes glide into a landing and melt on the warmed front window. I knew what I had to do.

I got out of the car and slowly walked toward Dorine's house. I heard the scrunching of the snow beneath my feet and knocked the snow off my boots on the gray wood porch. It created a rumble that sounded like thunder interrupting the quiet of that Christmas morning.

Dorine's husband, Pie, came to the door and announced in a gruff voice, "Ho, Ho, Ho! It's Stanice."

I had hoped for a quieter entrance. In the living room, where the front door emptied all guests, was Dorine and beside her on the gold corduroy sofa sat Francesca. I could hear a chorus of voices of more people spilling out from the dining room. And that, my friend, was where I wanted to head, but God helped me stand still in the moment.

Sheepishly, I said, "Hi, Dorine. Hello, Francesca." Then, I dropped my head to inspect the carpet.

"Stanice!" Dorine said with a nasty little twist in her voice. "Come talk to me in the kitchen."

I followed her into the small kitchen, "Dorine, I—"

"Stanice, I know all about what's going on here. Francesca told me everything. Baby, you got to deal with this thing straight-on. You can't keep running."

"You're right, Doe." I walked into the living room entryway. "Francesca, can I talk with you a minute?"

She got up and walked toward me. I was so tired of running that if she felt the need to beat me up on the spot, I would not have fought back. I felt like a slap or two might make everything all right between her and me. Maybe a few punches to my stomach or something and her money, of course, would make her day.

"I'm wrong, Francesca. I've ducked you, not returned your phone calls, not even made an honest attempt to pay you the rest of the money that I owe you for wrecking your car. Please forgive me. I will—"

"Stanice, listen—"

"No, Francesca. I'll start paying you again right now. I've got some money."

"No, wait a minute," she said, gently holding me back with a hand on my arm. "Listen. Yeah, you ducked me but I know everything that's been going on in your life. You know me and Dorine talk. I know things have been rough for you and I know you been struggling to stay on your feet. I'm proud of you and I love you."

"But Francesca . . ."

"No, listen. I don't want this money to come between our friendship. I've missed you."

I felt my eyes welling up with tears. Hers were too.

"Wait here." She went out of the kitchen and came back with her purse. She reached in with her dainty pink hand and pulled out a folded sheet of paper. She opened it and held it up to show me. It was the promissory note.

"Stanice, I was hoping that I would see you here today. This is the gift I want to give you for Christmas." With a swift motion, she ripped the promissory note into tiny pieces. I watched her release them, and they glided like snowflakes and disappeared into the kitchen trash can.

She reached out to hug me. "Merry Christmas. Consider the debt paid in full."

"Oh, my God. I don't believe this." I wept all over her shoulder. She wept all over mine. With the taste of the salty tears, I managed to say, "Thank you. Merry Christmas to you too, Francesca."

What dangers have you come up against and yet come out of unscathed? What dangers have we been averted from that we don't know about? For that matter, what dangers lurk around the bend? We have no way of knowing. However slowly, we come to believe that it doesn't matter that we don't know what we don't need to know. One thing we can be confident of—*God* knows everything that needs to be known. So, daily we must learn to trust God with each of the minutes that, when combined, make up our future.

Let us also take a moment to briefly look at what a mutated and degenerative web we weave when we duck, dodge, and deceive. We know what the right thing to do is and yet we try to get around doing it. We try to find an easier or softer way—but that way always results in unnecessary and self-inflicted pain. Even a great man of God, Paul, is quoted as saying, "The good I want to do I don't do and what I don't want to do I do." So we are in good company. However, like Paul, we don't have to surrender to living that way. We can look up and call on God to help us do what we, in and of ourselves, lack the power to do—the right thing!

Dear Heavenly Father: Right now, from where we are, take us to that place and space where truth lives, for you await us there. Thank you for the guardian angels that you've sent to protect us, even from ourselves every now and again. We love you, Heavenly Father, for making such provisions for us. We're glad that out of all the things you have to do in this universe and in your Kingdom, you still take care of us and love each one of us like we are the only ones you have to love. Above all, thank you for the gift of forgiveness. As you have graciously forgiven us and continue to forgive us, may we graciously forgive others? We're not perfect yet, nobody knows that better than you; but when we ask, we are forgiven, not by each other all the time, but always by you. Amen. So be it!

For he shall give his angels charge over you,
To keep you in all your ways.

PSALM 91:11 (New King James Version)

Therefore, as the elect of God, holy and beloved,
Put on tender mercies, kindness, humility, meekness,
longsuffering;
Bearing with one another, and forgiving one another,
If anyone has a complaint against another;
Even as Christ forgave you,
So you also must do.

COLOSSIANS 3:12–13 (New King James Version)

Amazed
by Grace

The long shiny black thin bent wire, which only minutes before hung in the closet with her starched white nurse's uniform, was now a makeshift surgical instrument. Her long dark fingers threaded the cylindrical tubing onto the wire as she held it up to the kitchen ceiling light.

"What's that?" I asked.

"Don't worry," she replied. "Relax and drink the nice hot tea I made for you." I lay there on the hard kitchen table cushioned only by a ragged white sheet.

I reached for the cup, drank the tea, and allowed my questions to drown in the bittersweet taste.

Fellow students told me she was a nurse and could take care of our "little problem" for the $300 that we managed to put together out of our college allowances. These same people said, "It'll be over before you know it. No pain. You'll be back in class on Monday."

I concentrated on those comforting words of well-meaning friends. I blotted out everything else, including the life that was about to die inside of me. I was fourteen weeks pregnant and a freshman whose dad had just paid second-semester tuition.

I felt groggy. The room started to spin. The bright overhead light bulb had spikes of reds and blues that darted about the ceiling like fireflies. It had to be the tea. I tried to rise from the table. My head felt like a block of lead. "What was in that tea?"

"Just lay back and shut up." Her words grabbed me by the throat and held me captive. "You college whores have your fun and then you come to me to help you get rid of your little problems."

This couldn't be the same nurse. Someone else must have come into the room; but I saw only one figure bent over me. I struggled to get up. I couldn't. With one hand she pushed down on my chest and with the other she probed my most private of parts. These were hands that were supposed to comfort the sick—now they were lethal weapons. She picked up the wire.

I felt excruciating stabbing pains deep inside me. I screamed, "Stop!" but something cold and clammy was over my mouth. The room faded to black.

How long I lay there I don't know. What happened after the wire? I don't know. The pain, I remember; it felt like someone had taken a red-hot poker and ripped my insides. The sheet was cold and wet with blood. The silence in the house, I remember. A note on the chair beside the table read, "Take these antibiotics; one every eight hours. Call your boyfriend. Be gone before I get back."

I felt so weak. My body screamed for painkillers. "God give me strength," I prayed. I tried to walk; but I couldn't stand up straight. I dropped to the floor and found that crawling was less painful. I pulled the phone to the floor and called my boyfriend. "Come and get me," I said.

He took me back to the dorm; then, he and a girlfriend tried to keep me quiet, but I was in so much pain. The pillow wasn't drowning my moans. They decided to take me to a motel. We checked into a room on the back side of the motel and they helped me in.

The room was suspiciously dim; yet the waterstained wallpaper was still visible. The ramshackle wood dresser sagged in the middle. Over the bed hung a picture painted on black velvet of a matador teasing a charging bull.

My girlfriend draped the bed with plastic dry cleaner bags and trash bags and laid me down. I rocked, reeled, cried, and hollered into a musty pillow for hours. Something was definitely wrong. My girlfriend, who had also experienced an abortion, guided us through the process.

"When will the pain stop?" I asked. I must have asked her that a hundred times.

"Soon. Soon," she said.

"Take me to the hospital. I don't want to die," I pleaded.

"No, we can't do that," my boyfriend said. Abortion was illegal.

Every few hours they would take me into the bathroom and have me sit straddled on the toilet seat facing the dingy, cracked wall.

"Push," my friend said.

I pushed. I felt pain in every part of my body. It hurt to talk, move, or breathe. I was also losing a lot of blood.

Exactly twenty-three hours after we left the nurse's house, they took me to the toilet seat again. I straddled and pushed. A pain hit me unlike all the others. It felt like my body was exploding from the inside out; then, I heard PLOP! in the water below me. Almost immediately, I saw the dead tiny brown curved baby floating in the little pond of blood and water. My knees buckled. My heart ripped. My mind took a

241

photograph that would be developed again and again for many years.

I learned at that moment what regret meant. It was no longer an abstract word but had substance and form, and a heart that would never beat again because of me.

If only my story ended there . . . but it didn't: It was only the beginning. If you've determined that a legal abortion would have eliminated my pain and suffering, think again.

Before that twenty-third hour, I knew no real pain. The real pain begins when the life is ended. Real pain lingers, night after sleepless night. When sleep comes, I revisit that straddle-stool in my dreams. Most days, I would rather be hit in the head with a hammer than to think about what happened that night; I would at least know that the pain would stop.

Often, I wonder, "What would my child look like?" "Was it a girl or boy?" "How old would my child be now?" Just seeing the father or my girlfriend reminded me of our secret. Passing the town or hearing the state's name brought back memories I wanted desperately to forget.

Those well-meaning friends didn't tell me how to live with the decision to abort. Parties, drugs, lovers, geographical changes, nor the passing years ever dulled the pain.

Then one day, I listened to a radio broadcast, a dramatic reading of a novella entitled *Tilly*, by Frank E. Peretti. The story is about a woman whose aborted child returns to comfort her. The little girl assures her that she's all right and with God in Heaven. She also tells her mom that when her mom asked for forgiveness a long time ago, God heard her and forgave her. Now she just had to forgive herself, and know that one day they would be together again. I listened and wept. My heart pounded and suddenly I recalled a verse that I didn't remember ever memorizing: "If we confess our sins, he is faithful and just and will forgive us and cleanse us from all unrighteousness." Later, I found out that it was 1 John 1:9.

At that moment, I felt that I had carried the emotional pain of my decision to abort long enough. My feelings about the abortion were bitter roots that had to be pulled up and thrown out. They were getting in the way of living my life to the fullest on this new road that I was determined to stay on. I knew that if I didn't let them go, I would eventually use drugs again to numb the pain. I knew that I would continue to have nightmares, and feel sadness whenever I looked at children. I knew that I could not be joyful in my present or future if I continued to cling to the things of the past. The deed was done. I did it and I could not undo it. But the story that I heard on the radio that day, combined with the verse that came into my mind, gave me hope and convinced me that God would forgive me, if I asked.

So, I got on my knees and cried out to God, "Please, forgive me."

In the next moment, I felt the burden I had carried in my mind and heart for over twenty years lifted. I knew He heard my prayer because the never-ending pain was replaced with a perfect peace deep down on the inside where my spirit resides that I had never known. I lingered there on my knees afraid that if I stood up the peace would dissipate. But God sealed His peace with assurance as I prayerfully talked to my baby, "Please forgive me for not allowing you to live a full life."

In the stillness of my mind, I replayed the story of Tilly but imagined my own child saying, "I forgive you, Momma. I'll see you one day and never have to say goodbye."

Still on my knees and with tears flowing from the slits of my closed eyes, I whispered, "How will I know you?"

"You don't have to know what I look like. You're my mother. I'll know you."

I knelt there and absorbed the love I felt like a thirsty sponge. It was as if she hugged me and then cradled my tear-stained face in her small soft hands and kissed my tears away.

I slowly stood up not wanting to leave the moment. But it's a moment in my life that will forever far outweigh the pain that I carried for so many years. A new peace was sealed with an image in my mind of a touch of assurance and a healing kiss from my aborted child.

I've not forgotten that night. Now and again, I think of my child in Heaven. Years later, when my son proudly strode across the stage to get his college degree, I whispered into my hand, "Aren't you proud of your brother?"

"Yes, Momma, I am."

I understand that some men and women feel no residual emotional trauma from choosing to abort, but for those of us who are still haunted by our past decisions—we can let go now. We can't undo what we did but we can go to God with anything and everything because He cares. We can ask for forgiveness, receive it, and then forgive ourselves so that we can move on with the plan that God has for our lives.

Also, I've found that because I had this experience, God brought many women and men along my path that I can share the answers and comfort that I found. As we are healed, we will be able to understand and empathize with others because we have been there. Thus, it gives our lives even more meaning and purpose. Our struggles will not have been in vain.

God has turned my hurts into compassion for others as well as given me joy in knowing that His forgiveness is real and lasts a lifetime. The same thing that God has done for me He is willing to do for you.

Dear Heavenly Father: We come to you believing that you can and will heal the inner wounds that the world can't see. We lift our gaping emotional and spiritual wounds up to you. Heal us. Make us whole and free. We are tired of carrying burdens that keep us from moving into the plan that You have in mind for our lives. Regrets only pull us down to the ground where we lie, moan, and groan because of the sheer magnitude of our past choices. We lay our hurts and our falling short of what you would have us to do at your feet. Forgive us and continue to take care of our children until one day you bring us home to You and we will see them again and never have to say goodbye. Thank you that you hear our prayers and that it is done as we have asked. Use us to comfort others as you have so graciously comforted us. Amen. So be it!

The Lord upholds all those who fall
And raises up all who are bowed down.
The eyes of all look expectantly to You
And You give them their food in due season.
You open Your hand
And satisfy the desire of
Every living thing.

PSALM 145:14–16 (New King James Version)

The Storm Is
Passing Over

As I drove down I-85 south, I looked over at my friend Claudia Holloway asleep on the passenger side. We had laughed, talked, and sang to the golden oldies cassettes that now littered the back seat. We were on our way to one of my favorite annual weekend conventions. The tall pine trees that dominated the woods along the interstate swayed and two hawks soared above in the cloudless sky as if to welcome me back to North Carolina. For the next twenty miles of the journey, I fought back painful memories of my previous life with John Smith there. Then I thought, *Maybe going back to Durham, North Carolina, is a part of my healing process.*

When we arrived at the convention hotel, the lobby was filled with groups of people milling around and talking. The first night's sleep came easy because I was long overdue for a little R&R. There's something about the fresh air of North Carolina that gives my overworked city lungs a respite.

The next morning as I walked with a group of friends I heard a man's voice shouting my name. I looked in the direction of the voice and there was Cary waving as he walked across the lobby toward me. Cary is a small, light-skinned guy who was John's first cousin.

"Hi, Cary."

"Hey, Stanice. Come with me for a minute. I want to talk with you about something."

I followed Cary outside and he sat down on the concrete step. I opted to stand a few steps lower than where he sat so that we could maintain eye contact.

He looked quite serious as he asked, "Have you seen your husband, John, lately?"

"No, I haven't. Not in over two years. I sent him a letter telling him I was about to file for a divorce, but he never responded." His question did make me think of the last couple of times that I had seen John.

Once, about two days after the protective order was granted, I sensed danger as I pulled into a parking space after work. Thoughts seemed to pop into my head, *"No, drive around the lot first. Don't park yet."* I drove slowly around the lot. As I was about to pass the apartment complex's large trash bin, the front end of a yellow car peeked out from the other side of the bin. A few revolutions of my wheels revealed John sitting in his yellow hatchback Escort with the motor off.

I was afraid. The pain was so fresh. *"Lord, show me what to do."* My eyes locked on John's for a fraction of a moment. His glare sent chills through my body. I knew I could not panic, so I talked myself through it as I drove around the lot: *"Get ahold of yourself. He's only a man. Remember, God is with you now, He never sleeps nor slumbers."*

I parked in front of my next-door neighbor's townhouse, jumped out of the car, and knocked on her door. She let me in. I called the police. When the police pulled up, John pulled off.

The very last time that I saw John was at the Durham County Library. I went to pick up a book that I had on reserve and as I walked into the lobby, there he was at the return desk. Although his back was toward me, I'd know that man if he were lying on the floor face down. I thought of walking back out the door but instead, with resolve and trembling, I walked briskly past him and wished that I could be invisible. I made it to the counter without incident and got my book. I waited awhile before leaving. It was dark but when I got to the well-lit parking lot, I saw John sitting in his little yellow Escort.

I walked to my car. *"Lord, please don't let him hurt me. Protect me."* I drove out of the parking lot first. John drove out behind me. I pulled over to the side of the road. He kept driving. I waited a few minutes and pulled off. He must have waited further up the street because his car ended up in front of mine. I could see him watching me in his rearview mirror. I passed my normal turn to go home because I did not want him to know where I lived. It was a one-way street with cars parked on both sides. He slowed his car. I had no choice but to slow my car. He picked up speed. I slowed down even more. I was so scared that I felt like throwing up. Then, suddenly, an idea came to me and I knew exactly what to do.

I knew North Roxboro Street and that there was a church up ahead to my right. I waited to make my move. I checked my rearview mirror. There was no car close enough behind me for me to put anyone in danger. I put my foot on the accelerator and pressed it to the floor. When John's car started to slow up ahead, perhaps to see where I was, it was too late. I hit my light switch and turned off all my exterior lights. It was pure-D dark. I made a quick right turn into the church parking lot. I stopped long enough to shout, "Yee haw, thank you, Jesus!" Then I turned the lights back on and drove out the other end of the parking lot onto the adjacent street going in the opposite direction.

"Stanice!" Cary's thick Southern drawl snapped me back to the present. "So you don't know, huh?"

"I don't know what?"

"I probably shouldn't even be saying anything to you but I like you. You know you were my friend before John came back into my life. And I never did understand—"

Cary could talk your ear off, if you let him. Plus, he had a reputation for taking a conversation where man had never voyaged before. Trying to keep up with his thought patterns was really hard; so it was best to stop him before he got all worked up.

"What, Cary? What is it that I don't know?"

He rested his elbow on his knee and cupped his chin with his hand. "Well, Stanice, John is dying."

It felt like Cary took a hammer, aimed for my heart, and slammed it into my chest. I gasped for air. I wanted to cry; but I was confused about what I felt. On the one hand, thinking of this man, known only to me as my estranged husband, brought back a flood of harsh emotions that bordered on hate. I realized that I had not forgiven him for the awful things he had done and said to me over the years.

On the other hand, the man that I was still married to and had known for many years was dying. My eyes welled up with tears but my wounded heart fought them back and dared them to drop.

Cary told me the details. As I struggled to grasp what he was saying and let the information filter through the bitterness that was in my heart, I heard Cary's explanation, in oddly shaped bits and pieces that floated and invaded the fresh North Carolina air. "Lung cancer—lost weight—living in a rehabilitation apartment house—doesn't like to see people—alone."

My mind wafted back, yet again. It seemed I couldn't stop it.

"Why, Lord, why did I have to see Cary and have to hear him tell me all this?" I hadn't dared think these thoughts for fear that

249

rage hid somewhere beneath them. But here they were in the forefront of my mind. I thought of the night that the deputies escorted him inside the townhouse to get the last of his belongings.

I recalled telling the sheriff's deputies, "Whatever he needs to get, let him get. I'll just stay downstairs."

"But, ma'am, it might be best to come up with us," the deputy said.

I still declined. The fight in me was gone. Things didn't matter. I just wanted him out of the house and out of my life! How much could he take in the ten minutes allotted him and with his little car? So I stayed downstairs, sat on the loveless seat in front of the fireplace, and prayed for the strength to get through all of this.

When John came downstairs on his way around to the kitchen, he taunted me and tried to provoke a confrontation. I had come to understand that it was just his way. So instead of playing into his hand, minutes later, I said, "Goodbye, John. Thank you, Officers."

"You're welcome, ma'am." They tipped their wide-brimmed trooper hats and closed the door behind them.

I latched the newly changed lock. I put on some gospel music and had a shoutin' 'n' praisin' good time. With the carpet tickling my bare feet, I danced all around that townhouse. All the tension of those last few weeks of living under emotional siege just oozed out of my body with each twist, turn, jump, and stomp.

Later that night I went upstairs and inventoried the leavings. There were three things that were gone that were classic-John moves—the jackets to all my suits, the cologne he gave me for my birthday, and for the absolute "give the man an Oscar"—my three-month supply of blood pressure pills. His last statement to me was clear: "You won't look good, smell good, or live long without me."

Suddenly, Cary's voice filtered through and pulled me back into the present.

"Stanice!"

"Yes, Cary, I heard everything you said. I want to call him. Do you have his phone number?"

"Yes, but not on me. I got it at home and I don't know it by heart."

So I asked him, "When are you going home?"

"I'm not going home until late tonight, after the dance. Are you going to the dance?"

I was a bit distracted because something was going on inside me—it felt like major reconstruction. I knew that I had to contact John. This was no coincidence that I was here talking to John's cousin Cary and finding out about John dying. So I tried to figure out how to contact John.

"Oh. No. Do you have John's address?"

"No, I kind of know where it is but I've only been there a few times and it was always at night. It's off of North Roxboro Street somewhere."

"Okay, Cary. Thank you for telling me all this."

"Don't tell him that I told you. He would probably be mad at me. You know you broke his heart. He told me everything. John doesn't talk to many people but he talks to me. You know, I thought it was—"

"Well, Cary. I'm going to catch up with my friends." I turned and started to walk away. "I'll probably see you before I leave North Carolina. Thanks again."

"I'll call you in the morning with the phone number."

I wondered, *How many John Smiths are there in the telephone directory?*

"Okay, you do that. I'll probably see you before I leave this weekend."

I thought as I walked, *John is dying—alone! I wouldn't want anyone to have to die alone.* I surrendered to the tears.

251

In the next moments, I beat myself up with a whole slew of "maybes." *Maybe I should have stayed with him. Maybe he was sick then and he didn't tell me. Maybe he was just scared, which would explain why he was so mean. Come on, Stanice. Get a grip. I know I did the right thing. Are you sure, Stanice?* When I start exchanging feedback with myself, I know that I'm in trouble. So I pulled a friend out of the workshop to talk to. Thad listened as I talked out all my feelings. Then, he shared with me his experience in a similar situation, took my hands, and prayed for me. I thanked him and went to my hotel room.

When I got to the room, I sat on the side of the bed, reached for the phone book, and started with the first John Smith. I dialed the number.

"Hello, Smith residence."

"Hello, is this the home of John Smith from Washington, D.C.?"

"No, I'm sorry, you have the wrong John Smith."

I dialed the second John Smith.

A raspy slow "Hello" came from the other end. It was my estranged husband. Even though I had not heard his voice in over four years, I'd know it even if he talked underwater.

"John, this is Stanice."

"What do you want?"

"John—"

"If you want a divorce you gonna have to pay for it yourself! I ain't giving you nothing, girl!" It was the same John Smith—nothing had changed.

I let him spew venom. And then—

"I called to ask you to forgive me for the part that I played in the breakup of our marriage and to see if there was anything that I could do to help you."

The conversation lasted about ten minutes. Mostly, I listened. He really didn't see that he had done anything wrong.

He expressed that I deserved everything that I got. He said he was happy without me, had a new car, didn't need nor want my help.

"I'm going to make it hard on you and I will never forgive you. Never!"

As I listened to him, I realized that this was a man who was sick, possibly dying, and evidently without a personal relationship with God. This was a scared man talking. He had probably yearned for years to tell me everything that came out of his mouth; but what he was saying just rolled off like water on a duck's back. In the past, whatever John said to me cut like razor blades but something was different about me. It was like God had reinforced me with protective armor.

I also realized that my call was not to tell him about what he did—he knew—even though he was in deep denial or just unwilling to look at his part.

However, in an instant, I knew that I had done this man a grave injustice. Regardless of what he did, I was convicted in my spirit for what I had done. I had married this man knowing that I did not love him. The fact that I did not love him had to show up in my attitude and my actions toward him. I've been in enough one-way relationships to know how empty and hopeless it feels.

I'd been there. I've known more than my share of relationships void of outward signs of affection. Void of kind and healing words. Void of any expression of love—seen and unseen. Void of knowing, gentle, loving touches. I know how it feels to be with a person that would rather not even be touched by you. I'd been there.

Being brought up in a loveless house, I know what it is like to just have a room and not feel part of a family. I know what it is to never see your father embrace your mother in a loving way. I know what it is to not be held and told, "I love you." I also know what it is to hear the words "I love you" but when you look into the eyes they are blank, cold, and austere. I'd been there—exactly where John was.

It was only after God found me as I was injecting heroin into my veins, desperate and alone in my apartment, that I found out what real love is—true unchanging—unadulterated love. In that moment, I understood that I was the one who didn't trust God enough to wait for the man He may have had for me. I jumped the gun because I was over forty and still husbandless. I took the reins from God and chose for myself. I was the one who was tired of being alone and figured in my head, *So what if I don't love him—he loves me—and it beats a blank.*

Yes, I asked forgiveness for the part that I played. Trust me, I did play a major role. John did what he knew to do; what he had done most of his life. Hurt people hurt people. I knew John's heart before I married him. I just ignored the fruit because of my own agenda. God didn't do anything to me; I did it to myself. I made my choice and I suffered the consequences of that choice.

I know that it was the grace and mercy of God, who loved me enough to save me from myself, that extracted me from what could have possibly ended up a deadly situation. And now here it was some four years later and I knew that it was God who was giving me the opportunity to make my peace so that I could move on with my life. So, I fell down on my knees at the side of the bed and asked God to forgive me for the harm I had caused John, and prayed for his healing. I also asked Him to forgive me for my disobedience and for not trusting Him.

As I lay there on the bed, I meditated on the verse "When we confess our sins, God is faithful and just to forgive us our sins and cleanse us from all unrighteousness." It brought me comfort, for unlike man, God not only forgives—He forgets. My sins go into the "sea of forgetfulness."

The next morning, Claudia and I went to Greater Zion Wall Missionary Baptist Church, the church I was a part of while I lived in Durham. I went up to the altar for prayer and Bishop Viril Myers laid her warm, gentle hands on my head. I closed my eyes, and she whispered in my ear, "This is what the Lord is saying to you, 'Put that old stuff to rest. Move on with your life. You can do nothing with it. You've done the part I had for you to do. Be at peace now. Drop it and move on. I have a mighty work for you to do.'" I wept and praised God for using Bishop Myers to speak to me words of comfort, peace, and promise.

After the service, encouraged, Claudia and I got in my car and headed toward the highway and out of Durham. I stopped at the gas station and called John one more time. I thought that maybe God had softened his heart during the night and that he would be ready to forgive me. That was not to be the case.

Again he said, "Never!"

I prayed for him anyway while he was still on the line and spoke in a heavenly language because I wanted to allow the Holy Spirit to speak to his heart since he did not receive my earthly words. Then I simply said, "Goodbye, John."

When I got back to the car, Claudia asked, "What did he say, Stanice?"

He said, "Never means never."

"Well, Stanice, you did your part. It's time to let it go."

I filled the gas tank and we drove off toward I-85 north. We talked and sang oldies but goodies all the way back to Washington.

That was July 19, 1998. Exactly two months and one day later, while I was at work, I got a telephone call from Cary.

"I thought I should let you know. John died last night."

I was surprised that the same hammer that struck me in the chest when I found out he was dying now struck again upon hearing that my husband was dead. I didn't go back to North Carolina for the funeral; but I wept for him. The words that I had received in the little Durham church echoed in my heart, *"Be at peace now. Drop it and move on. I have a mighty work for you to do."*

Sometimes we reach back into the past to pull into our present what needs to be left in the past. Reaching back can break your heart or the heart of another. God has provided all that we need for our present right here in the present and He is already setting into place what we need for the future that He planned for us a long time ago. I remember my mentor, Dorine, telling me one time, "Girl, you gonna mess around and miss your blessing. What if God wanted to bless you right now? It would shoot right past you 'cause you so jammed up reaching back and holding on to the past. Let it go!"

We would all do well to heed the words of this wise woman. But in spite of it all, it seems that the tougher our lives get, the stronger our faith gets—if we learn the lessons life brings us and move forever forward.

Dear Heavenly Father: We weep today for those who don't know you. Those people who have absolutely no idea how wonderfully satisfying being loved by you truly is. Remind us just how much you love us and that if we surrender our pasts to your care we will have more abundant lives and you can bless us right here in the present. We are learning that we didn't choose you—you chose us! You didn't have to choose us, Lord, but you just have that kind of love. And we thank you for it right now. Thank you too for your Spirit that convicts us when we are wrong; so that we can humbly come before your throne to ask for and receive your forgiveness. Amen. So be it!

"And whenever you stand praying,
If you have anything against anyone,
Forgive him,
That your Father in heaven may also forgive you
your trespasses.
But if you do not forgive,
Neither will your Father in heaven forgive your trespasses."

MARK 11:25–26 (New King James Version)

God Bless
the Child

Holding resentments is like stabbing yourself over and over again and waiting for the other person to bleed. I loved my daddy; however, coming to terms with our relationship was quite difficult.

I grew up in the 1950s and 1960s in Anacostia, a then-rural community in Washington, D.C. My family called me Neicy, but outside of the family I was known simply as "Mr. Anderson's daughter." I walked down the street and someone would shout, "Aren't you Mr. Anderson's daughter?"

Inside I shouted, "I have a name."

My dad had a "great man" image. Newspaper clippings and photographs on our walls at home chronicled his ascent from a Howard University graduate to D.C. city councilman. I always felt like I lived in his shadow and had to fill his shoes.

My family was meticulous about appearances; I was groomed to be with the "right" people, wear the "right" clothes, and say the "right" thing at the "right" time. In public, we posed as the "happy" middle-class Negro family.

However, in my father's quest for power and prestige, he was rarely home. If and when he came home, I knew that he had to go to the bathroom so that was why I left him notes on the toilet tank.

At sixteen, I got my driver's license, which was also my passport out of the county corridors of Anacostia to hang out in Uptown D.C.

At twenty-five, married, separated, and pregnant by another man, I worked where my father had been chairman of the board. One day, he called me and said, "You're scandalizing my name. They'll find you and that bastard in the Potomac River." I ran to the bathroom and threw up.

In the months that followed, I had very little contact with my dad; he skipped the birth of his grandson entirely.

Then, one day as I pushed my son in his stroller to the baby-sitter's house, my dad drove up, looked at us, said nothing, and sped off.

It would be thirteen years before I would see him again.

I sent my father letters for years; he didn't respond. However, with each year that passed it seemed less important that he accept me, because I gradually began to accept myself. Finally, I gave up.

Then one day—out of the blue—my dad called. My heart pounded as I asked him the one question that had burned like acid on my brain: "Dad, why didn't you respond to my letters?"

"I knew you were okay," he replied, "because your letters always had the same return address."

Still, he did not want to see me.

A year later, we agreed to meet. I watched my dad as he shuffled across the parquet floor of the lobby: He was leaning heavily on a cane, he was frail, and he was shorter than I remembered.

I remembered my dad as a giant.

How could this be?

As he got closer, I noticed that his eyes were dim. He attempted to smile. He was just a sad old man.

That's when I realized that I had changed.

We left the hotel and my dad drove us to his home, a small wood-framed house in the Annapolis, Maryland, beach community Arundel-on-the-Bay. Once inside, I saw moldy dishes in the sink. The smell of rotting food seeped from the refrigerator. There were piles of unread newspapers and mounds of unopened mail. Empty gin bottles were everywhere.

My dad cleared a place on the sofa for me to sit. I apologized for being such a horrible daughter. "Stanice," he said, "it's not your fault; you came from a very dysfunctional home."

All my life, I believed that I was the problem.

The arguments, resentments, secrets, jealousies, thrown lamps and spray starch cans, the merciless beatings, the parties with the grown-ups drunk, crying, cussing, and moaning while Ray Charles records played in the background—then going to church on Sunday?

This was all "normal."

My dad's statement was a major piece of the puzzle. It's easy to find the edges and corners of any puzzle; it's the heart of the puzzle that's more difficult to put together, especially the pieces with the same shapes, colors, and patterns.

My dad got up and disappeared into the back of the house. He returned with an armload of presents for his grandson and me; the once vibrant colored wrappings were now yellowed with age and the once festive ribbons were now sadly faded.

Perhaps I was not the only one who feared being rejected?

Another year passed. The following Christmas, my dad finally met his grandson. While I was ready to build a relationship, years of alcoholism, self-inflicted exile, and false pride left him unable to reciprocate. My dad chose not to be involved in our lives. I chose to believe that although my earthly father rejected me, my Heavenly Father never will!

I made a conscious choice to bury the resentments and forgive my dad. In the process, my broken spirit began to heal. I chose to move on with my life and stop torturing myself by dream-wishing his approval.

God approves of me; that is enough!

Just when I started to feel good about my new attitude about my relationship with my dad, I got a telephone call.

My dad was found alone in his apartment, dead.

My heart stopped. A silent scream exploded in my breast. The pain of a lifetime of unrequited love erupted within me. How I hurt for that last hug from my dad. My ears burned to hear my dad say, "I love you and I'm proud of you."

As my son and I sat arm in arm in the second row of the church facing the body that once housed my dad's spirit, a shiver ran through me. I realized that my dad did love his grandson and me—as best as he could.

Sometimes it's better to understand than be understood.

Perhaps the weight of his disappointments far outweighed his capacity to release them and embrace what he had—here and now. Perhaps the man that appeared not to fear anything feared the most important of things—love. But that does not mean that he did not love me—that he did not yearn to say the things every daughter is born to hear.

Maybe because my dad was who he was, I became who I am—in spite of it all—through it all—because of it all. I choose to pass on to my son a legacy of hope, humility, and love. I no longer live in the shadow of my dad's footsteps. I've learned that God created a pair of shoes that only fit me. I am my father's daughter and I have finally grown up to honor and forgive him, as the Lord instructs.

Our parents are only human. They want to love and cherish us but sometimes they get lost along the way to us. We want to be able to love them anyway, in spite of what they do or don't do; just as God loves us—unconditionally. We don't have the capacity for that kind of love; but with God's love shed abroad in our hearts the seemingly impossible becomes possible.

Dear Heavenly Father: We are learning that holding on to the resentments and bitterness only gets in the way of being fully used by you to bring joy where there is hurt and hope where there is only darkness and despair. We don't want to be the walking wounded, nor do we want to be crawling around in the dark of our own hearts. We want to grow up and learn how to walk upright in Your heavenly light. Help us, for without You we are lost! Amen. So be it!

"For if you forgive men their trespasses,
Your heavenly Father will also forgive you."

MATTHEW 6:14 (New King James Version)

Mortal Man

Bear with me, if you will, while I play a gentle melody of words on my keyboard. Excuse me while I tap out the rhythms that are not as familiar to me as the harsher chords of my life. Come with me as I search for the lost concerto of a daughter and her father.

My dad was just a man, not a god, as I looked for him to be in my youth. He had hopes like any other father must have for his children. My dad was just a man who was afraid to dream a dream for me for fear of disappointment. Perhaps his dream was too big for such a little girl who knew disappointment of her own along the way.

My dad was just a man who did not get much love and compassion from his father. My dad was just a man whom I believe did not set out to become the same kind of father that he had had.

My dad was just an educated man who thought children should be textbook true and when they weren't, not knowing what to do, he just lost his place among the pages, that's all. He loved the thought of loving the fantasy child, but I showed up instead.

My dad was a complex man I never really knew. He had hopes that were doused with the cold water of reality that lived within the walls of his house: a wife who appeared to be unable to free herself from the pain of her past and so she dragged it along with her wherever she went; a son hidden by the shadow of his dad's greatness and caught in the web of his mother's insatiable need to be needed; a daughter who rebelled and escaped into her own land of shadows after being raped at fourteen during a time when such tragedies were not even whispered in the dark. My dad did not know what to do with any of us—so he fled into his work—his community.

My dad was a social worker and city councilman who was swallowed up whole by the people he believed he could help rather than dwell among the wounded he could not help in his own house. Perhaps we reminded him of his own wounded heart. Some people have answers for everyone except themselves and their own.

My dad was a father with children he never understood, or perhaps he understood too well that the children would never be his clones. The girl-child in her own wonderland who he felt should have been the boy-child in his promiseland.

My dad oozed with titles, business cards, and nameplates that shouted to the world, "I am he that was promised." However, he was emotionally and physically absent from home most of the time and thus forfeited the titles he was born to have—father and husband.

My dad was a man of perseverance. He constantly reminded me that he was a self-made man who worked from the age of eight and wanted a degree so bad that he roller-skated at least twenty miles a day to and from Howard University. He reminded me how difficult it was to be a Negro in a white world and a dark-skinned Black man in a society of Negroes that preferred "high-yellow." He reminded me that he was a four-letter man who was not accepted by fraternities because of his dark skin. Yet these same light-skinned people shouted him on to victory at every track meet he ran, every touchdown, home run, and two-point basket. Rejection cuts deep and all the trophies in the world can't stitch it up.

My dad was a man who married a "beautiful high-yellow" woman against her parents' wishes. However, when he began to rise in his career and get media attention, my grandparents proudly introduced him as their wonderful son-in-law.

My dad was a man whose wounds were hidden from plain view but they festered all the same—there in the recesses of his soul. They were covered with titles, property, prestige; the best suits that money could buy. However, when I got real close to him, I could smell the open wounds. The older he got, the more he reeked with pain that to a novice might have smelled like Bacardi rum.

My dad was a man who wanted love but found it too risky. My dad was a man who desperately needed love but rejected it no matter what form it took. My dad was a man who sought adulation, denied his need for love, stumbled over his life, and fell into loneliness.

My dad died long before he was buried and I could not save him.

I still weep for my dad not because I miss him so much. I can't miss what I never really had. But I weep because my dad was just a man who, although a fighter of great and noble causes, failed to fight for the greatest and noblest cause—his family. Had he fought that fight then maybe he would have found himself and experienced the sweet taste of loving and being loved.

Bear with me if you will while I play the gentle melody of the last concerto of a daughter and her father on my keyboard. "Daddy, I forgive you. I have always loved you and I always will."

All of us seek the approval and acceptance of our parents—it's a birthright. But what if we don't get it? What if they can't give what they never had themselves? Where do you turn after all the back flips, jumping through hoops, tap dancing around criticism, and emotional unavailability? Who or what takes up the cause for us who are love-starved and esteem-thirsty? Drugs, money, alcohol, one-way relationships, property, degrees, chocolate, titles, worry, and other things we attempt to fill up our tanks with still leave our hearts on empty. Mortal man was not created to fill all our needs. Only the Creator can satisfy His creation. Only an intimate and personal relationship with God through Jesus Christ alleviates the vast chasm of our unfulfilled need for love and acceptance.

Where our parents, husbands, wives, other relatives, and friends may fail to give us the love we need—God never will.

Dear Heavenly Father: We thank you that in You, we are bathed in perfect love. So much so, that even when we are not shown how special we may be to someone, we know we can come to you and You will supply our need to be loved with pure unchanging love. We are learning just how deep and how high Your love is. Please fill all the voids that may be in our lives. We come like children to Your knee to be rocked in the bosom of Your love. We fall into Your waiting arms to receive Your peace and find the safety that we need to know is ours. Help us to forgive those who have hurt us and help those that we have hurt to forgive us. Have mercy on us because so many times we know not what we do. Amen. So be it!

Though I speak with the tongues of men and of angels,
But have not love, I have become sounding brass or a
clanging cymbal.
And though I have the gift of prophecy,
And understand all mysteries and all knowledge,
And though I have all faith, so that I could remove mountains,
But have not love, I am nothing.
And though I bestow all my goods to feed the poor,
And though I give my body to be burned,
But have not love, it profits me nothing.

1 CORINTHIANS 13:1–3 (New King James Version)

✳

PRAYER

✳

Somebody Prayed
for Me

Does God answer prayer? Do prayers take on a life of their own and live forever in the spiritual realm? Does God stack answer upon answer as with a spiritual Erector set? Does God reveal His answers over time like peeling layers of an onion until He gets us to the core of what He birthed us to be?

Attempting to answer the questions, I looked back over my life to two telephone calls placed over thirteen years ago. One call I received one evening:

"Hi, Stanice, this is Larry."

"Hi, Larry, what's up?"

"I'm organizing a retreat at Bryce Mountain and I would like you to speak."

"Is there a topic or theme, Larry?"

"We'd like for you to talk about turning your will and life over to God's care."

While I had no qualms with speaking and actually had grown quite comfortable doing so, I found myself answering with more than the normal yes. I went a step further, which I had not planned or even thought of before that moment.

"Well, Larry, how about I do something a little different with that topic?"

"Different?"

"Yes, instead of just talking, I can design a workshop complete with handouts and fun things for the group to do that will bring the principle of surrender alive."

The words flowed like I really knew what I was talking about. I had never tread in such waters.

Larry excitedly replied, "That's a great idea! You're on."

As I hung up the telephone receiver, I realized I had just jumped into the deep end of the pool and I couldn't swim a lick. I asked myself, *"Do you understand what you have just promised to do?"* And I answered myself, *"Yep! Something I have never done before—learn to swim in the deep end."*

I went to the hall closet of my tiny one-bedroom apartment and pulled my first-generation portable word processor off the top shelf. I sat it on the drop leaf warped wooden dining room table that was positioned in front of the living room window because I had no dining room. I typed in large bold letters: "Turning Our Wills and Lives Over to the Care of God." I centered the words on the page and double-spaced to begin the body of text. I looked at the screen and it looked back at me. I waited. Nothing. I typed letters just to hear the tapping of my fingers on the keys but the letters were not forming any words known to mankind. Silence. I backspaced, deleting every letter that I typed as I tried to convince myself, *"Girl, way deep inside somewhere . . . you can do this."*

Well, a few minutes passed, then a half hour of minutes and still not one idea flowed through my normally fertile brain. The canal locks were shut tight. I stared at the flickering white cursor on the word processor's screen and cried out, *"Lord, please help me. Where do I go from here?"*

After a few minutes, I got up from the table and picked up the telephone and called my mentor and friend Dot Tally in

Pittsburgh. I loved Dot. I remembered the first time I saw her. She had been introduced at the podium of a large convention banquet with over four thousand people in the audience. She was a pretty coffee-with-cream-shaded Black woman who strode across the stage showing no evidence of fear and with an air of confidence that I had seen only once before in my first mentor, Dorine. She had a sandy brown Tina Turner spiked haircut and her eyes seemed focus on each one of the banquet attendees like we were family and she was glad to see each of us.

The crowd hushed. She spoke into the microphone: "My name is Dot Tally and I'm a fifty-seven-year-old fox!" The audience laughed, some yelling, "All right Miss Thing!" and "That's all right!" I looked in amazement at this poised woman. Even though I was more than thirty years old, I said to myself, *"I want to be like her when I grow up."*

Later that day, Dorine introduced us and from that moment on we started to develop a friendship.

In the months to follow, I found out that Dot was a praying woman who loved God and graciously shared her walk with God with anyone willing to listen and learn. I remembered all this as her telephone rang.

"Hello."

"Hi, Dot. This is Stanice."

"I know your voice, baby. How's it going?"

"Dot, I just told this guy that I would design and facilitate a workshop at a retreat at Bryce Mountain but I don't have a clue where to start."

She shared her experience in a similar situation and how first times were always scary but necessary. "Stanice, when God gives you a task—and trust me it had to be God, because it was such a perfect thing to say because we tend to do the comfortable and no-need-to-stretch things—but when He gives you a task, He will give you just what you need to see it through and with excellence."

My sheepish next words were, "You really think so?" I really wanted and needed to believe what she said was true.

"Yes, as a matter of fact let's take it to Him now."

While I was wondering how we were going to do that, my friend prayed right there over the telephone—out loud. She talked to God like the two of them were best friends. Up until that point I had never experienced or imagined that kind of intimate relationship with a God that I couldn't see or touch. But in that prayer that night, Dot Tally reached out and touched the ears of God and the seat of my soul.

One thing that I have remembered from that night to this is her sweet contralto voice saying, "Father God, please get her creative juices a-flowing right now."

We chatted awhile longer, then I thanked her for praying with me before hanging up.

Minutes later I sat down at that dining room table and typed to the rhythms that flowed from my mind and heart. It was as if a celestial window in God's great house opened up and a host of ministering angels tossed out to me thought upon thought, idea upon idea, and word upon word. God seemed to pour into my brain ideas for games that would make the concepts come alive—directed me who to call, and what books to pull off my shelf to read for information that would bring together the rest of the pieces of the workshop. Within a week, I had everything I needed to conduct a two-hour workshop, including a new title: "An Exercise in Faith."

Well, I made it to the retreat and from the moment I opened my briefcase containing the workshop materials, I felt confident that God had sent me on this assignment because it was so in line with the secret desires of my heart to be a trainer. I knew that all would be well. There was neither fear nor trembling as I worked the room. I felt like I was swimming to the other side of the pool with the supple grace of a swan and the boldness of a beaver. I felt comfortable in the deep end.

Dot Tally believed in the possibilities for my life long before I did, and she had the wisdom to take it to the Possibility Maker. Even now, years after her death, whenever I face a new challenge and sit down to write—if I'm real still—I can visualize Dot with her Tina Turner haircut as she whispers into the heavenly wind, "Father God, please get her creative juices a-flowing right now."

Two telephone calls gave me answers to my questions.

Sometimes, after we decide to take a risk and come out of our comfort zone, and step into that new job, class, committee, or anything that we've longed to do for a while, fear tries to creep in and chastise us for saying yes to whatever our need-to-stretch thing is. Some of us are afraid to fail and perhaps even a bit afraid to succeed. When fear tries to get its debilitating grip on us, we can pick up the phone, or go into a quiet room, or to someone that we know has our best interest at heart to listen to us and pray with us; especially if we don't feel comfortable praying for ourselves. God hears all prayers and will answer them!

Dear Heavenly Father: Thank you for the gift of prayer. Thank you for sending people to us who are willing to share the gift and teach us how to open our own. We are grateful that you hear our prayers and the prayers of those who pray for us. Thank you that the prayers of your faithful people live on like a trail of sweet smoke from burning incense forever wafting up to Your Throne. We say "Glory" to the way you continue to answer the prayers until You extract the essence of what you birthed us to be. Amen. So be it!

Thus says the Lord: "Stand at the crossroads and look;
Ask for the ancient paths,
Ask where the good way is,
And walk in it,
And you will find rest in your souls."

JEREMIAH 6:16 (New International Version)

The Rough Side
of the Mountain

I drove down Route 66 west toward Bryce Mountain to present my retreat workshop on the twelve-step program's third step, "We made a decision to turn our will and our lives over to the care of God as we understand Him." The chalet the group rented was named Bears' Den. *Or was it Lions' Lair?* With my eyes on the road, I fumbled through my purse on the passenger's seat for the flyer with the directions. I felt a wallet, two tubes of lipstick, an aluminum foil package of rice cakes—everything but the flyer.

I slowed down and pulled over onto the shoulder. The sun was setting over the mountains ahead. It would be dark soon and I still had another twenty-five miles to go. I emptied the contents of the purse—still no flyer. I leaned over between the seats and looked on the back seat and the floor. I shifted a bottle of water and some papers to the other side—still no flyer.

I figured that even without the flyer I could find the chalet. I had been there the previous year for a retreat. *When I get to the area it will all come back to me,* I thought. I had already gone too far to turn around and people were depending on me to show up. *Yes, Bears' Den had to be the name of that chalet.* I tried to convince myself that I was right.

Maneuvering the car back into traffic, I increased speed to get back onto Route 66 and whispered, *"God, right now, I make a decision to turn my will and life over to your care. I'm not sure where I am going but you know exactly where I'm supposed to be. Please show me the way."* I continued driving toward Bryce Mountain.

As I entered the resort area, it was the few minutes between dusk and twilight. The headlights of the cars in the oncoming lane of the ever-winding-upward road signaled that night was just around the next bend. I turned on my headlights.

At night, nothing and everything looks familiar. There was no doubt in my mind—I was lost. I followed the signs to the "Ski Lodge." I hoped that someone there could help me with directions to Bears' Den. Or was it Lions' Lair? I pulled onto the gravel parking lot of the lodge. There were a few parked cars and sport utility vehicles. It was a quiet late autumn night. Ski season was a month or so away.

As I climbed the stairs to the lodge, the country and western music grew louder. The black-slate foyer emptied me into a huge, dimly lit room. The wood-paneled walls were lined with an odd mix of antlered elk heads and flickering neon beer signs. The smell of spilled whiskey wafted to my nose from the carpet of the main area. The bar semicircled the husky plaid-shirted white bartender. In the center of the bar that reminded me of an inner tube was a selection of liquors.

A young neatly dressed white man hovered over a woman on the barstool as if to protect her from the four other white men looming who sat at the other end of the bar. Everyone stopped what he or she was doing and stared at me with looks that I interpreted as, *"What is this lone black woman doing in this here neck of the woods?"*

Shoulders back and head up, I headed toward the bartender, confidently smiled, and said, "Hello, I believe I am
lost. Can you give me directions to chalets named Bear's Den
and Lion's Lair?"

"There are so many chalets up here, Miss. Not sure about
the names, though."

He turned to his patrons, "Anybody know where Bears'
Den or Lions' Lair might be?"

They whispered amongst themselves and came up with a
unified, "No."

As I turned to leave, a man with a gruff voice said, "Miss,
you should go to the ranger station. Hal looks after the place
all year round and he knows every nook and cranny of this
mountain."

"I'll do that. Where is the ranger station?"

"On top of the mountain." He took me to the window and
pointed. "Just follow that road there and it will take you right
to the top."

"Thank you."

"No problem. Now Hal might be on his rounds but just
wait there, he's got to come back to the station. Good luck."

As I headed to the front door, I looked back over my
shoulder. But there was no point in me telling him that luck
would have absolutely nothing to do with me ending up in
the right place.

I got back in my car and headed for the road that would
take me to the top of the mountain. The paved road turned
into a narrow gravel and dirt trail. I shifted my automatic car
into second, then first gear to take the steep incline. I went
slow and rocked and bumped my way up the mountain. I
passed a few houses but it was mostly woods along this dark
road. I kept driving up the mountain but along the way fear
and doubt must have crept in through the exhaust pipe.

As I pressed my way upward, negative thoughts taunted

me. *Suppose that man at the ski lodge lied? Suppose they all wanted to get me up here on top of this mountain so they could hang me? Nobody would find my body way up here.* I kept driving. If I slowed down too much, the car rolled back. I couldn't turn the car around on this narrow road. No way was I driving backward down the mountain.

The road leveled off. *This must be the top*, I thought. Through my headlights, I saw the sign on the side of the cabin—"Ranger Station."

I rose up in my seat and hollered out, "I made it!"

But there was no sign of Ranger Hal or his ranger truck. I recalled the bartender's words, *"He might be on his rounds, but he's got to come back to the station."* I backed up in front of the cabin with the car pointed in the direction of the roadway. I turned off the headlights and the engine. Silence waltzed to the light of a full moon.

The wind rustled the leaves on the trees and the ground. I heard the creaking trees swaying and the scamper of tiny paws of woodland creatures. It was all too much for this city woman to deal with; so my imagination took over.

I recalled every horror movie I ever watched or heard about and every Discovery Channel bear and mountain lion documentary. I imagined I heard sounds that were not human; but hisses, growls, and howls in obedience to the full moon. I turned on the headlights and saw slivers of eyes staring at me but my mind refused to acknowledge that they were attached to the small harmless body of a raccoon. The raccoon scurried to his hiding place. My gas supply was too low to keep the engine running. I didn't know what else to do but pray. *"Lord, help me. I'm cold, hungry, tired, scared, and all alone up here on top of this mountain."*

In the next moment, verses I had read at some time or another from the Bible came to mind. I spoke them repeatedly with the goal of chasing fear away. *"I lift up my eyes to the hills. Where does my help come from? My help comes from the Lord, the Maker of heaven and earth."* (Psalm 121:1–2, New International Version.)

As I looked to my right, there was a clearing in the woods I hadn't noticed before. The moonlight shimmered on the hills beyond the mountain. I was overwhelmed by the thought that God had put in my spirit, at the exact moment I needed it, a reassurance that He was right there on that mountain with me. I realized that there was no place I could possibly go that He would not be with me.

Tension loosened its grip on my body. I relaxed, laid my head on the headrest, and gazed at the beauty of the distant hills and surrounding sky. Reaching across the seat, I got my small Bible out of the glove compartment, turned on my overhead light, and read aloud. My tears fell onto the page as God's Spirit seemed to bathe me in His peace.

After about twenty minutes, I put the Bible on the dashboard, got out of the car, went around to the trunk, took out the blanket, and wrapped myself up in it. I got back in the car, reached into my purse, pulled out the rice cakes and ate. I reached around to the back floor of the car, grabbed the half-filled bottle of water, drank it, and thanked God for every drop.

Soon I heard the crackling sound of gravel and a motor growing louder. I turned on my headlights so that I wouldn't startle the driver. Yes! It was Ranger Hal in his official ranger truck. I turned on my overhead light and waved so he would know I was friend and not foe.

I told him my dilemma and he suggested that I follow him. In the wake of a cloud of dust and flying insects, I followed him each twist and turn of the way. He stopped. I stopped. He got out of his truck and came to my car.

"We're here." He pointed. "Bears' Lair is right through those trees."

"Bears' Lair? Not Bears' Den or Lions' Lair?"

"No. It's Bears' Lair. I remember when they built it. I suppose the owners wanted the name to rhyme more than they wanted it to make sense." He chuckled. He held his flashlight and lighted the path down to the porch.

Someone peered from the window. And then a masculine voice, "It's Stanice with the po-lice!"

"Thank you so much, Ranger Hal."

"Just glad I could help." He tipped his hat and walked back up the hill.

I heard a woman's voice. "She made it! I told you she was coming!"

I smiled as I reached the porch and whispered into the wind, *"Thank you, God, for always showing me the way."*

The door creaked opened. Light and an array of arms raised for hugs came spilling out. "You made it, girl."

It was late. *I'll tell them tomorrow just how I got here.*

Sometimes we wonder how we're going to make it through the many changes, blows, disappointments, and dark times in our lives. Sometimes, we think we know where we are going in life; but in midstream, we seem to lose our way. A job folds, a husband leaves, the children don't do what we want or expect them to do, the promotion doesn't come like we hoped it would, or a loved one dies leaving us alone. The joy of life seems fleeting and doesn't seem to outweigh the pain of living life on life's terms—terms that are sometimes hard—even a bit brutal. Like climbing the rough side of a mountain without a climber's pick and rope. We find that we can't fix the situation; we can't even fix ourselves; but when we get in touch with the One that has all power and is waiting for us to turn our will and our lives over to His care—miracles happen and wonders never cease.

Dear Heavenly Father: We want to praise you today just because *You are* and *forever will be* the Creator of Heaven and earth. We thank you that you neither slumber nor sleep; but instead watch our coming in and our going out. If we go to the tops of the mountains, you are there. If we go to the depths of the ocean, you are there. When fear overwhelms us, remind us that your perfect love casts out *all* fear. When we lose our way, find us and bring us nearer, my God, to Thee. Amen. So be it!

I lift up my eyes to the hills—where does my help come from?
My help comes from the Lord,
The Maker of heaven and earth.
He will not let your foot slip—
He who watches over you will not slumber;
Indeed, he who watches over Israel will neither slumber nor
sleep.
The Lord watches over you—
The Lord is our shade at your right hand;
The sun will not harm you, nor the moon by night.
The Lord will keep you from all harm—
He will watch over your life;
The Lord will watch over your coming and going
Both now
And forever more.

PSALM 121 (New International Version)

✳

HOPE

✳

Resurrected Dreams

My passion for writing started a long time ago. I recall being eight years old and writing on walls (in pencil, of course), toilet paper, notebooks, and anything else that was capable of holding the perpetual flow of words that cascaded from my brain. My first poem, "Beltsville Farm," was published in the school magazine when I was nine. However, I never believed that what I wrote was good. Other people said, "Stanice, this is wonderful." Teachers graded my efforts with a circled red letter A. But in my mind, I saw an underlined black letter, U, because everything I wrote appeared to me to be unsatisfactory.

The itsy bitsy spider went up the waterspout.

In my teen years and into my early twenties, I wrote poetry, love letters, journal entries, and stories. My writing changed as I changed. After I was raped at fourteen years old, everything I wrote became dim and grim tales of unrequited love, pain-filled poems, and the sun-is-shining-but-my-heart-is-dark stories. As my life became an endless string of drug-induced stupors, the writing turned into incoherent pieces of myself lost in a spiral of marijuana smoke that either escaped through my cocaine-encrusted nostrils, or plunged out of a hypodermic needle filled with heroin and the blood of my soul.

Down came the rain and washed the spider out.

In my thirties, some of my friends died from overdoses and gunshot wounds, but God spared me. Maybe because I was the weakest and most foolish.

Out came the sun and dried up all the rain.

In my forties, writing found me again. It helped shatter the chains of my painful and shameful past. Words fed my starving spirit and soothed my aching life. In spite of the fact that I abandoned the words and left them to die by the side of the road, they waited for me at the crossroads of life to point the way. "Just believe!" they insisted, "that we and you are one."

The itsy bitsy spider went up the spout again.

I believed, and thus took the first step toward life. A resurrected life filled with resurrected dreams.

Today I write because God has turned all my hurts into joys. I want God to get as much glory as supernaturally possible out of this life He so graciously spared. I write for others, who perhaps like me need encouragement and inspiration to press their way toward seeking God's purpose for their lives and developing the personal and intimate relationship with Him that is needed to fulfill the vision that He grants.

I write because I am free from the bondage of addiction. And to show that deliverance from and healing of the festering wounds that ooze into our todays and douse the hope of our tomorrows is possible. I write to celebrate the triumph of good over evil; understanding that even though Satan meant to kill me, God did not allow it. I also write because God promises He will turn *all* things—every experience of my life—around for the good of those that love Him.

I write because I applied the story about Moses to my own life. I stood before the Lord, opened my hands, lifted them up to the throne of Heaven, and prayed, "God, use to your glory whatever You have placed in my hands. Make me a beacon of light in a dark and dank world." Writing is one of God's answers to that prayer.

Even though writing is not easy for me, I'm glad it isn't because it keeps me God-dependent and not self-dependent. Because I know that what God starts in the Spirit I cannot finish in the flesh, I have to surrender to His leading every time I sit down with a pen or computer keyboard. I quietly ask or write on the fresh page, "Show me, Lord." I do this because I realize that I am only a tool—the ax in the wood-cutter's hand. It is not I who fell the tree but the woodcutter.

I don't know what people need. I don't even know what I need most of the time, but God knows. He knows who he assigned to read the pages that He allows me to produce. He knows the questions of our hearts, even the ones left unut-tered. God knows our fears, joys, hopes, thoughts, disappoint-ments—past and present. He, alone, knows the beginning and the end.

I also write out of selfishness because I believe that I receive far more than I give. For a woman that never lived up to her potential, finally, I am. Finally my life is not lived in vain and I'm not just taking up space or wasting the breath that God grants me.

Finally, I write to lead the way and show my son, Michael, and future generations that all things are possible when you offer up to God whatever He's placed in your hand.

What are our dreams? If we no longer have any, we need to ask God, the Dream Maker, to build us a dream from the ground up and from the inside out. That's why I believe sometimes we feel like there is major construction going on inside of us that sometimes we only recognize as restlessness, questioning, an unsatisfied desire to do a certain thing, and to be a certain place in our lives where we never seem to be at the time we want to be there. Like labor pains, a dream struggles to be born.

But then, some of us, when blessed with a dream, allow fear to keep us from moving forward to realize the dream. We allow our negative thoughts to drag us back to our past failures: *"How dare you even try. You know that's beyond you."* Or *"Where do you think you're going? You can't do that! Remember what happened the last time you tried to step out there? What makes you think that it's going to be different this time?"*

We must not listen—they are lies from the bottomless pit of lies! Instead we must come to believe that when we ask God for a dream or a vision for our lives, our prayers will not only be answered with tailor-made dreams prepared in advance for us; but we will also be given absolutely everything that we need to realize the dream. We can do all things through the God who strengthens us. And we must act on our dreams now, because if not now—when?

God hears our cries in the stillness of the night and in the busyness of the days. Before we even finish praying, help is already on the way. I know because He did it for me. The same thing He does for one He will do for another. Unlike human beings, God doesn't play favorites; but He does reward those who diligently seek Him.

Dear Heavenly Father: Give us the progressive vision that You have for our lives. Protect our minds against the invasion of negative and nonproductive thoughts that seek to defeat us. When the harshness of life seems to wash us out, remind us to get up and look up to You. Help us to inch our way back up the spout again and claim Your victory with every step we take. Thank you that our lives do have meaning and purpose! Breathe life into our dry bones and fan the flames under our smoldering dreams. Help us to believe that it's never too late to follow that dream and vision for our lives. Order our steps and show us that we can do all things with You as our Helper. Thank you for creating talents and gifts within us that we may we use them to your glory. Amen. So be it!

Having then gifts differing according to the grace that
is given us,
Let us use them:
If prophecy, let us prophesy in proportion to our faith;
Or ministry, let us use it in our ministering;
He who teaches, in teaching;
He who exhorts, in exhortation;
He who gives, with liberality;
He who leads, with diligence;
He who shows mercy, with cheerfulness.

ROMANS 12:6–8 (New King James Version)

Always Check
the Fruit

Storms can rage quietly within the human heart and go unnoticed until that first clap of thunder and then—BAM. John's words struck like a bolt of lightning parting the night sky of our marriage. "If you don't give me one thousand dollars, I am going to make your life a living hell!"

"What are you saying to me, John? I'm your wife!"

His eyes were glazed over with a veil of hate, and his face was framed with gray and black three-day-old patches of stubble. "I know you have a secret bank account." He took a few steps toward me and waved a small white piece of paper. "I found this ATM receipt last week."

"John, you've lost your mind. Secret? There's nothing secret about that account. I work just like you do. But the fact that you can stand there and threaten and blackmail your own wife, now, that's scary!"

"Stacey, you ain't seen scary yet. But you will, if you don't give me the money."

I had to get out of that kitchen. My back was against the window and there was only one way out and John was standing in it. I slowly moved toward the doorway. John put his arm across the doorway preventing my exit.

"John, move!"

His cold stare pierced through me like a poisoned-tipped arrow into my soul. My heart beat rapidly against my chest and my throat constricted, but I stood my ground. I looked directly at him, as if to dare him to NOT let me pass. Finally, he lowered his arm and I walked into the dining room. He followed closely behind.

"Do you understand me, Stacey?"

He hurled my old nickname at me like a spear with the intention of nailing me to our sordid past.

I kept walking and said nothing. I turned the corner and walked toward the powder room.

I could feel his warm breath on my neck as he said, "I know you heard me. You ain't got to say nothing. I know you understand me and you know that I am quite serious."

I went into the powder room and attempted to shut the door; but he pushed into the door with the palm of his hand. I leaned my body into the door and managed to shut it.

"That's all right, Stacey. You can run; but you can't hide. Remember, I live here too."

With my hands and head resting on the door, I cried. Suddenly, I heard the front door slam shut and the lock clank. I came out of the bathroom, ran to the kitchen window, and peered through the slit in the curtains. John got into his yellow Escort, started the engine, and backed out of the parking space. I breathed a sigh of relief as I watched him drive off and out of sight.

I cried out to God. *"Why did I marry this man? I feel so stupid. I know what he is capable of. What do I do now?"*

I went into the living room, sat on the blue love seat facing the fireplace, and stared at the neatly stacked logs. I tried to figure out what had been going on with me that resulted in such a bad decision.

I knew John Smith before I stopped using drugs. He had been "my man," or reasonable facsimile. His job was to keep me supplied with drugs, and my job was to keep him happy, no matter what the cost. During that two-year relationship with John, he beat me, raped me at will, and verbally abused me whenever he needed to feel better about himself and his life. I'm not blaming him for the tormented condition of my soul at the time. After all, I chose to stay with him, in spite of his treatment of me, because I had a greater desire to stay high than anything else.

When John came back into my life, I hadn't seen him in over ten years. He said he found my number in the telephone directory and when he saw my name, he realized that he was still "in love" with me. He asked to see me and I said yes. When I asked him about his present life, he said, "That's all changed now. I've changed. I don't use drugs anymore and, like you, I'm a Christian. As a matter of fact, I believe it was the Lord who allowed me to find your telephone number because I prayed for a wife."

Perhaps my self-esteem was still low even though I had surrendered my life to God's care and been off drugs for over ten years. Perhaps I was just lonely. I knew what the Bible said about having sex outside the confines of marriage; but I still desired sexual contact. So I convinced myself that if I got married I could at least have sex in peace.

Other than the sex, could I have possibly believed that John loved me? No. Did I love him? No. For someone like me who had been verbally and physically abused for most of my life, perhaps I had also convinced myself that I was worthless and destined to marry an abusive man—that it was an impossibility to expect anything more. I already had one failed marriage to my credit because of my seeming inability to show love and receive love. Whatever the case, getting married again meant that at least I would not have to be without a man's touch any longer—and—at forty-four years old, it beat being alone.

And then, I thought, *Maybe God did send John back to me. Since God had changed my life, then He could have definitely changed John's life.* I convinced myself that a relationship with him could and would be different this time. I felt that I owed John because, while in the grip of our drug addiction, I was far from the perfect woman to him (not that he was anywhere near the perfect man to me either). So, we could make amends to each other and we could be to each other—now— what we couldn't be to each other—then.

So, after talking all this over with myself, I reached back into my emotionally dysfunctional past and pulled this man into my present.

However, I didn't check the present fruit. I mean, let's get real, cherries just don't grow on a lemon tree. I knew that cherries were red, but as I interacted with the "new" John, I never took the time to answer my own questions, *Why am I seeing yellow? Where is all the anger coming from? The fits of rage that made me shudder? The grabbing and shaking just to get a point across?* The truth about who we really are shows in the way we live.

After all, I knew the signs. I've been in abusive relationships too many times before. Everyday thoughts would echo in my brain, *"Danger!" "No! This ain't right!" "Get out now! Let him go!"* However, I ignored the warnings. Instead, nine months after allowing John back in my life, I literally moved him out of a rooming house in Washington and drove him to North Carolina. Two weeks later I married him.

Again, I was on a self-destructive course—this time without the use of drugs—but destructive nonetheless. I was certain that God opened the door that led me to North Carolina, but He didn't say anything about taking John. I made that decision.

On my wedding day, it rained so hard and for so long that I thought Noah was coming back. As I stood there at the altar of the First Baptist Church in Chapel Hill, North Carolina, I knew in my heart that I was out of place and out of my mind. When the preacher said, "If there is anybody here who thinks this couple should not be wed, speak now or forever hold your peace," everything inside me wanted to shout, "Stop the wedding! I cannot do this!" But I said nothing. I stood there miming the words "I do" like a puppet on twisted strings.

That night we did what a married couple is encouraged to do—but—I still had no peace. Plus, I felt desolate—like I had slammed the door in the face of my future. Any possibility of ever loving and being loved was gone. Hope froze to death between the sheets of our marriage bed that cold and rainy night.

About six months into the marriage, I saw that my decision to marry John was not just adversely affecting me but also the one person that I truly loved the most—my son.

My eighteen-year-old didn't live with us but one day the three of us were riding somewhere in my car. My son was in the passenger seat and I was driving. John hollered at me from the back seat after I told him I lost my sunglasses. My son turned around in his seat and looked at John and commanded, "John! You WILL NOT talk to my mother like that!" I looked into the rearview mirror. John shut right up and sat back in the seat.

I had gotten used to the hollering, threats, temper tantrums, and the bruises from John grabbing me. It all became a way of life—once again. As long as I tiptoed around my husband's feelings, didn't bring up certain sensitive subjects, said nothing about him calling me at least ten times a day at work, and allowed him his sexual perversions—all was peaceful. Even though I had worked ten years to get my life back and find my place in the world, I reverted back to life as a nonentity in the relationship.

But when I witnessed my son demand respect and defend his mother's honor, something stirred inside me and woke up. My precious son turned and looked at me with eyes that spoke to my wounded heart, *"Momma, why? Don't you know that you don't have to live like this anymore? God freed you a long time ago."* In that moment, God used my son's eyes to deliver to me the courage and the resolve I needed to take the first step to righting the wrong. In that moment, I silently asked God to help me get out of the mess that I had made.

A week later on a sweltering hot and sunny North Carolina day in June, I had the movers on standby awaiting my call. Fearing reprisal, I waited until my husband went to work before I sprang into action. Without a clue, he returned from work that day to a nearly empty apartment. I had moved out.

Even after I moved, John called me excessively, stopped by my job, and tried to convince me that he was getting help through counseling with our pastor and that he would be different this time. By September, worn down and believing that even though I made a mistake marrying him that I was committed now and had to try again, I moved him out of the apartment I had left him in and into the townhouse that I rented in a neighboring town.

Disgusted with myself, my mind snapped back into the present—sitting on the love seat facing the fireless fireplace. Already sleeping in separate bedrooms, here it was one month after I let John move back in with me, and he threatened me again. I put my head into my hand and sighed at the incredible situation. I cried, got down on my knees and prayed, *"My Lord, help me. I can't live like this anymore. Forgive me for the part I played in all of this and please show me what to do now."* I went to the bookcase, slid my Bible off the shelf, and read to fortify my heart and spirit for the battle ahead. Before I zipped the purple book cover and put the book back on the shelf, I felt assured that everything was going to be all right—in spite of the circumstances that surrounded me like armed hostile soldiers. I made a decision to trust God to guide me, direct my steps, show me what to do and when to do it. I was ready to trust God with the details of my future and I believed that more would be revealed—in God's time not mine.

John didn't come home till late that night. The bedroom door creaked open. I pretended to be asleep. I heard his footsteps trail off as he went across the hall into his bedroom and shut the door. The next morning, I knocked on his door. "John, I'm not giving you any money and you've got to go. I will not live like this anymore. You have until November 30 to move out."

He opened the door. "Stacey, I plan to leave anyway but not until April or May. November 30? You must be crazy. You can forget that. And I wouldn't sleep too hard from now on if I were you."

I waved my hand in front of his face with one sweeping movement. I could feel the strength and power of God welling up inside me as I said, "If you have a problem with November 30, you need to take it to God because that's where I got the date. And as far as me sleeping at night, the Bible says, 'No weapon formed against me shall prosper.'" I walked away and proceeded to get dressed for work.

Weeks passed. We barely talked. He stayed in the guest bedroom—which had become his room—most of the time. For days, he stopped shaving and barely ate. Sometimes, when I got home from work, I'd get a glimpse of him sitting on the side of his bed staring at the wall. I also smelled evidence that he was drinking liquor again. As I watched his behavior deteriorate, it got harder for me to sleep at night. I propped chairs against the two doors of the master bedroom where I slept. Each night as I lay in bed, I repeated over and over, "No weapon formed against me shall prosper" (Isaiah 54:17, New King James Version) until I fell asleep.

Three days before John's November 30 moving deadline, I heard him talking on the telephone. When he saw me pass by, he spoke louder into the phone, "Man, she don't know who she's messing with. I'll drag her out in the woods, and then file a missing person report on her." John was not going to leave on his own. I knew it was time for me to take the next step.

At work the next day, I called the Durham County domestic violence hotline and talked with a lawyer. I explained my situation and asked her what my options were. She explained that I could petition the court to issue a domestic violence protective order that would have John immediately removed from the home by the sheriff's office. This would be followed by a hearing a week later to determine if the order would be continued. "However, because your husband hasn't hit you it's highly improbable that the judge will grant you a protective order."

I explained my husband's history of abuse and that his present behavior indicated that it was just a matter of time before he started beating me again. I had to help her understand. "Let's say that my husband hasn't hit me—YET—and the operative word here is 'yet.' He is already verbally and emotionally abusive."

"Mrs. Smith, the law—"

"Look, it doesn't matter whether it's a hit upside the head or words that cut like a knife—pain is pain. You've got to help me—NOW—before it's too late. I refuse to become a statistic for your domestic violence death chart."

"Okay, write down everything that has been going on in the household. Bring that with you tomorrow. I'll help you file and we'll see if the judge will sign it."

I hung up and called the rental office. I explained that my husband would be moving out tomorrow and I needed them to change the locks on the door after the sheriff escorted him out. Since my husband's name was not on the lease, they saw no problem in granting my request. One down—one to go.

On the morning of November 28 at 8:30 as I headed toward the front door, I turned to my husband, who was watching cartoons in the living room. "Goodbye, John."

He probably assumed I was going to work. "Okay. Whatever." He never took his eyes off the television.

I parked and before getting out of the car I took a moment to pray, *"Thank you that you will extract John from my life, no later than November 30. I will trust and not be afraid."* With my head held high, shoulders straight, and believing that the angelic hosts of Heaven were with me, I climbed the steps of the Durham County Courthouse. As the security guard searched through my purse, I asked for directions to the Domestic Violence Office.

As I walked into the office, I heard someone say, "Are you Mrs. Smith?"

"Yes." It was the lawyer I had talked with over the phone. She introduced herself and went over the forms with me. As I sat listening to her, I noticed, sitting with her back pressed to the wall, was a pale white woman with bruises on her lovely young face, dim swollen and lifeless eyes that wouldn't take the chance of missing who might come through the door next. I could smell the fear. She had a John somewhere too. It was clear that she hoped he wasn't making his way down the hall and through that door.

I focused, again, on what the lawyer was saying to me. I filled out the application for the protective order and handed it back to her.

"Mrs. Smith, don't get your hopes up. Like I told you

before, the judge probably won't grant the protective order because your husband hasn't physically abused you."

"I don't mean any disrespect, but you did consent to represent me. Right?"

"Yes."

"Okay. I've done my part by showing up and filling out the papers. Now you go and take the application wherever you need to take it so that the judge can sign it."

"I can't promise you it will be signed."

"I know that you can't promise me anything, but God promised me that John would be out of that townhouse before November 30. Therefore, since it is clear to me that John is not leaving on his own, that means the judge WILL sign. I will walk out of here today with a signed court order."

She looked at me like I was crazy, turned around, and shrugged on her way down the hall to the judge's chamber. When I turned around to sit down, I noticed that the young woman was gone. I silently thanked God for the peaceful resolution of my situation and for the woman that I never got a chance to meet.

About five minutes later, the lawyer came out of the judge's chamber with a bewildered look on her face. "She signed! The judged actually signed the protective order."

I hugged and thanked her for her cooperation. Looking at her pale face, I knew that she had just witnessed the awesome power of God to make a way out of what seems to be no way. I gave her a moment to get it together and then asked her what the next step was.

At 10:30, I proceeded downstairs to the sheriff's office, gave them my address and a physical description of my husband. At 10:45, the sheriff dispatched a car to remove my husband. At 10:50 I called the rental office. "This is Mrs. Smith, I talked with you earlier this week. Well, today is the day. As soon as you see the sheriff escort my husband out of 1733-C, change the locks." I also called the telephone company and arranged to have the telephone number changed.

At 11:10, I paid the parking attendant, and drove off toward I-85. Next stop? Greensboro, North Carolina. A short forty-five-minute drive away. I was treating myself to lunch.

While driving down I-85, I noticed that the previous storm clouds had been replaced with billowy white ones that looked like cotton candy swirling in the sky. I opened all the windows in the car. The chilled wind blew through my hair. It was a beautiful brisk North Carolina day that smelled like freedom.

I never allowed John back into my life. Three years and ten months later, I received a telephone call informing me that John had died during the night of lung cancer.

Sometimes it seems like war is raging all around us—sometimes even within us. We wonder how we got ourselves into such precarious situations.

Do you remember the commercial where a man sits on the side of a bed and appears to be bloated and miserable? He looks into the television camera at us, reaches for the Alka-Seltzer, and says, "I can't believe I ate the whole thing"? Well, that's how I feel sometimes when I look back over the choices that I have made and still make in my life. It sickens my spirit and even the look I see on my friends' faces seems to say, "I can't believe she ate the whole thing."

I know that I am not alone. There are many of us who can relate to that feeling. Unlike the man in the commercial, however, burritos and jalapeño peppers ain't the problem—it's us—and the choices we make. Maybe we feel so overwhelmed because there is no one to blame but ourselves.

Plus, we have to live with the consequences of our actions. However, it is so good to know that we are not alone and that when we make mistakes, we can pick ourselves up, dust ourselves off, and keep moving forever forward.

Thank God, we don't have to keep making the same mistakes over and over again. My mentor, Dorine, told me more than once, "Baby, it's all right to be a fool but don't keep being the same fool over and over again. If you gonna stumble—stumble forward." I've always been amazed how God will use that woman to tell me things that I may not *want* to hear but *need* to hear.

Some decisions that we make are irreversible—others are not. It is in knowing the difference between these two that marks maturity. It is acting on that knowing that courage is found. We must come to understand that courage is not the absence of fear but going on to do what needs to be done in spite of the fear.

Dear Heavenly Father: Thank you for your promise that no weapon formed against us will prosper. We thank you for taking us by the hand and lifting us up and out of the messes that we create when we are left to our own devices. Help us to not reach back and drag into the present what you have already freed us from. We thank you that you look beyond our faults and see our needs. So sweet is your unconditional and unchanging love for us. When we make the wrong choices, you still love us and gently call us back to the path that you know is best for us— Your path. Your promise to give a future and a hope that is far beyond anything that we can even ask, think, or imagine is the heartbeat of our faith. We're grateful that you wouldn't love us any less today with our imperfections as you will love us in one of your tomorrows without them. Amen. So be it!

Jesus asked the boy's father, "How long has he been like this?"
"From childhood," he answered.
"It has often thrown him into fire or water to kill him.
But if you can do anything, take pity on us and help us."
"If you can?" said Jesus. "Everything is possible for him
who believes."
Immediately the boy's father exclaimed, "I do believe;
Help me overcome my unbelief."

MARK 9:21–24 (New International Version)

Never Too Late to Dream—
Part I

My brother, Stan, and I sat at the dining room table, while he shared news from back home. He had just moved to Durham, North Carolina, and into the little townhouse I rented. It had been about five months since the courts continued my protective order and with it my husband had been extracted from my life like a decayed tooth. It was so refreshing having my brother there with me. His arrival was like a tall, cold glass of water on a stifling hot August day. We laughed and talked about days gone by.

"Hey, Sis, are you still writing poetry?"

"Honey, I haven't written any poetry in years."

"Girl, you used to write some great stuff."

"Look, Stan, I asked Momma a few years ago, 'Momma, do you remember the poems I used to write?'" I stood up and emulated my mother with all her drama. "She said, 'Lord, yes! I used to listen to you reading those poems to me and I'd ask God, "What's wrong with my baby?"'"

"Momma, you asked what was wrong with me. I don't understand."

Again I mimicked my mother, "Yeah Stanice. You see, everything you wrote just seemed to be sooooo depressing. Rain and tears. Falling into the abyss and stuff like that. So I prayed for you, 'Lord, help my baby she's in trouble.' But I never told you what was running through my mind when you read your poetry to me. At least so far as I can remember I didn't tell you."

By this time, my brother had laughed himself right out of the chair onto the floor.

"Neicy, you so crazy."

I like to make my brother laugh. He makes these throaty he-he-he sounds. He just gets so tickled until tears run down his face. It was a two-way street because he would make me laugh just looking and listening to him laugh. So I just kept on with the dramatization.

"Stan, I was shocked when she said that they were 'soooo depressing.' Actually, I thought they were quite good until she got that blank look on her face and she'd say, 'That's real good, baby.' But I could tell that she just didn't get it. I always wondered why the look on her face didn't quite match her words. When she told me all that—I knew."

My brother insightfully offered, "I know you, Neicy, better than you know yourself. You hear what you want to hear sometimes. Momma never said that your poems were not good, she just said that they were depressing. But not all of them."

"Well, I just wrote what I felt and how I was living on the inside. Hey, that was just where I was."

My brother got really serious. "I never told you this and I vowed that I never would. I don't know. Maybe I shouldn't . . ."

"No, Stan. What? Come on and tell me."

"I will tell you this, your poetry was better than you thought. As a matter of fact as I recall you never thought any of them were good; but I loved them and so did a whole lot of people."

"A whole lot of people? I only showed them to you, Momma, and Daddy, if I could get him to stay still long enough."

"Maybe I shouldn't go on and tell you. But . . ."

I playfully poked him in the chest. "Come on now. Don't play with me. Tell me."

"I used to read your poems in class and I didn't tell them that my sister wrote them. As far as they knew, I was the author."

"What?"

"Yep. Remember when Mom and Dad sent me off to that boarding school? Well, I copied your poems in my own handwriting and took them with me. The kids at school loved them—especially the girls. They would walk up to me and say, 'Boy, you may be silly sometimes, but you sure can write!'"

"You've got to be kidding."

"No, I'm not. As a matter of fact, I would always sign up for the talent show at school and I would memorize your poetry. That was my act. Your poetry!" He stood up and pretended he was back on stage. "I patted to perfection my little Afro that I had just loosened up with my blow-out comb. Of course, my color-coordinated outfit was starched and pressed. They lowered the lights in the auditorium. I walked onto center stage, followed by the spotlight. I raised my arms and spread them like I was Marvin Gaye pleading to Tammy Terrell and recited, 'Nalunga! My sweet and Ebony Princess. Nalunga! Tall, and sleek, and strong my Ebony Princess. Nalunga! The forms you take in the depths of my mind are as infinite as your beauty. But not without reason. No, not without reason. Nalunga! You are the golden sand of the African shores. You are the stars on a clear and cloudless night. You are the Sahara Desert's burning sun. You are Mt. Everest, the Sphinx, the Taj Mahal. But not without reason. No, not without reason. Nalunga! Proud, fertile, and regal my Ebony Princess. You are the music flowing from Coltrane's golden horn. You are the thoughts that leap from Nikki Giovanni's mind. You are the agility of Abdul-Jabbar. The courage of Malcolm X, the eyes of Stevie Wonder. But not without reason. No, not without reason. You are life, you are love, you are mine!' The audience loved it! I had to change that 'Prince' you had written to a 'Princess.' Couldn't ruin my fly player image."

I laughed. "You ought to be on HBO. You're funny!"

Stan was full of drama, like my mother and probably myself, even though I was in denial about being anything like my mother. Now that's another story. But he worked that poem! I hadn't heard that poem for at least twenty years. As I listened, I had a revelation: It was quite good. My brother continued to describe his performances.

"Neicy, look, the audience would always be so quiet you could hear a roach crawl across the floor. Every now and then a girl would holler out, 'All right now!' I was hurting them—I was so smooth. The girls were mesmerized. I moved all over that stage like I owned it and the whole night was mine. I talked and walked the poem out, girl. I'm telling you, now."

"Yeah. Right."

"Hold up, hold up! As I got toward the end, I took them to the hoop with my sharp delivery, slam-dunked them starting with the last verse, and then WOP! The end. Consider it done. The lights came up and the people went off! They whooped and whistled. And the girls went wild! I blew kisses and raised my hands in gratitude like a star, Sis, like a star!"

As I sat there watching and listening to him, I wasn't sure how I felt. I couldn't help but laugh because the boy was funny. But I also felt angry and betrayed at the thought that my baby brother had palmed off my poetry as his. Or was I angry with myself for not believing in my own work? I thought of the years I had wasted by not pursuing what had always been my secret passion—the written word. Had I given up on myself five minutes before the miracle happened?

It's said that as human beings we are more alike than different. Have we given up five minutes before the miracle happened? Some of us wonder, "Is it too late?" No, we can't go back and undo the opportunities that we have let pass us by but we can grab hold of the ones that present themselves from this day forward. Yes, we get tired sometimes. We may even feel like we are going nowhere or that things are not working as fast or as we envisioned they would—but we have got to hold on and dare to dream anyway.

To realize a dream or a hope may mean that we have to untie our boats from the safety of the shore and launch out into the deep waters. However, we don't have to do it alone. God will be with us whether we opt to stay on the shore or head for deeper waters. As a matter of fact, if we allow Him to steer our boats—especially since He sees forever and has the power and vision to guide us around the typhoons and lead us through the shark-infested waters of this world—we will make it to the other side, where dreams reside and hopes are fulfilled.

Dear Heavenly Father: Thank you that you have the answers to the piercing questions that cut through to our hearts. We cling to You like weary and thirsty travelers in the desert, knowing that You alone are the Thirst-Quencher. You give us rivers of Living Water, comfort and peace in the midst of our struggles, and you give us the strength to go on, in spite of how we feel or how little we know. But this one thing we are coming to know more and more with each passing day—You love us! Those of us who don't have a dream for our lives—give us one and help us to realize it. Those of us who do have a dream, strengthen us, guide us, make the way clearer and steer us to its fruition. And help us all to encourage one another. Amen. So be it!

So, I restore to you the years that the swarming locust
has eaten,
The crawling locust,
The consuming locust,
And the chewing locust,
My great army which I sent among you.
You shall eat in plenty and be satisfied,
And praise the name of the Lord your God,
Who has dealt wondrously with you;
And my people shall never be put to shame.

JOEL 2:25–26 (New King James Version)

Never Too Late to Dream—
Part II

My mind snapped back to Stan's performance.

"And, Sis, without fail I always got a standing ovation. I'm telling you, they hollered, 'More! More! Do one more, Stan!'"

As I sat there, the tears just seemed to come from nowhere. It was not anger that I felt; it was sadness. Sadness for what might have been.

"Neicy, what's wrong?"

"I want to be angry at you, but I can't, I'm not. I'm just—"

He stood there and looked at me. The joy on his face turned to shame, as he looked down at the floor.

"Stan, all these years, and you never told me my writing was good."

His eyes were pleading. "I told you but you never believed it. You are the one that has to believe in your own talent."

"You're right, I never did. I never—" I got up, ran out of the living room up the steps into my bedroom, and shut the door. I fell across the bed. Now I really was depressed. Seeing myself as I really was depressed me.

"Lord, I never knew. I never believed. Help me sort through this. What do I do now? Is it too late?" I must have cried myself to sleep. A knock on my bedroom door woke me.

A voice came from behind the door. "Neicy, are you all right?"

"Yes, Stan. Come on in."

He sat down on the bed next to me. "I'm sorry, Sis. See that's why I didn't want to tell you. I knew what I did wasn't right. I'm sorry."

"It's okay, Stan."

He put his arm around my shoulder and drew me close to him. "You were good, Neicy, and talent like that just doesn't evaporate. Only God could take a gift like that away and I don't believe He did."

"You know what, Stan?" I looked over at him. "I'm glad you're here and I'm glad that you told me. I needed to hear that now. I mean at this point in my life. I've been writing, although not poetry; but I write lots of stuff and then just hide it in a drawer. Fear of failure looms over me like a foreboding sky. It keeps me from sending my work out into the world."

"It's okay, Sis."

"No, it's not okay. I know now that I've got to grow past this."

"You will."

"With God being my helper and you being my brother, maybe I can do it."

In a tender moment that I will never forget, my little brother held me as we sat on the edge of the bed, and we swayed side to side.

"You're going to be all right. You're my big sister. I've always believed in you and I've always been proud of you. I guess I should have let you know that before now."

"Now is all we have, Stan. And right now, now is enough. I love you."

"I love you too."

Later that night, as I said my prayers before going to bed, I held my hands up to God and dedicated them to Him. I whispered the words of a hymn that always gives me comfort and a sense of surrender of my plans to God's plan for this life that He spared. "Have your own way, Lord. Have your own way. You are the potter. I am but clay. Make me and mold me into your will. While I am waiting, yielded and still."

Every one of us has some talent or ability that God has given us for the good of the world. For some it's singing, dancing, encouraging others, writing, or administration, and some may bake the best pies on the planet—or so every one who tastes them thinks. Whatever our talent is, we have a responsibility to share what God has given us, so that we might bring comfort and joy to another human being.

Our gifts will surface if we ask God to show us and then diligently search them out. How do we search? We try to do something. We sing in the shower, take a class, pick up a pen, look at our job evaluations, and we can even ask our family and friends, "What do you see as my gifts?"

You don't have to give an account for how others may use their gifts, but you will have to give an account to God, someday, for how you used the talents that He has entrusted to you.

Once we identify our talents, we must believe that they exist enough to hone them and then share them with the world. Yes, in spite of the fear. We must remind ourselves that God does not give us a spirit of fear but of power and of love and a sound mind. When we step out on faith, the fear must flee.

Dear Heavenly Father: Thank you so very much for the new beginnings that you make possible through your Mercy and Grace. What you've done for us no one can do and who you are to us no one can be. You are the Lord God Almighty, the Great I AM—all that we need and all that our souls thirst for is to know you and be known by you—to love and be loved by you. No thing, no person, no concept, nor any idea can fill the void that you created to be filled—*only* by *You*. Amen. So be it!

"And it shall come to pass afterward
That I will pour out My Spirit on all flesh;
Your sons and your daughters shall prophesy,
Your old men shall dream dreams,
Your young men shall see visions,
And also on My menservants and My maidservants
I will pour out My Spirit in those days."

JOEL 2:28–29 (New King James Version)

In the Cellar
of Afflictions

I decided that I was going to live my dream to write—no matter what! Doubts came—I expected that and continued to write in spite of the doubts. Times were good and I was feeling pretty good about myself, so I started writing a novel. My writing coach, Tom Fuller, warned me that my first novel would not be publishable but writing it would be a good learning experience. But what he didn't tell me was how to keep writing when all hell breaks loose in your life. How would I continue to write under adversity? That was a question and a lesson only God could teach.

It all started with a leisurely trail ride on a ranch in Raleigh, North Carolina. It was a gorgeous cloudless day. There were about fifteen riders, including me. As we rode out of the clearing and into the woods, the smell of moss, packed fallen leaves, and the rich brown earth met me. The clopping of hooves on the rocks provided the rhythm. A canopy of tall pine and poplar trees provided the shade on the riding trail. It was cooler in the woods and my mind bathed itself in refreshing thoughts.

The lady who rode a horse in front of me turned on her saddle, pointed, and softly said, "Look! A deer! Right over there."

"Well what do you know? The lie is dead—Bambi lives!" I offered, hoping to draw a smile from her tense face. She was a new rider who must have gotten her hands on a western wear catalogue and ordered everything but the spurs.

With just a pair of faded jeans, a gray sweatshirt, and riding boots given to me by a friend, I confidently rode Foxy Lady, a seasoned mare for this not-so-seasoned rider. As the group was about halfway down a steep embankment, I heard a commotion that came from the group of riders in the front of the equestrian convoy.

"What's going on?" The lady's face contorted in her first step to terror.

"I don't know."

Then a chorus of shouts, "Bees! They're stinging us! Bees!"

I tightly held Foxy Lady's reins. I tried to maintain control but the horse reared up like she was in center ring at a Wild West show. The next thing I felt was the cool, hard ground coming up to meet my face. I tasted the dirt in my mouth. As if by instinct, I rolled further down the embankment in an attempt to steer clear of the deadly bucking hooves of all those two-thousand-plus-pound animals. I pulled my sweatshirt up around my head, got up, and ducked and dodged hooves until I was clear of the danger.

The sounds echoing in the forest escalated to a crescendo of horses neighing, hooves slipping and sliding on the rocks, air whizzing from the horses' kicks, hundreds of bees buzzing, and the thuds of my fellow riders hitting the ground.

After what seemed like at least an hour, one by one my fellow riders found me in the clearing of the woods. We took stock of one another's injuries. No one was seriously hurt.

I had a splitting headache, my glasses were gone, and I felt the burn of abrasions on my face and arms; but I could walk! I thought of Christopher Reeve, who hadn't been so fortunate when he was thrown from a horse. I abandoned myself to the moment, lifted my hands toward Heaven, and shouted, "Thank you, Jesus!"

My comrades looked at me and took a few steps back. So what! I didn't care. After we gathered our composure, and some of us our nerve, we rode back to the stables.

Monday, I went back to work. I walked with a bit of a limp, my arm and wrist hurt, and I never did find my glasses.

A week later and before I fully recovered from the trail ride fiasco, Hurricane Fran struck the Raleigh-Durham area with full force. I was without electricity for two weeks; but I was more determined than ever to keep writing. So, with the flickering light of a borrowed oil lamp, I sat at my desk every night and worked on my novel.

Not quite a week after living through the hurricane yet another adversity struck. I was washing the dishes when my hands started to ache. I took them out of the water, dried them off, and looked at them. As I watched, welts started to rise from under the skin of the insides of my hands. They were the size of quarters but shaped like little jagged islands. I touched the welts and pain shot up my arms. Now, I was mad! I stomped my foot on the kitchen floor and said out loud, "Right now, the Lord rebukes anything that is trying to come against me! No weapon formed against me shall prosper! I will finish my novel!"

After my fit of, let's call it, righteous indignation, I lifted my hands up toward heaven like a child with a boo-boo runs to Momma for her to make it all better and prayed, *"Lord, I know that the enemy does not want me to write but you do; so I praise you right now for the victory you will give me in this situation. I refuse to let whatever happens stop me from praising you and walking in the vision that you have given me. Like Job, I know that my Redeemer lives! I will keep writing as long as there is breath in this here body. Amen."*

With my "Amen" said, I walked briskly to my desk in the bedroom, grabbed my notebook, eased on my jacket, and painfully drove myself to the Duke University Medical Center emergency room.

While I waited to be seen, I ever so gently placed the pen between my index and middle fingers and without bending my hand, because the pain was too great, I let the pen glide my words across the paper. Each word and punctuation mark was painful; but I kept writing.

Several doctors looked at me and suggested that I had developed an allergy to the dishwashing liquid that I had used for years without incident. They injected me with Benadryl and gave me a prescription that I immediately took to the pharmacy. With pain and tears, I scribbled out the check to pay for the medicine and drove home.

Once there, I took the medication, and ten minutes later I slowly started to break out in hives from my face down to the bottoms of my feet. I itched and burned all over. Again, I painfully drove myself back to the emergency room. It seems the doctors didn't hear me when I told them that I was allergic to penicillin. The medication that they prescribed had penicillin in it.

Over the next three weeks, my hands cleared up but only to react again and again with the same type of welts. This happened three times—even without using the dishwashing detergent. But I never stopped writing, as painful as it was for me to hold a pen or strike a keyboard.

Several days after my third visit to the emergency room, about 4:00 A.M., welts started popping up on my legs. Back I went to Duke University Medical Center. The doctors were baffled but the explanation they offered this time was just as baffling to me. They dubbed my case "allergic reactions due to the effects that Hurricane Fran had on the water supply." Through it all, I kept praising God and writing.

Before I left North Carolina, I finished my first novel. It's like a lot of other writers' first attempts at a novel—not a Pulitzer Prize entry, but that didn't matter to me. The victory was in finishing it, in spite of all the circumstances that surrounded me, and everything that came against me. God being my Helper, I finished the task that was set before me, and to His glory!

We all have times in our lives when it seems like everything is going against us. Problems mount, illnesses come, frustrations multiply, and we feel like we can't take one more bit of bad news and live! However, if during those times we take our focus off the horrible circumstances that are surrounding us or the feelings of despair that are welling up inside of us and focus on what God has already brought us through in the days and years gone by—we come to believe He will work it out for us again and again and again! We have to set our faces like flint to walk by faith—to believe like my mentor, Dorine, always tells me, "Baby, it's gonna be all right!"

I truly believe that nothing happens to us that isn't already sifted through the hands of God first. And because of that He knows and will give us just what we need to get through it. Sometimes, life is just like a master archer with a bow: To hit the target the bow has to be stretched way back to the absolute limits, but when the archer releases the arrow—WHOOSH—the arrow goes right where the master archer aims—the target! Had it not been stretched, the arrow would have fallen to the ground, limp and defeated, having missed the mark.

Dear Heavenly Father: Thank you that you have given us the victory! Help us to not focus on the situations that face us or the circumstances that surround us; but help us to stay focused on Your love for us. Stretch us, if you must, so that we can be finely tuned instruments of Your Love in Your Hands. Amen. So be it!

My brethren, count it all joy when you fall into various trials
Knowing that the testing of your faith produces patience.
But let patience have its perfect work,
That you may be perfect and complete,
Lacking nothing.
If any of you lacks wisdom,
Let him ask of God, who gives to all liberally
And without reproach, and it will be given to him.

JAMES 1:2–5 (New King James Version)

Purified
by Fire

It appeared to be an ordinary workday at the Duke University Medical Center; however, I couldn't keep my mind on my work. I had been in North Carolina for what seemed like two of the longest, hardest, and darkest years of my adult life. My mind was like a video cam as it replayed the abusive marriage that I had run for my life to get out of about eight months prior.

Facing the fact that I actually married John Smith made me sick to my stomach. When we were together someone would ask him his name and he'd reply, "John Smith." Then they would smile and say to me, "I guess that means you're Pocahontas?" I hated that. If they only knew what life was like at home for *this* Pocahontas.

After securing the restraining order that got him out of my life, I only saw him at stoplights, the library, or other chance-at-a-glance sightings. Whenever I saw him or thought of our marriage, I felt an overwhelming disgust with myself for making such an awful mistake. My mouth would involuntarily salivate like I was about to throw up.

The negative thoughts were like darts thrown at my head and the game board was already too crowded. Every thought brought with it yet another burden too heavy for me to bear.

I thought of the longest night of my life just weeks prior, being alone during Hurricane Fran, in a house in the middle of the woods of Hillsborough, North Carolina. Between the hurricane, the marriage, getting thrown off a horse as bees stung it, and constant visits to Duke University Medical Center's emergency room with painful allergic reactions that the doctors attributed to environmental conditions left behind by the hurricane, life was all too much! I felt that, this time, God had surely given me more than I could possibly bear.

With thoughts like these, this day was far from an ordinary workday at Duke. Overwhelmed by life, emotionally drained, and spiritually dry, death started looking good to me. I thought if I died I could be with God in an indescribably beautiful Heaven. There would be no more pain or tears. Nothing would be too hard and everything would be good. I could even shed my tormented brain for a heavenly version that was not capable of thinking negative thoughts. I laid my head down on my desk and cried. I knew I was in trouble. My past work experience in the field of drug addiction taught me to never take lightly talk or thoughts of suicide.

In the next few moments, I felt an overwhelming urge to go to the chapel over in the next building to pray. I walked there briskly. When I got there, with no one else around, I fell down on my hands and knees at the altar and cried out to God, *"You've got to help me. Guide me. What do I do now?"* I continued to pour my heart out to God.

Leaving all my burdens on the altar, I went back to the office and dialed the telephone number of my friend Dorine in Washington.

The dreaded voice mail informed me, "I'm either away

from my desk or on another line." I hung up and dialed a friend in Maryland.

An answering machine, complete with the voices of children in the background, "We're not in right now, if you leave—".

I hung up. I needed to talk to a human being. I dialed another number.

"Hello."

"Delphine! I feel overwhelmed by life. Everything is wrong and bad. I actually thought of dying and it scared me." For the next few minutes I cried and spewed out all that was going on in my life. Finally, I stopped talking. Dead silence.

"Delphine, are you there?"

"Yes."

"Well, tell me something."

"You want me to give you feedback?"

"Yes, why do you think I'm calling you long distance. You've got to help me."

"Well. Okay."

Dead silence.

"Delphine! Breathe or something!"

"Well, Stanice, actually all I have is one question for you."

"Okay, what?"

"Why are you still there in North Carolina?"

Dead silence—this time on my end. A chill went through my body. That question pierced to the heart of my conundrum like a scalpel in the hands of a skilled surgeon.

"Delphine, I have absolutely no idea why I am still here."

From that point on, I'm not sure of another word she or I said. We talked and I'm only half sure of that. It felt like God was chiseling her question into my soul.

Later, in the stillness of the night, truth took me again to my knees. Suddenly, it was clear! I knew why I was still in

North Carolina. Pride! It was my pride that kept me there. Determined that North Carolina would not defeat me, I was not going home to D.C., no matter what anyone or God for that matter said until I had "things" and "position" to show the people back home. I could not go back home a failure.

"Father, forgive me." As my tears soaked my bedcovers, I knew it was time to go. Questions bombarded my mind. *How? When?* Another thought quieted the questions. *You'll be home before Christmas.* It was already the end of October.

The next day, I went to a support group meeting. I told everyone that I would be going home soon.

"I want to sincerely thank each of you for your love and support during my stay in the Durham area."

"We love you, Stanice," a few of them shouted out.

"I love you too and I'll miss you."

After the meeting, a rather handsome Black guy, about thirty-ish, came over to me. "Hi, my name is Charles. You probably don't remember me but I remember you."

"Hi, Charles." I wished I remembered him; but he was right, I didn't.

"I live in D.C. I'm here visiting this weekend. My fiancée's family lives here and I'm here for a while."

"Oh, okay."

"I heard you say you were moving back to D.C. Can I help you with your move?"

"Help me?"

"Yeah. Years ago, you helped me. I've heard you speak on several occasions and what you say always gives me a lot of hope. So it would be good if I could finally do something for you. If you need help that is."

"Well . . ."

"Where's your calendar? Just pick a day and LaBarry and I will rent a truck and come to Durham to move you back home."

The keyword for me was "LaBarry," a friend from D.C. I pulled out my calendar and picked the weekend after Thanksgiving. I thought that very appropriate.

Well, the following month, as scheduled, Charles and LaBarry rented a van and drove to Durham, North Carolina, to move me back home to Washington. I sold and gave away all my furniture. I knew that God would replace things. I took only what fit in the van and my car's trunk. Charles and LaBarry paid all the expenses of the move. They finally agreed to let me at least buy them donuts and coffee.

I followed the van, in my car, up I-95 north. When we drove around the bend and across the 14th Street Bridge on into D.C. and I got my first glimpse of the Washington Monument, I wept, prayed, and praised!

As of the writing of this story, I've been back in D.C. over three years. From my balcony and bedroom window, I can see the Washington Monument. Even now, if I look at it and take a moment to reflect, I still weep, pray, and praise! All I need now is a pair of ruby slippers and a dog named Toto!

Sometimes we have to leave home to find out that home is where we really belong. But in the meantime, God will do a new thing with us wherever we are to prepare for His plan— once we finally yield to His plan. Which, I might add, speaking from experience, is a far better plan than we could ever even dream of for ourselves. He's just got that kind of love. Coming to believe this, we no longer feel like giving up five minutes before the miracle happens!

Dear Heavenly Father: Just like You promised—weeping may endure for a night but joy does come in the morning! Thank you for speaking to us through Your Word, our friends, and circumstances, although we are sometimes slow in receiving Your message. We thank you for your patience and your grace. We are eternally grateful for the hard places and seasons in our lives. For it is in them that we learn to come to You and lay our burdens down at Your feet. Amen. So be it!

"But now," thus says the Lord, who created you, O Jacob,
And He who formed you, O Israel:
"Fear not, for I have redeemed you;
I have called you by your name,
You are Mine.
When you pass through the waters, I will be with you;
And through the rivers, they shall not overflow you.
When you walk through the fire,
You shall not be burned,
Nor shall the flame scorch you.
For I am the Lord your God,
The Holy One of Israel, your Savior;
I gave Egypt for your ransom,
Ethiopia and Seba in your place.
Since you are precious in My sight.
You have been honored,
And I have loved you."

Isaiah 43:1–4 (New King James Version)

※

LOVINGKINDNESS

※

A Friend
in Need

It was early one sunny North Carolina morning. I lay in my bed trying to squeeze in fifteen more do-nothing minutes. The telephone rang. I hesitated answering. For anonymity's sake let's say that it was Grace on the other end of the line. I hadn't heard from her in a while.

"I've been praying for you. I've been hoping that you would call. Are you all right?"

"No, Stanice, I haven't been doing too good."

"Where are you?"

"My daughters and I had to move in with my mother. I couldn't make it out on my own anymore. I hate that I had to come home. I really miss my apartment."

"What's going on with you?"

"I'm full-blown now. I have AIDS."

"Oh sweetie, I'm so very sorry to hear that. But I'm glad you had a home to go back to."

We talked on for a while and then I found myself asking, "Have you been to church since you've been up there?"

"I went one time, but I felt so bad. I've lost my hair and it just felt like folks kept looking at me. Whispering about me."

"I know what it's like to lose your hair," I felt the need to tell her.

"You do? But you've got gorgeous hair."

"Yeah, now, thank God. But once I had alopecia and my hair came out and left large bald spots. Finally, I just shaved it all off."

We related to the feelings awhile. Her voice got lighter as the burden of uniqueness fell away as we talked.

"Actually, I still have two of the wigs I wore during my hairless period. You can have them if you want."

"Wigs?"

"Yeah, I didn't like the idea myself at first. But a woman's got to do what a woman's got to do. Nobody even knew these were wigs unless I told them. One is braids and the other one is jazzy with a fly cut. It looks like you just got a fresh perm."

She laughed and said, "Hey, I'm game. Bring them on."

Grace was waiting for me at the door of the gray single-wide trailer. We hugged and I handed her the bag of wigs. She was only thirty-five and yet she appeared to have aged greatly since I last saw her. She had a bright red and yellow scarf tied tightly on her head. Her short brown body was thin. She walked like a ninety-year-old arthritic woman, stopping every few steps to catch her breath.

Grace told her mother and two teenage daughters to sit down in the living room because she had a surprise for them. She pulled my arm and led me to the back of the trailer like a high school girl about to show me some boy she had a crush on. She sat down on the side of the bed and took the wigs out of the bag. She tried both of them on but she was really partial to the shoulder-length braided wig.

She looked in the mirror and the sweetest, widest smile greeted her. She was absolutely radiant, as the tears crept down her cheeks.

"You are a beautiful Black woman, Grace."

She reached out and hugged me around my neck. "How can I thank you?"

"You go to church on this coming Sunday with your head held high and you thank God."

Our moment was to be shared because from the living room voices, almost in unison, shouted, "Momma, we're waiting."

Grace gathered what strength she had left, took a deep breath, and walked the walk. Hands on your hip don't let your backbone slip kind of walk down the short, narrow hallway. Slinging braids off her face in her own makeshift summer breeze. I hung back in the hallway. This was Grace's moment.

"Grandma, look!" they yelled out the front screen door like a fire had erupted. "Grandma, come see Momma."

"Ooo wee, Momma, you look so good." The girls fought for first place with hugs around Grace's waist.

I heard the aluminum door spring open and slam shut. "Oh, baby, you look beautiful." Her mother almost sang the words.

I sat down on the sofa forever imprinted with the shadow of God's pure love.

Later that same day, as we sat and talked she asked me to tell her more about God. "I want to know I will go to heaven when I die." I went out to my car, got my Bible. When I came back, we read verses filled with God's promises. Afterward, we prayed together as she asked God to be the center of her life from that point forward. Thus began her new personal relationship with God as she learned how to walk by faith and not by sight.

Grace along with her two daughters and her mother went to church when Sunday came. Two weeks later I got a call from her mother. Grace had passed during the night from this life to the next.

As I sat on the side of my bed listening to her mother give me the details, my mind filled with Grace's feeble but sweet voice reading aloud, "O, Death where is your victory? Where,

O, Death where is your sting?" (1 Corinthians 15:55, New International Version).

A week later, as she requested, they laid her body to rest with the braided wig on her head; but her spirit had departed at her last breath here on earth. I knew that now she had a brand-new imperishable body—one that would never wear out. Grace had no more pain, no more sluggish body, no more AIDS, no more stares laden with pity—only the perfect peace in the presence of the Ultimate and Perfect Friend—God.

Still, I miss you, Grace, and I will never forget you nor the love you gave me.

I'm reminded of the song "No Man Is an Island." Its message is so obviously true that no man, woman, or child can stand alone. We all need someone—at least one friend. We need someone to listen to us even when we ramble. There is comfort in knowing that we can pick up the telephone and call someone, or e-mail someone, or hop in the car or train to go talk to someone. Someone that allows us to cry on their shoulder if we need to. Someone who loves us and treasures our uniqueness. Someone who lifts us up when the burdens of life stoop us. Someone to share our victories as well as our disappointments. No man is an island—no man stands alone.

However, it starts with you and me. We've got to take the risk and let someone in. That means becoming vulnerable, which can be scary to some of us. However, being vulnerable, although it may mean opening up to hurt, also means being open to love. If we close down in hopes of shutting out the hurt, we can't possibly receive the other greater and more wonderful thing—the love.

In addition, I have found that to have a friend, I have to be a friend. I believe that beneath every selfish and self-centered person is a lonely and scared person. I know because I've been there—done that. However, I made a conscious decision that I didn't want to live like that anymore—life is too short—and love is too important.

So important that a burden shared by a friend is a burden halved. It seems that God created us with each other in mind. No man is an island—no man stands alone.

Dear Heavenly Father: How can we ever thank you enough for the wonderful, awesome, and magnificent grace and mercies that you give us every day? How can we show you enough just how much we appreciate your lovingkindness? How do we attempt to verbalize the indebtedness we feel toward you for loving us and putting people in our lives to love us and call us friend. Help us tell others about the way you've made for us countless times too numerous to mention in a single prayer. How do we sleep in the stillness of the night without shouting in our dreams, "Thank you, Heavenly Father?" Help us to see with our limited vision that we are no longer cursed but *blessed beyond measure* with whatever is going on in our lives because You promise to work absolutely all things together for the good of those who love you. Help us to trust you more—lean on you more—seek your guidance—love you more. Help us be a friend and receive a friend with the same friendship that you extend to us. Amen. So be it!

He gives power to the weak,
And to those who have no might He increases strength.
Even the youths shall faint and be weary,
And the young men shall utterly fall,
But those who wait on the Lord
Shall renew their strength;
They shall mount up with wings like eagles,
They shall run and not be weary,
They shall walk and not faint.

ISAIAH 40:29–31 (New King James Version)

Compelled
to Fly

It was a wonderful Friday evening at HR57 Jazz Preservation Center. Wednesdays and Fridays are jam sessions where any musician can bring his instrument and play. I went to support a new friend, Dude Duckett, a jazz guitarist.

I walked through the door of the dimly lit club and waited in line to pay my $6 admission. Off to the side and toward the back of the club sat Dude surrounded by his black guitar case and amp. I watched as he squirmed in his seat. I realized at that moment that I was right where I was supposed to be—supporting a friend.

Not long after my arrival, I gently urged him to a table toward the front of the club along the exposed red-brick wall. As he anxiously waited for his set, he twitched, turned, and tuned up his guitar. Every few minutes he looked up from his guitar strings and smiled with eyes that seemed to search for assurance.

"I know I'm going to be all right; but I tell you this—if you were not here beside me, I would probably be stretched out in the middle of the floor sweating it out by now. I'm glad you're here."

"I'm glad I'm here too, Dude. You'll do well. You have been prepared for such a time as this."

"Yeah? But, Stanice, suppose my amp doesn't come on. It's an old amp from the '50s with tubes inside that need to warm up. I mean, this light here has to make it from white to blue to purple. It's got to be purple to be ready. Now, once it's purple, then my jazz thing is on!"

I leaned over in my seat and put both hands on the unplugged amp and prayed over it. Afterward, I looked into Dude's eyes and said to him, "It's gonna be all right because God's got it now. That amp ain't our business no more. You just do what you been born to do, God will take care of the rest."

That night signified a milestone for him. He is the son of an accomplished jazz singer mom and jazz guitarist dad. His dad died not long ago. His uncles and cousins are all musicians. But this was Dude's maiden voyage in a club where no one knew his parents and none of his uncles or cousins were present.

Before this night, he had lived his musical life in the shadow of greats; but Dude never considered himself worthy of playing with them.

The air around us was rich with the sounds of saxophones, violins, and trumpets as the musicians tuned up and ran scales anticipating their five minutes in the spotlight. Dude took his amp to the stage and plugged it in. He came back to our table.

At the edge of the yellow-twilight-lit stage sat a lone regal-looking conga player draped in a flowing African mud cloth robe. With mastery and precision, he pounded out a rhythmically hypnotic beat that served as an underlayer to the snatches of conversations I heard coming from each table. Perhaps they wondered like Dude and I who the next musician to play would be.

Shh! The announcer approached the mike. "And now, ladies and gentlemen, tonight our next performer's first time playing at HR57, let's give him a warm welcome. Mr. Dude Duckett!"

Applause filled the room and reverberated off the walls as he walked through the standing-room-only crowd. He found his place, strapped on his guitar, and plugged the cord into the newly anointed amp. The pianist started with a run of sophisticated chords, followed by the drummer sealing the beat, then the conga player mixed in some cultural flavoring, then a bad young white boy on bass plucked out his territory, and then without missing a beat in came Mr. Dude Duckett on guitar.

From where I sat, I saw the amp light shining a brilliant passionate purple. Dude hit the ground running and strummed up a sound so wonderful that his hero, Wes Montgomery, had to be turning in his grave.

As I watched Dude pour his body, mind, and spirit into that guitar, I saw that he and jazz were one entity. Either one without the other would have been left wanting. I hoped that he would hear in the rhythm the Holy Spirit whispering a confirmation to him that he was to do more than sit on a couch and play for himself and me. That every day of his life thus far had been preparation for this maiden voyage when he would see that he could fly! That moment when he came to believe that it was his God-given responsibility to share his gift with the world—the jazz that only he was born to play—to bring forth *that sound* that only he can make.

Dude was awesome! Applause exploded in the club. He started his triumphant walk back to our table but the piano man interrupted. "No, no, no. Where you going? Come back here. We need you on this next song." More applause.

When Dude finished playing the second song, he came back to the table not the same as he had left. Like Moses coming down off the mountain after being given the Ten Commandments, Dude's face shone like a man who had been in the presence of God. He and I broke out in praise and thanksgiving to the Lord right at the table.

"I believe that God and my Dad are both smiling right now. I feel like I am walking on cotton candy, Stanice."

It was a glorious night. God ordered our steps. We even met a young Black girl singer with a neat African print head wrap. She stopped at our table after hearing Dude to tell him how much she enjoyed his performance and to find out if he would play for her set. He agreed. She wasn't sure what she should sing.

"How about giving us a little Billie Holiday," I suggested.

"I know lots of Billie!" Her face beamed with the radiance of a twenty-something confident that her big dream was possible. Encouraged, she walked toward the stage, turned back to our table, and said, "Thanks, I'm singing this song for you."

After HR57 closed, Dude walked me to my car still talking in his excitement of the evening. He had taken his leap of faith . . . and landed dead-center!

He called me when he got home and we talked more about the evening and he thanked me for being there for him.

"Stanice, tonight wasn't about commercial. Tonight was spiritual! It was God showing me who I am in Him. Now I know that my family's jazz legacy will live on through me."

"I feel you, Dude! I'm blessed to have been a witness. Perhaps, one day I'll be given the opportunity to say, 'I was there when Dude Duckett broke loose and made his own jazz.'"

We talked some more, and then he said, "Well, I know it's late; but I got to call and wake up my family and tell them what God did for me tonight."

As I reflect on that glorious night at HR57 of Dude's solo flight, I'm reminded of how it was for me when I finally made a decision to believe in my gift and work hard to be the writer I was born to be. These gifts that God tailor-makes just for us are not ours to keep to ourselves or ignore, but they are to be honed and shared with others—especially in these last days. People need what God put in our hands to bring to the table of life. What is in your hand? Offer it up to God and watch what He can and will do with it. He will bless you to bless the world.

Yes, it's always a wonderful and most holy thing to watch as butterflies break out of their self-woven cocoons. Perhaps it is in the cocoon that the individual flavor and soul of the gift is born and we find ourselves compelled to fly—free at last!

Dear Heavenly Father: What is in my hand that can be used for your glory? Assign to me the gifts that you prepared in advance that I should bring to the world. Please forgive my selfishness in not using them to your Glory and my lack of belief that I even have gifts that you can use. I know so little but I'm growing to love You so much that I am compelled to come before you today offering myself and all You've created me to be. Let my light so shine that people may see my good works and glorify You in Heaven. Thank you for providing whatever it is that I need to go to the next level in my relationship with You and the world around me. In Jesus' name, Amen. So be it!

"So the Lord said to him, 'What is that in your hand?' He said,
'A rod.'
And He said, 'Cast it on the ground.'"

EXODUS 4:2–3 (New King James Version)

"Now may the God of hope fill you with all joy and peace in believing,
That you may abound in hope by the power of the Holy Spirit."

ROMANS 15:13 (New King James Version)